Stefan Ramaekers • Naomi Hodgson
Editors

Past, Present, and Future Possibilities for Philosophy and History of Education

Finding Space and Time for Research

 Springer

Editors
Stefan Ramaekers (iD)
Laboratory for Education & Society
KU Leuven
Leuven, Belgium

Naomi Hodgson (iD)
Centre for Education and Policy Analysis,
Department of Education Studies
Liverpool Hope University
Liverpool, UK

ISBN 978-3-319-94252-0   ISBN 978-3-319-94253-7   (eBook)
https://doi.org/10.1007/978-3-319-94253-7

Library of Congress Control Number: 2018953048

Printed on acid-free paper

This Springer imprint is published by the registered company Springer International Publishing AG part of Springer Nature.
The registered company address is: Gewerbestrasse 11, 6330 Cham, Switzerland

Preface: Paul Smeyers and the Dutch Connection

Connections and Friendships

When I first met Paul Smeyers, in Leuven in the early 1980s, he had been working on his dissertation at the London Institute of Education. His supervisor, Prof. Cyriel de Keyser, had sent him to the UK to sort out what analytic philosophy of education was all about, just as he had sent Jan Masschelein to Germany to do the same concerning German *Allgemeine Pädagogik* and critical theory. At that time, PhD projects at the Catholic University of Leuven had a stronger international orientation than at my own alma mater, Utrecht University in the Netherlands. I was asked to teach two of De Keyser's undergraduate courses in fundamental pedagogic from 1981 to 1982. It was my first opportunity to teach in another country, and it was an invaluable experience. To foreign ears, it may sound like we speak the same language, but for the rest, Flanders and the Netherlands are significantly different. My experience in Leuven was not only professionally rewarding, however; it was also the start of a unique friendship and a very productive professional partnership.

In those early years of his academic career, Paul was quite isolated as an analytic philosopher of education in the Dutch-speaking context. Luckily it was quite easy for me to create a Dutch connection. In order to introduce him to Dutch colleagues in theoretical pedagogy who shared his interest in Anglo-Saxon philosophy of education, I started to organise regular meetings in Utrecht in which we would present and discuss our work. Among the participants in the meetings we held over the next few years were Ben Spiecker, Jan Steutel, Wouter van Haaften, Ger Snik, and Wilna Meijer. We would go on to collaborate further when, in 1988, Paul invited me to join the editorial board of *Pedagogisch Tijdschrift*, a Dutch-Flemish general pedagogical journal. The reader should keep in mind that, in the Continental tradition, pedagogy has a much broader sense than in the Anglo-Saxon part of the world, where it tends to be restricted to what is going on in schools or, even more narrowly, to teaching methods. During his editorship, the journal flourished as a lively forum for discussions on important pedagogical issues. Through his experience at the London Institute, Paul had become a member of the Philosophy of Education Society of

Great Britain. In 1994 Paul introduced me to the society and its annual conference. Previously held in London, it had moved to a new venue at New College, Oxford, and since then has developed into one of the main international conferences in philosophy of education. New College became the place to meet colleagues from all over the world. It was no mean feat to get there at that time. I will never forget the 5-hour boat-trip from Zeebrugge to Folkestone. On one particular occasion, at the dinner table on the ferry of the Belgian company Sally, Paul advised me strongly to savour the food. Over the next few days, I should not expect to be served one single decent meal, he warned. Staying alive in England proved much less of an ordeal for me than for him; the standard of Dutch cuisine was still pretty low in those days too. And when we returned after the conference and I tried to pay the bill in a restaurant in Zeebrugge, he grabbed it out of my hands exclaiming: "But Bas, on Belgian soil!" Paul is world-famous for his hospitality and generosity.

Collaborations

Until then, the majority of our publications had, naturally, been in Dutch. In the 1980s, however, things had begun to change. Paul and I started to discuss the publication policies at our universities. Paul had always said that Belgium was always about 10 years behind the Netherlands and that when the changes came they were always less extreme. In the late 1990s, the shift of emphasis toward publications in English and in English only had reached the policy statements of the Flemish universities too. We wrote an article defending scientific writings about education in the Dutch language, for obvious reasons. Many of the publications in pedagogy are related to what is going on in specific national institutions. Educational systems differ profoundly from nation to nation in many respects. It makes no sense to write about the Dutch or Flemish context in English. Many core concepts simply cannot be translated without losing essential elements of the meaning. Furthermore, counting publications creates a perverse stimulus to divide publication into smaller parts and publish them in different journals. What a waste. (I still regret that I did not succeed in convincing Paul to include in our article the recommendation to implement a points system in which there would be a limit on how many publications one could have in a year, with points deducted if that is exceeded.) The irony of our plea for scientific publications in the Dutch language was that we published that article in the *British Journal of Educational Studies*. (Paul's Dutch-Flemish journal *Pedagogisch Tijdschrift* had to stop in 2005 because of a shortage of submissions; unsurprisingly, given that Dutch and Flemish pedagogues had to publish in English and in English only).

Our collaboration concerned not only pedagogy but also research, a sustained concern throughout Paul's writing. In the late 1990s, we published an introduction to interpretive research methods, *Opvoeding en Onderwijs Leren Zien* (1999) (*Learning How to See Upbringing and Education*), comprised of contributions from Dutch and Flemish authors. The volume was unique at that time as every chapter contained an elaborated example of a research project with the use of the method at stake. Paul has used this format again recently as the basis of an international collection, the *International Handbook of Interpretation in Education Research*. Paul managed our project with extreme accuracy. One of the problems with those big projects is that while the first invited contributor has delivered his or her chapter months ago, the last one has yet to start writing. It is – for most of us, arguably – impossible to complete such an editing job on your own. Collaborating on such a project is really a pleasure, however; at least when Paul Smeyers is your coeditor.

It was while celebrating the publication of that book, over dinner at *Comme Chez Soi* in Brussels, that the plan for an even more ambitious project was made. Paul and I considered the core introductory text on different schools of thought used in undergraduate courses at Dutch universities to be outdated. The collection, edited by Siebren Miedema (Leiden University), was updated edition after edition but had been in use for 15 years by that point. The postmodern revolution had shown that the resemblances between the modern schools of thought were more relevant than their differences. So, in 2001, we published *Grondslagen van de Wetenschappelijke Pedagogiek: Modern en Postmodern* (2001) (*Foundations of Scientific Pedagogy: Modern and Postmodern*). Miedema was one of the contributors. Our text went on to be used for at least the next 15 years, gradually replacing Miedema's.

Taking the critique of postmodernism seriously, I had pleaded in the late 1980s for an essayistic approach to writing about pedagogy. It is quite silly to think that pedagogical truth is something that can be falsified by one counterargument. Pedagogical truths should be underpinned by arguments-pro without too much consideration of possible arguments-contra. Pedagogical truths should be *essayed* (tried out). Good practice is unthinkable as mere application of theory. Practitioners have to be convinced instead of to be told what to do. Hence, Paul came up with the creative plan to publish a collection of pedagogical essays. Indicative of how he paved the way for his PhD students, Paul proposed that we include two younger colleagues in our essay project. But we agreed that four names on the cover of a collection of ten essays were too many. So, as a subtle comment on the endless lists of authors we find on many research articles, we decided to use a pseudonym. E.A. Godot published his first collection of essays on societal problems that are not pedagogical at first sight in 2003, entitled *Hoezo Pedagogisch?* (*Why pedagogical?*). The second collection, published in 2006, reflected on the actual meaning of the seven deadly sins and was entitled *Zonde van de Tijd*. (The phrase is not directly translatable. It carries the double meaning "sin of the time" and "waste of time.")

Research Community

The themes of pedagogy and the practice and conditions of research have recurred not only throughout Paul's work but also in the themes and discussions of the research community over the last 20 years. Arguably it has had little impact in turning the tide of changes in academia and the status of philosophical and historical research. In 2009, for example, I was invited by Paul to teach in Ghent to keep a chair in fundamental pedagogy warm for a younger colleague. In 2011 it transpired that this had been in vain; the chair was reallocated to a field with better research metrics. The research community did, however, provide initiation and opportunity for younger colleagues and established an international community of scholars whose work and appreciation of those events are reflected in the chapters that form this book.

The international conferences Paul Smeyers hosted in Leuven were always extremely well organised. The importance of good facilities is often underestimated, but never by Paul. The meetings of the International Research Community "Philosophy and History of the Discipline of Education," for which he and Marc Depaepe obtained funding from the Research Foundation Flanders, have been held in Leuven since 2000 to form a separate chapter. In this volume, other colleagues report about the success of that extraordinary enterprise.

Utrecht University   Bas Levering
Utrecht, The Netherlands

Contents

Contributors

David Bridges University of East Anglia, Norwich, UK

St Edmund's College, Cambridge, UK

Homerton College, Cambridge, UK

Nicholas C. Burbules University of Illinois, Urbana-Champaign, Champaign, IL, USA

Stefaan E. Cuypers Centre for Logic and Philosophy of Science, KU Leuven, Leuven, Belgium

Marc Depaepe Faculty of Psychology and Educational Sciences, Kulak Kortrijk Campus, Kortrijk, Belgium

Lynn Fendler Department of Teacher Education, Michigan State University, East Lansing, MI, USA

Naomi Hodgson Centre for Education and Policy Analysis, Department of Education Studies, Liverpool Hope University, Liverpool, UK

Bas Levering Utrecht University, Utrecht, The Netherlands

Jan Masschelein Laboratory for Education & Society, KU Leuven, Leuven, Belgium

Michael A. Peters University of Waikato, Hamilton, New Zealand

Stefan Ramaekers Laboratory for Education & Society, KU Leuven, Leuven, Belgium

Frank Simon Ghent University, Ghent, Belgium

Maarten Simons Laboratory for Education & Society, KU Leuven, Leuven, Belgium

Richard Smith School of Education, University of Durham, Durham, UK

Paul Standish University College London, Institute of Education, London, UK

Lynda Stone School of Education, The University of North Carolina at Chapel Hill, Chapel Hill, NC, USA

Jean Paul Van Bendegem Centre for Logic and Science-Philosophy, Vrije Universiteit Brussel (VUB), Brussels, Belgium

Chapter 1
Introduction: Reminders Assembling a Picture of Paul Smeyers

Stefan Ramaekers ⓘ and Naomi Hodgson ⓘ

Abstract To introduce this volume, we offer a picture of Paul Smeyers as a researcher, one who clearly fits the description of the excellent researcher of the research-intensive university today. But the metrics and descriptors used to define research in this way do not capture what is educational in Paul's educational philosophy, his approach to it, or what it has contributed to the field. Taking a selection of the Wittgensteinian *Leitmotifs* that have recurred throughout his work over the last four decades, we provide an (admittedly, wilfully selective) account of his work, its formative influences, and enduring relevance. We situate this within the wider context in which philosophy and history of education exist today, in a university system much changed since Paul's own doctoral study, to pave the way for considerations that follow of the various ways in which the time and space of and for research might be recollected, understood, and defended.

A Picture of a Research Career

Paul Smeyers has been a very prolific academic, with writing published in each of the last four decades. Some metrics (correct as at October 2017). Articles in international peer-reviewed journals: 90. Articles in internationally accessible journals and in other journals: 55. Chapters in books (published by internationally recognised publishers and other publishers): 75. Books (as author): 7. Edited books and special issues: 45. He published not only in English but continued to write in Dutch, despite changes in academia and pressure for "internationalisation", although the balance

S. Ramaekers (✉)
Laboratory for Education & Society, KU Leuven, Leuven, Belgium
e-mail: stefan.ramaekers@kuleuven.be

N. Hodgson
Centre for Education and Policy Analysis, Department of Education Studies, Liverpool Hope University, Liverpool, UK
e-mail: hodgson@hope.ac.uk

© Springer International Publishing AG, part of Springer Nature 2018
S. Ramaekers, N. Hodgson (eds.), *Past, Present, and Future Possibilities for Philosophy and History of Education*,
https://doi.org/10.1007/978-3-319-94253-7_1

has shifted in favour of English since the mid-1990s. The majority of his publications are single-authored. And when they are not, they are co-authored in the true sense of the term, i.e. co-*authored*, partly written by himself. Not just proof-read, or checked, or commented on with track-changes. Not just adding his name out of some "acquired right" that comes with being the promotor of a PhD-student, or the promotor of a project, and hence becoming an even more prolific "writer". (Aren't so many "great researchers" of today prolific in that sense?) this is just not his style. He really felt, and defended throughout his career, that a writer's thinking is that writer's thinking. (A selected list of his publications is included as an appendix to this volume.)

So, according to this research profile, Paul is eminently "REF-able", as those of us working in UK academia like to say. That is, he does if anything fit the description of an excellent researcher: he has not only published widely in high-ranking international journals, but also successfully applied for external funding, supervised doctoral students to successful completion, and shown leadership in his field. But such metrics and descriptors can only give us a superficial account of his scholarship and his career. They say nothing of the educational value of all this, why he does it, and what it leaves behind. In this opening chapter we give a (willfully partial) account of his work and his approach to researching education philosophically throughout his academic career. Reading this introduction together with Bas Levering's Preface, and the chapters by Marc Depaepe and Frank Simon (Chap. 2), Richard Smith and Paul Standish (Chap. 3), and Nicholas Burbules and Lynda Stone (Chap. 10) readers will gain a fairly comprehensive account of Paul, his work, and its development. The themes we raise here are also echoed throughout these and the other chapters of this book, a volume that is not only intended to celebrate the career of Paul Smeyers, but also to offer perspectives on the state of the fields of philosophy and history of education that he leaves behind.

These fields have been the focus of the Research Community for Philosophy and History of Educational Research, convened by Paul Smeyers and Marc Depaepe, for over 20 years. In that time, significant changes in the governance and status of universities and publicly-funded research, in Europe at least, have placed significant pressures on, and raised new questions for, these fields. Jan Masschelein and Maarten Simons detail this context in Chap. 4 and articulate how the university's public pedagogical form must be defended against the demands of today's intensively research-driven environment. We have a clear sense that this phenomenon is not restricted to Europe, however (see Burbules and Stone, Chap. 10). The occasion of Paul's retirement offers a timely opportunity to consider these questions and challenges through the lens of his work and the themes with which it has continually engaged.

As far as research in the foundation disciplines of education is concerned, philosophy and history perhaps have to work harder to justify themselves than their more obviously empirically focused cousins. As researchers in these fields, we find ourselves, perhaps, in a tension between pictures of research: one, the picture as "research profile", constituted by making ourselves visible as researchers through (self-)promotion in terms of our outputs, public engagement, social media, ensuring measurability via various metrics; and two, the picture of the world itself constituted by the philosophical approach one takes. The latter becomes the means by which to question and resist the former. In his work, Paul has engaged with the scholarship of writers as diverse as Israel Scheffler, R.S. Peters, Paul Hirst, Alasdair MacIntyre, Charles Taylor, Peter Winch, Michael Oakeshott, Raimond Gaita, Jacques Derrida, and others, in the interest of such philosophical questioning. But if there is one philosopher who has informed – or, more strongly and accurately, shaped – Paul's philosophical approach, it is Ludwig Wittgenstein. (This is hardly a surprise for anyone familiar with his work, or acquainted with him personally. So, readers are fully entitled to say "duh" at this point.)

Wittgensteinian *Leitmotifs* feature prominently in his writing, meaning not just that these are explicitly discussed and brought to bear on philosophical issues of education and educational research, but also that their presence is felt, is traceable, even when not explicitly worded. The most conspicuous of these are: the idea that a picture held, holds, can hold us captive; the invitation for assembling reminders for a particular purpose; the problematic of (the philosopher's, or more generally the human) longing for crystalline purity; the notions of family resemblances, private language, perspicuous representation, putting things side-by-side; the idea of philosophy as therapy, and of philosophy providing (only) description (the descriptive method); the epistemology of following a rule; and, of course, the much-used (but not always accurately) notions of form(s) of life, language-game(s), and grammar.[1]

That many of these Wittgensteinian notions reappear in the chapters to come, either explicitly addressed or just mentioned in passing, is not pure coincidence, of course. It is indicative of what is shared among the contributors (as scholars as such, and as members of the Research Community for Philosophy and History of Educational Research in particular) and, probably more importantly, of what contributors find so typical of Paul and his work. In what follows, we use some of these *Leitmotifs* as a way of ordering, for ourselves, a few "reminders" of Paul's work and its importance to the field of philosophy of education and the people in it.

A Picture Held Us Captive

The initial groundwork for what was quickly to become Paul's philosophical frame of reference – the philosophy of the later Wittgenstein – that would accompany him throughout his academic career, was laid in the MA theses[2] he wrote as a student at

---

[1] We will not provide specific references for these expressions. We do not mean to discuss these concepts per se, but rather are using them to sketch a particular picture of the perspective that has shaped Paul's research over the last few decades. For those familiar with the concepts, we trust these are sufficiently familiar to make sense in this context; we also trust our use of them is acceptable. For those unfamiliar with these concepts, we hope our use of them will trigger an interest in getting to know them.

[2] At the time, universities in Flanders did not yet have (what are now called) BA's and MA's. Students started a so-called "candidature" (a two-year university degree), followed by a "licenti-

the Catholic University of Leuven. For the program in Educational Sciences he wrote an MA dissertation titled "Analytische filosofie van opvoeding en onderwijs: De bijdrage van R. S. Peters" ("Analytical philosophy of education: R.S. Peters' contribution") (1976), and following that, when studying philosophy, he wrote his MA dissertation on Gilbert Ryle, titled "Een kritisch onderzoek naar de vooronderstellingen van Ryle's opvatting over filosofie" ("A critical investigation of the presuppositions of Ryle's conception of philosophy") (1982). His work in these dissertations was continued and culminated in an in-depth study of analytical philosophy of education leading to his PhD dissertation, which he submitted in 1984 under the title "*A picture held us captive*. De analytische 'philosophy of education' tussen Ryle en Wittgenstein: Hersituering en onderzoek van haar relevantie voor een wijsgerige pedagogiek" ("*A picture held us captive*. Analytical philosophy of education between Ryle and Wittgenstein: Resituation and investigation of its relevance for an educational philosophy").[3]

We want to emphasise here, and hope to bring out in this introduction, that what is at stake in Paul's adoption of Wittgenstein's later philosophy goes deeper than can be captured by saying Wittgenstein has been "inspirational" for him. The sense we have from his writings is that this "inspiration" is more aptly taken as a finding of words to express educational concerns that, before "having" (or owning) these words, were perhaps already there, but could not be articulated, or at least not as clearly, or lucidly, articulated.

His doctoral thesis already testifies to this. It not only opened up Wittgenstein's later philosophy to a wider audience of (specifically) philosophers of education in the West of Continental Europe, but also this work began a thread that can be traced through the decades of work that have followed. Without ignoring the very specific thing Wittgenstein meant to say by "a picture held us captive", we feel confident in saying that if anything has pervaded Paul's work, and has motivated his thinking and writing, it is an enduring interest in, and concern for, registers of this particular Wittgensteinian *Leitmotif*. What is the picture that lies before us? Or alternatively, what picture lies in our beholding of the world? His work on the many concrete issues and themes in education and educational research he has addressed revolves around variations of this very matter: what is it that makes us do certain things in

---

ate" or "licence years" (2 or 3 years, depending on the degree). See Toscano and Smeyers (2018) for more on this. See ibid. for a detailed account of Paul's specific position on (the nature of) educational research.

[3] There is a translation issue here. "Wijsgerige pedagogiek" can hardly be translated in English. See Ramaekers (2018) for a conceptual exercise on this. The idea expressed in the title is an assessment of (a certain position in the tradition of) analytical philosophy of education and to evaluate its implications for advancing philosophical reflection on education (schooling, childrearing) in another tradition, i.e. the Continental tradition of "wijsgerige pedagogiek" (or in German: Algemeine Pädagogik). That may perhaps seem a bit odd to contemporary, especially younger, readers. But bear in mind that this work was done before the pervasive globalisation – meaning, in our cultural history, Anglicisation – of academic research that, sort of, started off in the early '90s. Paul's research was timely, groundbreaking, and new: it attempted to introduce ways of thinking and philosophising in an area of scholarship predominantly influenced by Continental philosophy and philosophy of education.

education and educational research, and not others? What urges us to go in this or that direction and not another? What incites us in certain ways, and not in others? What enthuses us into a specific vein, and not another?

Assembling Reminders

The inevitable *companion de route* of the idea that "a picture held us captive" is that other familiar Wittgensteinian *Leitmotif*, "assembling reminders for a particular purpose". There is a natural relationship between these two, drawn out throughout Paul's work. He assembles reminders in order to get a clear picture ("a perspicuous representation") of the picture that holds one captive, to identify its determining contours, in order to show (remind one of) other aspects of education and educational research (which he, thereby, often shows to be inevitable, or necessary).

For example, Paul has assembled multiple reminders about what has befallen educational research over the last few decades. Many of his articles, chapters, and books address this theme. Indeed, his 2006 article, "'What it makes sense to say': Education, philosophy and Peter Winch on social science", explicitly opens with Wittgenstein's paragraph 115 of his *Philosophical Investigations*: "A *picture* held us captive. …". In his untangling of problems surrounding educational research, in the 2006 article in particular, he is "assembling reminders for a particular purpose" to remind his readers about something that is somehow, somewhere, familiar (known, perhaps), but not (or not sufficiently, or not sufficiently clearly; or perhaps no longer) articulated about matters of educational research, i.e. that in fact there is no better alternative in educational research than to embrace a pluralistic interpretive position, an argument Paul has defended extensively. He is reminding his audience what the *real* stakes are in educational research: what it is that educational research is *actually* capable of; what demands educational research can *honestly* and *earnestly* satisfy. David Bridges takes up this theme in Chap. 6 to remind us what philosophical research is and, perhaps more importantly, what it isn't, and hence to suggest that the more honest response to the charge that philosophy "leaves everything as it is" (Wittgenstein, 1953 #124), is to agree, rather than to frame this as a failing, as our current concern with "impact" and "implications for practice" might suggest.

But this is not to say that Paul's work is not concerned with practice. Quite the contrary. Philosophy of education should, in Paul's understanding, have a bearing on educational practice, both in the sense of finding its questions there as well as in returning there hoping to "improve" that practice. A misunderstanding Paul has taken care to unravel, however, is the perception that any kind of educational research, hence also philosophical research, should be able to spell out its implications for practice in fairly direct and straightforward ways. Hence, in our invitation to the authors featured in this volume, we addressed the issue of philosophers "leaving everything as it is" and raised the question of whether or not this was indeed an issue for our own contributions to the philosophy and history of education. Arguably, to expect philosophical research to directly impact educational practice misunderstands what both philosophy and education are.

Philosophy having a bearing on practice means, for Paul, not providing clear ways to deal with things, or solving problems for practitioners. It means, at best, but also most honestly, offering the practitioner a vocabulary to help her think for herself within and about her practice(s). Philosophical work does not and cannot lead to educational practice in a *direct* sense. It can, however, lead to a heightened, or deepened, sense of educational reflection. So here, again, a very Wittgensteinian thread can be discerned. The application of a rule cannot be spelled out *by* a philosopher *for* a practitioner. The application of a rule is exactly what the concept entails it is: an application. That is, it is in need of a very concrete person applying it herself. It needs to be done, by someone; tried out; testing both rule and practitioner. What a philosopher of education can offer in this regard is a particular understanding, i.e. of possible conditions of applicability, potentialities, invitations to try. Whatever "solution" that philosopher of education has conjured up cannot, however, be imposed, but only offered for trying.

Paul addresses, therefore, the question of what philosophy can and cannot do for education – philosophy's potential and limit for (understanding, researching, improving) education – or more generally the question of the relevance of theory (philosophy being a specific form of theory) for education, of its rightful place. Given his insistence on the real bearing of philosophy of education on educational practices, it should not come as a surprise that he never shies away from arguing that it is, cannot be otherwise than, always a kind of "political" research. The seriousness with which Paul has treated all of the areas he has attended to in his research should suffice to indicate that philosophy of education for him is no *Spielerei*. That is, as educational researchers (and philosophers of education being a subspecies of these) we cannot avoid taking a particular stance.

It may seem obvious to say that a practitioner will always implement a practice, an idea, herself, in her own way, in her own particular context; or that an educational researcher cannot but take a political stance, in that her values will have a bearing on what she does. But, the concern for "best practice" and with finding "what works" in education seems to require the form of "reminder" that a Wittgensteinian approach provides. What Paul often draws attention to in such reminders are that certain aspects of our practices are inevitable; that there are *human* beings involved in their execution and constitution. In both education and educational research, Paul has always evoked registers of what it makes sense to say and to do, and such evocation always implies a reference to, or an appeal for, a community, to some form of inter-subjectivity, or to a set of meanings that are shared (the extent of which cannot be grasped in any analytically clear way). (A theme Paul finds in Wittgenstein's later work, and which has deeply influenced his outlook on the world, is what he always defended as a subtle balance between I and community: Wittgenstein, he argues, brings out an understanding of meaning that is not a form of pure inwardness (subjectivity; primacy of the subject), nor of pure outwardness (objectivity; primacy of the collectivity), but that delicately, but to an important extent unfathomably, balances a simultaneous belonging of "I" and "they".) Understood in this manner, his way of "assembling reminders" could easily be – and sometimes is – misinterpreted as a form of conservatism. Instead it should be seen as a form of reticence and tactfulness: the act of assembling reminders serves to offer educational practitioners and researchers the necessary (or minimal) "friction" or "rough ground" (which is different from "the ground") they need, as anyone does, to actually act, to actually do something, and to actually (try to) change something.

Here we want to draw attention to a further dimension of what we have referred to above as Paul's "adoption" of Wittgenstein's later philosophy. Paul has been known to defend, at times, the position that philosophy of education is a form of applied philosophy. And for this reason, possibly, the idea of the "application" of a Wittgensteinian "framework" comes to mind to some readers. His own account of the work of Wittgenstein, precisely in terms of a "Wittgensteinian frame of reference" or "perspective", may have contributed to such understanding. That is, it may have suggested that *here* there is a framework (Wittgenstein's), and *over there*, there are educational issues and issues of educational research that can be approached "through" that framework or perspective. But "application" denies the depth of the impression that Wittgenstein's work made on him even more than the idea that it was "inspirational". The sense we have from a (re)reading of his work is rather that, in "seeing" education and educational research in Wittgensteinian terms, the stakes of education and educational research cannot be articulated by recourse to something called a "framework".

Wittgenstein's work has *shaped*, that is, formed – in the German sense of *Bildung* – his thinking, and, we carefully dare to say, his entire being. Perhaps his being introduced to the work of Wittgenstein (and the secondary accounts of that work) is more akin to the process of initiation (of children in language and world), and the obtaining of a world-picture thereby – a conception of education Paul has defended throughout his career – than he himself might be willing to concede.[4] Granted, this would have to be called something like a "second" initiation. Our point is, the impression of his getting acquainted with the work of Wittgenstein, of this style of thinking and writing, seems to have been almost as impressive and indelible as the introduction into a world-picture provided by a human being's first educators. Melodramatic as this might sound, perhaps it is fair to say that "Wittgenstein" is the picture that holds Paul captive?[5]

In this sense, his "use" of Wittgensteinian *Leitmotifs* is not (just) to be seen as an antidote to claims of a fashionable nature ("what works", "best practices", …) but as *performing* his concerns. For Paul, it seems to us, there is no other way to *respond* to these issues – which is a way of saying that what has deeply *formed* him always inevitably *informs* his way of addressing and responding.

---

[4] This is a point that deserves further philosophical elaboration, especially with Paul himself, since we have had our differences on this issue.

[5] We thank Bas Levering for his insight and offering this way of phrasing to us.

The Longing for Crystalline Purity

Paul's engagement with the problem(s) of the longing for crystalline purity so typical of human desire comes across most clearly in his dealings with (dominant pictures of) educational research. As Paul's writings unfold, he gradually, and
convincingly, unfolds why and how educational research cannot be modelled along
the paradigm of the natural sciences. Educational issues cannot be adequately – that
is, respectfully – addressed or rendered meaningful in terms of "explanations" and
(positivistically conceived) "predictions".[6] As he puts this in his own words: "To
claim that educational research favors nowadays a particular methodology and the
use of particular methods is an understatement. Though it loves to refer to itself as
embracing 'post-positivism', it can be asked whether it really has parted from a
logical empiricism characterised by the invariance of perception, meaning and
methodology … There is a tendency to mark out limited areas of investigation that
are relatively uncontaminated by broader questions (possibly in the name of 'objectivity')" (Smeyers, 2014, pp. 239–240).

A recurring focus not only of Paul's work but also that of the wider Research
Community has been the tension between the scientific paradigm of research and
philosophical approaches to, and questions about, education. This not only pertains
at the level of methodology but, today, also the ways in which the quality of research
is measured, e.g. in terms of its societal impact, its implications for (effective) educational practice. The issues or themes Paul has addressed in relation to educational
research itself range from the intricacies of the dichotomy between quantitative and
qualitative research, the nature of these forms of research (i.e. their genuine possibilities for understanding and improving education), the registers of understanding
(*Verstehen*; reasons) and/versus those of explanation (*Erklären*; causes); the necessity of an interpretive stance in social science; the nature of prediction in social
science; causality and (in)determinism in educational research; the very relevance
of educational research and the demand that research needs to be "relevant"; the
implications of internationalisation (c.q. Anglicisation) of educational research;
publication pressures and the fixation on citations and impact factors; homogenisa-
tion of educational research; the importance of irony, evocation, expression, and
more generally, the literary in educational research; narrative research and its importance for understanding education; commitment on the part of the educational
researcher, her engagement with practice and real educational issues; representa-
tionalism and non-representationalism in educational research and theory; educationalisation; material culture in educational research; and the relevance and place
of philosophy and history of education for educational research.

Expressing these in Wittgensteinian ways, Paul's work not only criticises the still
dominant positivist hold on educational research, but also tempers the perhaps more
radical counterparts to this positivist predominance; specifically, the critiques of the

---

[6] The recent wave of psychologists populating research units in educational sciences and studies
must surely sadden him.

state and status of research and the university that have tended to be informed by the poststructuralist and postmodernist schools of thought (i.e., authors such as Foucault, Lyotard, Lacan, Derrida, Agamben, and so on). His engagement with these authors, developed in collaboration with, among others, Nigel Blake, Richard Smith, and Paul Standish, does not seek to deny the major contributions this thinking makes to philosophy, nor is it questioning the many ways in which these authors have been (and still are inspirational) for philosophy of education. Indeed, he writes:

> In some sense I had embraced the Wittgensteinean stance and even the analytical approach of philosophy of education, yet at the same time I was tempted by the Continental position and it seemed obvious to me that what they argued for was not only interesting and relevant but moreover profound. All of this came together in a particular reading of Wittgenstein's work, who is for many not only an analytic philosopher *pur sang* but as well someone who introduced several Continental themes and who set the agenda for a good part of the discussion in philosophy in the second half of the twentieth century (Smeyers, 2014, p. 234).

The development of Paul's interest in poststructuralist and postmodernist thought and his contribution to educational thought in that vein are recollected in Richard Smith and Paul Standish's discussion in Chap. 3.

Paul's bringing Wittgenstein to bear on the influence of poststructuralism on educational research can be seen in the way he writes about – cautions his fellow philosophers of education about – *being carried away* by these poststructuralist writers' profundity, to the point that accounts of education and educational research become one-sided and ignore the flesh and blood of real educational practices that feature real persons. His writings about these strands in philosophy of education can in a genuine sense be called true to the Wittgensteinian project. He likens the movement of those inspired by such strands to that of the traditional philosopher who is Wittgenstein's interlocutor in the *Philosophical Investigations*. Wittgenstein asks: "is the word ever actually used in this way in the language-game which is its original home" (1953, #116). Similarly, Paul raises questions to the very effect of trying to "bring words back to" their ordinary use, and hence helps to sketch the contours of a/the picture in the eye of the philosophical beholder. Of course, this is not to say that we do not always picture reality in a certain way. But sometimes that picture gets a hold of us, instead of the other way around, and we seem to be "bewitched" by it, to use another Wittgensteinian expression, and hence unable to see anything other than what is offered through the framework of that picture.

In the face of a particular picture of what research is today, this seems to take on a double importance: to be both reminded of the constitution of that picture and our place in it, and of the tools we use to describe, understand, and resist it. It is often assumed that it is the tropes of postmodernism – subjectivity, the end of grand narratives, and the exposure of "truth" as constructed – that are at the root of what is currently termed "post-truth". In Chap. 7, Michael Peters provides a timely reminder that various theories of truth have been contested in the history of philosophy and not only in and by the Continental tradition. Peters provides an account of this history and of the ways in which Paul and others were involved in developing an account of postfoundationalism for education. As the quote from Paul, above, suggests, this enabled the articulation of the Continental themes in Wittgenstein's work as well as, importantly, a tempering of the more extreme tendencies in the application of those themes to educational thought and practice. If the "metaphysical" that Wittgenstein struggles with in his philosophising can be paralleled with the hyperbolical – something Cavell describes as "speaking outside language-games" (1979, p. 207) – the questions Paul raises ("Is this really the case?", "Can x really be understood as …?", etc.) work to temper a philosopher's excitement, not to the effect of ending up with some unsatisfying moderateness, but with the effect of invoking a register of the real, that is, real for us, as human beings, of flesh and blood.

Family Resemblances

This last point in particular speaks to Paul's philosophical interest in the human condition as such, seen in his writings about skepticism (and living with it), desire, irony, authenticity, the importance of the aesthetic, care for the self, etc. in line with the works of Cavell, Nietzsche, Heidegger, Foucault, Lacan, and, of course, Wittgenstein – an interest shared by many of his colleagues in the Research Community. This wariness of extremes is evident in his taking seriously not only the implications of Wittgenstein's thought for formal education and educational research practices, but also for education in its broadest sense, from raising children to what Cavell would call "the education of grownups" (1979, p. 125). Paul writes:

> Following Wittgenstein education has to be thought of as an initiation into practices. And being part of this shared social practice constitutes the subject being inscribed in the intersubjective order; it characterizes as well knowledge and epistemology as what is right to do and ethics. Embracing a 'view from nowhere' as well as 'giving up justifying what I do' are developments exemplifying an unwillingness to live the 'scepticism' which characterizes human existence (Smeyers, 2014, p. 235).

Here, and in his tempering of the claims of poststructuralist-influenced accounts, the political dimension of (his) scholarship comes to the fore; acknowledging the constitution of our conditions and reminding his audience of the "rough ground" needed to at least get somewhere (some real place) rather than adding to – or simply rejecting – calls for radical overthrow of the status quo, which he sees as an abdication of our responsibility.

Paul has written about schools and families, about teaching and (what is now predominantly called) parenting, addressing and entangling that specific human activity we call "educating" children (in a broad sense), its inherent challenges and the ways it has been challenged because of the changing conditions in which educators and children have found themselves over the decades. In this respect Paul has written about the justification of an educator's (parent's, teacher's) intervention in a context of increasing pluralisation of values, and about the possibility, limitations, but also necessity of initiation (in and after postmodernism; cf. e.g. Lyotard's loss of grand narratives); about initiation's so-called conservatism; the very possibility of an educational project; the educational relationship as an inherently ethical relationship; about love, care, trust, and power (and the unavoidability of the latter) in educational relationships; about paternalism; about education as a "practice"; about nihilistic readings of raising and educating children at the *fin de siècle*; about the particularity of the pedagogical relationship; the integrity of the educator, the "I" of the educator, her authenticity, engagement and commitment (the unavoidability of it) against the background of postmodernism's and poststructuralism's over-throwing of the subject and its intentionality; about government intervention in families; the intrusion of an expert discourse in matters of childrearing; the idea of risks in education; the rights discourse in matters of parent-child relationships; about the limitations of empirical educational research in the area of raising children; about the lure of neuropsychology in childrearing, and about neuroeducation; about relativism and skepticism in contexts of education; about cosmopolitanism and the self; about performativity in matters of education; about moral education and values education; about the necessary corrective of currents such as progressivism and utopianism for a traditional hierarchical understanding of the pedagogical relationship, but also about their (necessary) limits.

Clearly, then, on a formal level, the family as a pedagogical institution, educational relationships, and what is at stake in these, have been an ongoing concern of his research. What always figures at the background of his position is his stance on the educational relationship, which is, for him, always a personal and ethical relationship, a relationship between real persons, of flesh and blood, with all their virtues and vices, with their inevitable inheritances and individual intentions.

His concern for the personal and ethical has not been merely an abstract concern or performed only in his writing, but also is evident in how he worked, and indeed how he initiated his students in to the field of philosophy of education and into this form of life we call academia. As a doctoral promotor, Paul passed on his belief that one's years as PhD student are formative ("vormend"; cf. the German *Bildung*) for the rest of one's life. Paul was deeply convinced that what you study and learn during your doctoral years will stay with you for the rest of your career/life, will always be part of how you will approach issues to come. No doubt him saying this was prompted by his own experience – the depth of the impression Wittgenstein's work made on him and the way that that work, the thinking performed in it, shaped his view on things – but, having been doctoral students ourselves, looking back on this, it is, simply, true. The imprint of the philosophers we studied during our years as doctoral students on our world-picture is immeasurable. We cannot really remember what it was like to look at the world before, or imagine what it would look like without, those insights that collectively make up the frameworks provided by their writings. (This, arguably, is why we might more properly call it educational philosophy, not philosophy of education.)

At that time, as students, we were not only initiated into ways of seeing the world but perhaps, held captive by a certain picture of what it meant to be an academic, to work in a university, one embodied by our doctoral supervisors and the older generation of academics who formed the philosophy of education community more generally. In the intervening two decades, however, much has changed, a feature not unacknowledged by Paul himself:

> Whether it be for tenure, promotion, or funding applications, the paradigm of successful research from the natural sciences surfaces in the areas of psychology and educational research. It is almost impossible to row against that stream and it is young colleagues who suffer the most. Looking from the inside the sub-discipline is thriving … But the explosion of the dominant approach in educational research and the vast amounts of money that such research is allocated signal a different story. The gradual world-wide disappearance of philosophy and of philosophy of education from the university curricula cannot be misinterpreted. My concern could be seen as a nostalgic longing, yet I would argue that this diagnosis cannot be escaped (Smeyers, 2014, p. 243).

This is a very real and tangible concern and one reason why this volume is not a work of "nostalgic longing" but an opportunity to take account of Paul's work, of philosophy of education, of what has been passed on, of what we want to defend – the space and time of and for research of a particular kind – as academics today.

Finding Space and Time for Research

It is tricky – wise people would advise against it, we are sure – to try to "capture" a scholar's work in such a short introduction. We have tried to sketch a few characterisations, realising these are partial and only broad strokes. In the chapters that follow, however, the contributors offer not only substantive analyses of educational issues and questions, but also help to offer a more perspicuous picture of a number of matters we have only touched upon here. In different, but still related, senses, each of the chapters narrates one or more aspects of the idea of space and time for educational research: the space and time occupied by Paul, his work in the many collaborations with his colleagues and friends, and his formative role in the development of philosophy of education as an international field (Depaepe and Simon, Chap. 2; Smith and Standish, Chap. 3; Peters, Chap. 7); the space and time of a development of Wittgensteinian scholarship and its legacy in education (Cuypers, Chap. 8; also Peters, Chap. 7); the space and time of philosophy *pur sang* (Wittgensteinian style) (Van Bendegem, Chap. 9); the space and time for the "useless" educational-philosophical deepening of concepts (such as "hospitality", Fendler, Chap. 5) and the wider educational-philosophical import of these and similar undertakings (Burbules and Stone, Chap. 10); and the wider question of finding space and time for research (Bridges, Chap. 6; Masschelein and Simons, Chap. 4). The contributions also bring out what was valuable in the space and time that Paul, with Marc Depaepe, created as convenors of the Research Community in Philosophy and History of Educational Research: a space and time of collaboration, conversation, and collegiality.

We are grateful to all contributors for their wonderful and insightful chapters for this collection and for offering so many reminders, of different kinds and nature, about what mattered to Paul for many decades.

References

Cavell, S. (1979). *The claim of reason. Wittgenstein, skepticism, morality, and tragedy*. Oxford, NY: Oxford University Press.

Ramaekers, S. (2018). Childrearing, parenting, upbringing: Philosophy of education and the experience of raising a child. In P. Smeyers (Ed.), *International handbook of philosophy of education* (Vol. 2, pp. 995–1012). Dordrecht, The Netherlands: Springer.

Smeyers, P. (2014). A kind of spiral thinking: Philosophy of education through the eyes of a fellow traveller. In L. Waks (Ed.), *Leaders in philosophy of education: Intellectual self-portraits* (pp. 231–244). Rotterdam, The Netherlands: Sense.

Toscano, M. & Smeyers, P. (2018, Forthcoming). Paul Smeyers and a perspective on educational research: In dialogue with Maurizio Toscano. In J. Quay, J. Bleazby, S. Stolz, M. Toscano, & S. Webster (Eds.), *Using theory and philosophy in educational research*. Abingdon, UK: Routledge.

Wittgenstein, L. (1953). *Philosophical investigations* (3rd ed., G. E. M. Anscombe, Trans. ed.). Oxford, UK: Basil Blackwell.

Chapter 2
At the Intersection of Anecdotal Stories and Great Narratives: Reflections on the Cooperation Between Educational Historians and Educational Philosophers

Marc Depaepe and Frank Simon

> *The quantitative and anti-anthropocentric orientation of the natural sciences from Galileo on forced an unpleasant dilemma on the humane sciences: either assume a lax scientific system in order to attain noteworthy results, or assume a meticulous, scientific one to achieve results of scant significance.*
>
> (Carlo Ginzburg, 1992, p. 124)

Abstract Partly based on our publications in the series of Smeyers and Depaepe, but also on our experiences and discussions within the underpinning Research Community, we present in this chapter some meta-reflections on the potentialities of the history of education as a scientific discipline. First, we focus on the cooperation of educational historians and educational philosophers in the Research Community. What did we learn from each other? One of the things we hoped to acquire from the dialogue with philosophy was more theoretical depth – an argument that is further developed on the basis of the concept "grammar of educationalisation". However, the openness towards more theory in history should not exclude attention to the specific and unique in the always changing nature of the historically conditioned situation. On the contrary, as is shown in the final paragraph, the awareness of "presentism" in educational discourse is one of the lasting values of educational historiography.

M. Depaepe (✉)
Faculty of Psychology and Educational Sciences, Kulak Kortrijk Campus, Kortrijk, Belgium
e-mail: Marc.Depaepe@kuleuven.be

F. Simon
Ghent University, Ghent, Belgium
e-mail: Frank.Simon@Ugent.be

© Springer International Publishing AG, part of Springer Nature 2018
S. Ramaekers, N. Hodgson (eds.), *Past, Present, and Future Possibilities for Philosophy and History of Education*,
https://doi.org/10.1007/978-3-319-94253-7_2

By Way of Introduction

The authors in question have always regarded a *Festschrift* as a good opportunity to discuss their joint track record with the academic being honoured. While Marc Depaepe's relationship with Paul Smeyers, who has never concealed his interest in this type of *petite histoire* or anecdotal story, has been more long-standing than Frank Simon's, plenty of common reference points can still be found. Without a doubt, the source lies at the end of the last century, when the *Research Community: Philosophy and history of the discipline of education* was first convened. It met for the first time in Leuven from 18 to 20 October 2000. Subsequently, similar intensive seminars were organised on an almost annual basis, and it is ultimately as a result of these that the initiative arose for this *Festschrift*.

The idea for such a Research Community (RC) was conceived in the Department of Educational Sciences at KU Leuven, largely on the initiative of Paul Smeyers. Smeyers and Depaepe had first met here in the early 1970s, initially as students, subsequently as colleagues, as members of academic staff. They also worked together on the editorial team of the now defunct *Pedagogisch Tijdschrift* (1976–2004), the last generalist periodical on educational research in Flanders. This was the successor of the legendary *Vlaams(ch) Opvoedkundig Tijdschrift* (1919–1955), subsequently renamed *Tijdschrift voor Opvoedkunde* (1955–1975), after success-fully merging with more or less like-minded Dutch journals. As researchers and lecturers in the philosophy and history of educational sciences, respectively (and as the occasional co-organisers of the Belgian-Dutch days for pedagogues, which existed for these two foundation disciplines), they witnessed first-hand both the fur-ther breakthrough of the empirical approach as the dominant idea in educational research and the associated marginalisation of the philosophical and historical approaches. Incidentally, this scientific evolution was discussed in great detail in the, also since-abolished, specialised courses in the philosophy and history of edu-cational sciences, for which they had also been responsible in Leuven.

It was precisely from within this context that the idea was conceived to re-establish a dialogue between the history and the philosophy of education. These two approaches fortunately remained on the Leuven curriculum as general courses, but they were continuing to grow ever further apart at the international level, not only in terms of scientific organisation (associations, conferences, etc.) but also in terms of paradigm developments (Smeyers & Depaepe, 2015). As we will discuss in more detail below, the history of education had become increasingly "historic" and less "educational" from the 1970s onwards, whereas the philosophy of education seemed much more "philosophical" than before, especially in the minds of historians. This was manifested not just in the language used and the questions raised, but also in the method(s) that were applied. This may also explain why "thoroughbred" philoso-phers were involved, in 1999, in the establishment of the Leuven-based research community, all the more so given that the application for the required grant from the Research Foundation Flanders had to be submitted by various Flemish universities.

Specifically, the application was filed by Jean-Paul Van Bendegem, a philosopher of science at the Vrije Universiteit Brussel.

Mutatis mutandis the same could be said about the historian Frank Simon of Ghent University, were it not for the fact that he had specialised in the history of education from the outset and had worked together with Leuven from the 1970s onwards in this regard (see Depaepe & Simon, 2009 for further information). The establishment of the RC, for which Frank Simon had taken the initiative with others on behalf of Ghent University, served to lend this cooperation even more depth and lustre, after more than 25 years. Indeed, following Paul Smeyers' transfer, on 1 October 2007, to Ghent University, Frank Simon became his direct colleague in Ghent, albeit only for a couple of years, as he had to retire on 1 October 2009. That did not however prevent him from participating actively in the RC's research and activities, but in more of an advisory capacity.

The RC certainly did not aim to develop a general educational sciences model in line with the German model, founded on a "historic-systematic" method (i.e., with a historical and a theoretical component), which we believe was nevertheless subsequently misunderstood in Germany to be the case (Tenorth, 2015). Nor did this renewed dialogue between educational historians and educational philosophers solely and exclusively limit itself to combating the intrusiveness of the empirical "evidence-based", let alone the psychological research paradigm, even though in some circles it was perceived in that way (compare e.g. Phillips, 2013). In this context, a critical review of this scientific evolution using the tools that both disciplines intrinsically have at their disposal seemed more than sufficient. In addition to this however, there was the fervent hope that all parties could learn from each other even though everyone continued to do his or her own thing; taking account nevertheless of the sometimes great differences in approach within the same discipline, which, given the composition, certainly did not have to be regarded as a monolith. In the realm of the so-called new cultural history of education, for example, there were not only proponents of the "history of the present" model (Popkewitz, 2011, 2013; Priem & Fendler, 2015), which conceives of history in the Foucauldian sense as a discursive strategy, in this new-fangled cultural historiography. But also there were more pragmatically-oriented researchers, who, while going along with the so-called contemporary "turns" in cultural history in general (the visual, the sensorial, the material, the emotional, etc.), attempted to incorporate them critically and heuristically as part of a more sophisticated interpretation, rather than following them slavishly. For all intents and purposes, we regard ourselves as belonging to the latter group (Depaepe & Simon, 2009) although this by no means prevented us from sympathising with the former group, who, with their more theoretical choice for the "grand theory", sometimes came very close to certain educational philosophers (Masschelein & Simons, 2008).

On the contrary. Through the exchange of these diverse points of views between educational philosophers and educational historians (not to mention everything that might lie in between), we were counting on the history of education, traditionally starved of theory, being able to benefit on the theoretical level in a number of ways: for example, regarding the conceptual framework, the concepts used, the underlying relationship with the theory (including on the sociological level and in terms of the relationship with society), a reflection on how best to deal with the past, the mapping out of historiographical developments and of theoretical and methodological trends and debates, and further interaction with the history of science and knowledge (e.g. Lässig, 2016). These were all matters in which we had already expressed our interest, also outside the RC. In terms of philosophical research in the educational sciences, we above all looked forward to the authors studied being placed in context and possibly also for their claims of absoluteness to be qualified as a result. Such claims do not just colour the "great narratives" of these authors and their theories, but also, often, albeit subconsciously, seem to confer a superior status to philosophy over history.

Did all of this amount to anything? This also appears to be the key question for the editors of this *Festschrift*, to which they also link the hypothesis that the RC's objectives were barely achieved. They posited in their invitation to contributors that the RC was not capable of influencing mainstream research in the educational sciences. In fact, what happened was worse. Both of these so-called sub-disciplines were further marginalised due to all kinds of developments in science and society – not least those relating to the material conditions in which philosophical and historical research must be conducted in educational institutions. Chairs in both of these disciplines continued to be abolished and they were deemed ever less relevant to and sometimes disappeared altogether from the curricula of teacher training programmes – which have historically always been the cradle of teaching in both these disciplines. Not only did this involve a narrowing of the educational sciences, it also paved the way for the further monopolisation of educational research by the evidence-based paradigm.

Below, we will devote the first part of our reflection to this hypothesis. The editors' interest, however, extends beyond the occasional contemporary failure of the historical and philosophical approaches in the educational sciences. They also wonder what the lasting value (and therefore also the legitimation of the raison d'être) is of history and of philosophy in education, with a view to safeguarding the future of both of these disciplines. We have also thought and written extensively on this subject, concerning its historical aspect of course, (see e.g. Van Nieuwenhuyse, Simon, & Depaepe, 2015, on which we will base ourselves further for the last part). In a second part of this text, we endeavour to recapitulate a number of our points of view, correlating them with more recent trends in general, cultural historiography, naturally also in relation to the developing social context. The issue of presentism, which is almost inextricably linked to the practice of history, is at the heart of our reflection.

On the Cooperation Between Educational Historians and Educational Philosophers in the RC

Previous writings have already speculated at length on the initial objectives of the RC. We are of the opinion that a distinction should be made between the ambition of enriching one's own research on the one hand, and the ambition of reorienting mainstream research across the entire field of educational sciences on the other. The latter aspect has never really been on the agenda, certainly as far as educational historians are concerned. At least, not as an effect to be pursued directly. Probably because, as mentioned, educational historiography has found much more of a common ground with social and cultural historiography. In that sense, defining the history of education as a "sub-discipline" of the educational sciences continues to be difficult – although this is something that "pedagogues" usually do. It is possible that the same question can be raised about educational philosophy, but it is not up to us to answer this question. Something we as education historians can do, however, is refer to the 1970s again. As a consequence of the large number of students who enrolled, in Leuven too, in the educational studies programme in the wake of the symbolic (and revolutionary) year of 1968, academic staff worked tirelessly to develop an encyclopaedic structure of the educational sciences. Following such prominent German examples as Friedhelm Nicolin (1969), Smeyers' supervisor Cyriel C. De Keyser was the great pioneer in Leuven in this regard. In that context, it is also worth comparing his admiration for the much talked about attempt of Wolfgang Brezinka (1972) to transform the largely humanistic *Pädagogik* into an empirical-analytical *Erziehungswissenschaft*, to which educational history was made subordinate, like a sort of "reservoir of hypotheses". This obviously significantly impeded its pursuit of "emancipation" (cf. Tröhler, 2017). Under such an arrangement, it was not merely hypothetical that a blind spot would develop around the important work that historians themselves had carried out. The history of the child and of youth, which was developed in France among other countries, thanks to "mentality historians" such as Philippe Ariès (see Dekker & Groenendijk, 2012; Van Damme & Simon, 1988/1989), who drew on the *Annales* School for inspiration, is probably a good example of this challenge as it took quite some time before the domain was "appropriated" as such by pedagogues.

Nevertheless, this is not yet any reason to contract out the history of education for good to general, social, and cultural historians. It goes without saying that educational historiography – possibly a better name for the old-fashioned "historical pedagogy" that is still in current use in various Germanic languages – must at least pay attention to the "educational" view. Even though the question of who actually conducts the research, in terms of his or her professional background and training, continues to be very relevant, all things considered. In this regard, we have advocated for many years now (see the arguments of Depaepe, 2010) in favour of more interdisciplinary cooperation, not just with historians but also with many others, such as anthropologists, sociologists, theologians, literature scientists and … of course also pedagogues (in all their various sub-specialisms, such as educationalists, special education professionals, social workers) and philosophers (including educational philosophers). It is also important to note that we have *de facto* tried to make this cooperation a reality, and as a result have at the same time demonstrated that historical research does not have to be an individualistic undertaking in and of itself, but can also and equally validly be the subject of real teamwork!

Interdisciplinary cooperation is much more than a buzzword. The history of our discipline shows that substantive and methodological innovations mostly originate from the cross-pollination of various approaches. It hardly need be mentioned that Michel Foucault greatly contributed to a better understanding of the history of education by introducing genealogy in philosophy as a method to underpin critical analysis; not in the least by studying the historic forms of exclusion that coincided with a discourse of normalisation and/or disciplining. Elsa Roland (2017) recently proved how inspiring this can be for the study of educational developments in Belgium in general and those in Brussels in particular. In our view it goes without saying that there is more to this story besides this, for educational historiography. Ultimately, historical educational research involves much more than filling in pre-established frameworks, or whipping up a Foucauldian variant of well-known matters (a practice that is unfortunately seen in South America, where history of education is currently flourishing, as well as even among our own doctoral students now and again). Because these heuristically often very interesting but nonetheless very granular frameworks can often take on a completely different perspective from the viewpoint of history (and of the history of science of educational historiography!). This is especially the case if the handwork that necessarily precedes any development of a historical theory shows that these frameworks are not quite right, and should preferably be replaced with new, more finely-meshed frameworks, that are developed out of educational historiography itself (Tenorth, 1996).

And it is precisely in this regard that the *petites histoires*, for which Paul Smeyers likes to attribute the competence to educational historians, may possibly crop up again. In our opinion, the life and work of less prominent pedagogues – the Ghent lecturer Jozef Emiel Verheyen (Depaepe, Simon, & Van Gorp, 2006), or his colleague in Leuven (and possibly also rival in the struggle over the educational legacy of Ovide Decroly, who will be discussed below) Raymond Buyse (Depaepe, D'hulst, & Simon, 2013), to name but two, are a good example of such anecdotal stories. Often their opinions are connected with very specific events in their lives. Ten years ago, Depaepe (2007) attempted to demonstrate this, on Smeyers' request, regarding the relationship of educational history with educational philosophy, also on the basis of Foucault's biography (including his relationship with the above-mentioned Ariès). History's statements do not primarily focus on the timeless (or non-contemporary) and therefore potentially "nomothetic" aspect of things. Quite the opposite in fact: it zooms in on the contemporary, the specific or (unique) and therefore always the changing nature of the historically conditioned situation. That is why it also prefers an ideographical approach (following the centuries-old dichotomy that Wilhelm Windelband and, in his footsteps, Wilhem Dilthey, established between the *erklären* of the natural sciences and the *verstehen* of the humanities (see Kleinberg, 2016 and further regarding the implications of the research in terms of education, Smith & Keiner, 2015)). In this context, the acceptance of a scientifically weaker status, as indicated in the opening quote by Carlo Ginzburg (1992), does not so much constitute a logical consequence as an implication that must be socially defended. After all, the reputation and prestige of a scientific discipline are not first and foremost related to processes that are internal to science, but to factors that are social and therefore *de facto* external to science, such as a person's professional status and career. This can also be illustrated with the emergence of the seemingly very successful empirical movement in the educational and educational psychological sciences (Depaepe, 1993).

But we digress. Let us return to the more finely-meshed conceptual frameworks of educational history, which we hoped would acquire more theoretical depth as a result of the confrontation with educational philosophers in the RC. One of these frameworks related to the "grammar of schooling" – a conceptual key developed at Stanford by Larry Cuban, David Tyack, and William Tobin – to better understand the resistance to innovation in education. When applied to the history of primary education in Belgium, from the end of the nineteenth century to well into the twentieth century, we had developed an educational complement for this – "the grammar of educationalisation" (sometimes also translated as "grammar of pedagogisation", and possibly even most precisely as "grammar of educationalising") (see Depaepe & Smeyers, 2008). In brief, the possible added value of both these "grammars" resides in the fact that their starting premise is educational practice in schools. The difference between the first and the second is primarily related to the aspects they cover. "Schooling" refers to the hard cores and patterns of the formal educational game that the teacher and the pupil play every day in class, whereas educationalisation is much more interested in the underlying moral-educational meaning that must be used to explain behaviour in school.

Our question about a more substantiated use of the concept of "educationalisation" in any event lay at the basis of one of the RC's meetings. In addition, we published a themed issue of *Educational Theory*, as well as a book in the RC series. We consider the fact that the concept thus became more commonplace, thanks to the intervention of David Labaree (2008), in the USA and more particularly at Stanford as our own modest contribution, which may serve to qualify the idea of "grammar of schooling" developed there. For all clarity, we must nevertheless add that this "educationalisation" has been interpreted in many different ways right up to the present day, despite the demand for further theoretical reflection (Bürgi, 2016; Heinze, Witte, & Rieger-Ladich, 2016; Tröhler, 2017) and is still for the most part used as an umbrella term. But the fact that the introduction to that themed issue was recently translated into Portuguese (Depaepe & Smeyers, 2016), demonstrates that the RC's activities did not go entirely unnoticed, at least within the boundaries of its own disciplines. This claim can be easily demonstrated with the themed issue that the *Zeitschrift für Pädagogik* devoted to the Leuven initiative. Besides the reflections of the initiators and the above-mentioned commentary by Tenorth (2015), RC members also published a further two articles on the subject (Priem & Fendler, 2015; Smith & Keiner, 2015). Indeed, Priem and Fendler (2015) refer to the same relationship between educational history and educational philosophy – a relationship which, according to the title, probably oscillates somewhere between a rational divorce and a *mariage d'amour*. Regardless, their essay argues strongly in favour of more "permeability" between the two. That greater permeability must help understand the historical entanglement of the methodologies and analytical instruments used by researchers, including among others our representations of "transfer", "adaptation", "hybridity", "translation", etc. At the same time, it can also inspire us to make a more balanced and ethically responsible choice between these methodologies, from a philosophical point of view. Masschelein and Simons (2008), for example, called on educational historians to start their reflections from a specific philosophical, i.e., ascetic ethos, because of discontent and discomfort about the current situation, in a themed issue of the RC in *Paedagogica Historica* (Smeyers & Depaepe, 2008). As a result, philosophy is conceived as an intrinsic educational objective (and not as a doctrine, meta-theory, or method that educational historians should use as a starting premise).

"Proving" that our own research has become more aware of theory thanks to the dialogue with educational philosophers is of course difficult, but we do think this is the case. In any event, this dialogue has encouraged reflection and self-reflection, also in terms of establishing an educational history. When asked how both our disciplines provide arguments, develop rationales and an argumentation, we purposefully chose to take the readers on a visit of the "workshop" of the historical-educational researcher (Depaepe & Simon, 2009). We took a walk down the path that we have covered together since the 1970s, which undoubtedly further increased attention for the possibilities and boundaries of the methods used and for the chosen source material. We considered the intensive RC seminars to be *de facto* intellectual training of the highest level – and we suspect that educational philosophers may have come to the same conclusion. In the themed issue of *Paedagogica Historica* that we mentioned above, Paul Standish (2008) attempted to refute the criticism of the educational historians on the claims to absoluteness of philosophy (perhaps he was arguing against Tröhler, 2007, rather than Depaepe, 2007 – who can say?), by pointing out that the claims system targeted by philosophy was much more differentiated and indescribably more complex than is suggested in this criticism. Others, including Paul Smeyers (2008) himself, meanwhile, seized the diversity of "genres" in educational research as an opportunity to argue in favour of methodological pluralism. The study of education covers various forms of knowledge, depending on its objectives. And, as far as the interpretative aspect is concerned, to which educational history and educational philosophy belong, a possibly educational focus on the optimisation of practice does not in any way absolve researchers from taking a hygienic approach to empiricism: "The writing of research may be seen as what prevents us from being absorbed in the chaos of unmediated complexity. It allows us time to think and is performed at some distance in the interests of perspective and justice" (Smeyers, 2008, p. 705; see also Smith & Keiner, 2015).

We can only endorse such ideas. In view of the complexity of the problems analysed on the one hand and the limited nature of our knowledge and expression skills on the other, we have always argued in favour of multiple perspectives on educational history. Furthermore we also learned – something that undoubtedly is also the RC's merit – that scientific debates should preferably be stripped of their evangelising, yes, often even missionary, aim to disseminate the "conviction that only we are right". A dialogue with others does not always have to be aimed in the first place at convincing the other, let alone converting him or her to one's own viewpoint. Listening is an option too. And learning to live with the diversity of opinions and points of view. Anyone who demonstrates understanding for the perspective from which a certain conviction arose, even from a theoretical-methodological viewpoint, learns to qualify the major debates and also to relativise them. Such an approach does not have to culminate in relativism, it can also result in wisdom. After all, the path that leads to a given paradigm encompasses more than a rational reconstruction of arguments. It also involves countless opinions about how knowledge operates in society.

This constant change in perspective constitutes, at least in our opinion (Depaepe, 2005), an added value that can be obtained through historical educational research. Since the dawn of time, understanding the notion of diversity of points of view has led to wisdom, in the sense that one can understand these viewpoints without having to share them unconditionally. This applies in particular to the history of the science of the educational field, which we have attempted to demonstrate extensively in the RC by focusing on Ovide Decroly (1871–1932) (following from Depaepe, Simon, & Van Gorp, 2003). Thanks to many of our interventions, we succeeded in demystifying the discourse that to date has often been exaggerated regarding this educational innovator. Our aim was not to ridicule him, but precisely to make him more human. Something that was extremely appreciated within the RC by our colleagues from the University of Brussels but also beyond (Roland, 2017). Such a critical voice is very rare in the glorification of the pre-war interest in the child and the innovations in education that followed from this and which were often conceived as the result of a predominantly German-speaking *Reformpädagogik* – as rare in fact as attention to the contribution of French-speaking educational psychology (see e.g., Barz, 2017; Németh, Stöck, & Vincze, 2017).

Mutatis mutandis we have attempted to do the same in regard to the now very popular heritage education in general and the commemoration of the war in particular. Here too we estimate that historical research can help deflate many myths and much rhetoric, although one still often runs the risk of stepping on people's toes when working in the field with the custodians of this heritage. The handling of the "matter" of the museum of education in Ypres, which was painful for us, and which ended with its closure in spite of our arguments within the RC to maintain it (Depaepe & Simon, 2016), abundantly proves this. And indeed so does the answer about the term "dark tourism", which was formulated outside our discipline, and rejected by the heritage supporters as being disrespectful and even offensive to the many "pious pilgrims" (Dendooven, 2017).

We think that the historical-educational discipline's lasting value for the future resides in the critical-constructive corrective against such contemporary discourses, which usually rely on the political, social, and cultural self-interest of certain groups and individuals in society to gather steam. We will discuss this shortly. Like every other historical approach in and of itself, it can act as a dam against the dangers of any presentist attitude whatsoever (Rüsen, 2017). It goes without saying that such a presentist attitude is rife in times of post-truth and a so-called "alternative" view of the past. The reference to the very simple, ahistorical, and atheoretical way of thinking, which suits sponsors and politicians like Trump in equal measure in a neoliberal setting (and which therefore also encourages one-sided "fact"-oriented research, see among others Depaepe, 2017) is sufficient for the time being. With Latour (2017, p. 53) we can qualify this as "post-political" disdain for the world, including the denial of the effective problems that threaten our planet. This, in turn, according to Latour, appeals to the role of the historical researcher as a public intellectual. He or she should engage in the public debate – more than is customary – something that philosophers (including educational philosophers) probably find utterly normal (Masschelein & Simons, 2008), but which causes reticence in a large number of historians (including educational historians). And yet they too can anticipate historical anniversaries, be alert to current issues that require a more global context, and make themselves heard through social media, with critical remarks and questions ... not least when the often complex historical background is mocked, whether consciously or not. Which seamlessly brings us back to the problem of presentism.

The Awareness of Presentism in the Educational Discourse as One of the Lasting Values of Educational History

While the notion of "presentism" can ultimately be qualified as "slippery, amorphous and polyvalent" (Walsham, 2017), this "problem" (Hartog, 2012, 2013), historically speaking, is very closely linked to the almost unshakeable belief in social progress (Coss, 2017). Since the emergence of a largely Eurocentric idea of "modernity", (Western) society has constantly changed, an idea that was above all propagated and achieved in the eighteenth century. Whereas continuity especially was the norm under the *Ancien Régime*, change became the main characteristic of the moderns. Awareness of the huge fracture between past and present took shape in a new understanding of reality, which was no longer seen as virtually timeless and unchanging, but rather as a process of constant evolution and even revolution. The consciousness of the fact that there was a gaping gulf between the past and modern times gave rise from the end of the eighteenth century to a "modern" "historical consciousness", or consciousness that the past has ended for good and is thus different from the present (Tollebeek, 2002).

The pace of this change increased constantly during the past 250 years. Moreover, according to Rosa (2005), this process of permanently accelerating change is driven first and foremost by the economic logic of capitalism in which time is money, and money a scarce commodity. There can be no excuse for losing time and so it must be used "productively". At the same time, however, the capitalist system creates a feeling of alienation, or at times even unease, uncertainty. The wave of economic, social, and cultural change creates a rift with the familiar world view and brings with it a loss of footing. This sets the scene for a harking back to the past, and it does so in numerous ways. It can take the form, for example, of a nostalgic, fervent, and comforting desire for the past, or of a *historia magistra vitae* for the present, a past from which lessons must be learned, or a past recoverable through heritage to serve present political, social, and educational ends. In other words, the past is used in an instrumental manner to draw "lessons" for the present, or to form good citizens rather than critical disciplinary thinkers. As we have already mentioned above, we have demonstrated this in various publications, both in the framework of the history of the origin of the traditional history of education and in the framework of today's history education (compare Van Nieuwenhuyse, Simon, & Depaepe, 2015 whose key ideas we will use below).

Nevertheless, we would like to briefly discuss this in more detail, to refine the discussion with educational philosophers further. Because the complaint that the (for the most part recent) past is mobilised and reformulated in presentism *"selon les urgences du jour"* (Rousso, 2012) possibly still applies to some approaches in education. Take, for example, the notion of creativity, which is understood in today's neoliberal society more and more as "entrepeneurship". On the other hand – and Lynn Fendler (2008) strongly emphasised this in her contributions to the RC based on an approach founded on a *history of the present* – presentism may also have a positive side. As the influence of the present on the view of the past is a *conditio sine qua non* that the historical researcher cannot ignore, we must first and foremost be aware of this problem. Such a "strategic" presentism, which "consciously" considers the contemporary assumptions in their literal sense can undoubtedly raise questions about the complacency or the self-declared evidence of certain pedagogical interventions that are deemed natural. Moreover this puts the various technologies of the pedagogical intervention (which not only manifest themselves in educational practice but also in the language used and in the associated *ways of thinking*) into perspective. We can, after all, walk back down the path from the present to the past. This is called to *"reiterate"*. And this is the number one key verb we use to indicate how we must find out which path was covered, against the chronology of time, to arrive at the present. And how it became "genealogical". But such a "strategic" presentism, in any event, can in principle always be distinguished from what we can call "crude" presentism, which starts from a simplistic, linear and/or finalistic relationship between the past, present, and future. Unlike the strategic approach, this crude or, perhaps better said, unconscious presentism takes no account whatsoever of the complexity with which these three dimensions of time in human life are linked to each other.

It's true that people live in the present, but that doesn't mean that they're unaware of their past. They constantly carry the traces of the past with them, while so-called plans for the future are often constructs that are attributed to the present or past, albeit *a posteriori*, precisely because they want to introduce coherence and rationality in their own life histories. Through memory, individuals store not only knowledge, but also experience of things that have happened, and they incorporate these memories constantly in the living of their life. Every individual, and by extension society as a whole, approaches the past from some perspective or other, then attempts to reconstruct it and, in doing so, attribute meaning to it (Jenkins, 2009). One significant dimension of a "complete" historical consciousness is therefore that one learns to recognise the status of knowledge of the past and use of the past, and learns to assess its value. In the end, a historian works not on the past as such, but on "time", as Bantigny (2013) contended a few years ago, and this category has an inherent leaning towards the constant interplay of the past, present, and future dimensions.

In that sense it is certainly good to know that working with historical *exempla* (initially taken as positive, but after the two World Wars often also as negative examples, opening the "hunt" for the "blemished" past) in academic historiography, including in educational historiography, was purposefully eschewed in the last decades of the previous century (Jensen, Leerssen, & Mathijsen, 2010). Gradually researchers turned their backs on the nineteenth-century "utilitarian" perspective (which, in the history of education as such was above all interested in citizenship building in the emerging nation state, whereas the formation of "educatorship" would have played a central role in that same context in the history of education, cf. Bruter, 2012; Gautherin, 2002). First and foremost, they traded it in for a more "realistic" perspective, which attempted to approach history again on its own terms and in its own right; subsequently, under the influence of post-modernism, for an increasingly expanding epistemology of "multi-perspectivism", in which knowledge of the past was inevitably regarded as interlinked with the historian's current perspective, both with the perspectives and the cultural representations of the historical actors themselves (Munslow, 1997).

The fundamental problem, however, is that the historical culture as a whole in society did not follow or barely followed the academic historiography in that self-reflective, multi-perspectivist discourse. This has created an increasingly large gulf between the two as the *common sense* continues to swear by a utilitarian epistemology (Rosenzweig & Thelen, 1998; Samuel, 1994). The prevailing discourse of the ordinary man in the street, and of policy-makers, who rely on them for their vote in the short term, stopped short at a profitability aimed at utility and profit. As a result, in-depth cultural-historical research was perceived by society perhaps not as ballast but as a superfluous luxury. Judging by the flourishing remembrance sites on the internet, we might even say that remembering now appears to have become more important than the writing of history. Besides personal remembrance, collective remembrance is growing strongly in importance. Since the fall of Communism, and increasing globalisation and associated migrations, governments around the world have been giving an ever more prominent role to a shared knowledge of the past, for the purposes, yet again, of citizenship and identity formation. Here too in Flanders, this trend currently takes shape in the requirement, in the above-mentioned cross-curricular attainment targets, of what is known as "remembrance education" and "heritage education". This trend has also become the subject of a genuine heritage industry and remembrance or commemoration management. Heritage experts, who come together in heritage units, search out on our behalf the things that need to be preserved, the sites of our archaeological heritage that are deserving of protection. This planned and ready-made "remembering" (and its correlative, planned and ready-made "forgetting") naturally implies the cultivation of a sort of public history. Consciously wishing to remember is part of the development of the new identity-formers' dispositive power. We mustn't lose the things that are important to our cultural identity. Or that can help develop a desired framework of standards and values. This reduces our interaction with the past once again into a very selective and instrumental event, based on current objectives. Only those aspects of the past that are of service and of use today are retained, or so it seems. The logic used in the process of giving meaning to the past is a present-oriented logic, which is not that of the past itself. This leads not only to a highly selective, but also a very context-bare interaction with the past. This is because past events are no longer studied in their own space and time, but only for their use to modern society, where the historic context no longer plays a meaningful role (Van Nieuwenhuyse & Wils, 2012). Also, concern for heritage and the act of remembrance associated with it is mainly a strategy in, of, and for the present – a regime of temporality that is omnipresent in our society (compare Hartog, 2012, but also Patrimoine, 2018), partly through fear of an uncertain future, that we naturally create ourselves.

Nevertheless, historical understanding, also in relation to education and teaching, precisely goes, in our view, beyond the limited view of present time by making it clear among other things that the prevailing impulse towards utility is still part of the lengthy process of modernisation. As a result it also holds open the door, albeit theoretically, to the above-mentioned "critical correction", which could exist from the cultivation of the culture of the non-utilitarian. All in all this amounts to the construct of a historical science "with a human subject that discovers the past as people construct it" (after Barros in Depaepe, 2005, p. 57) – which again involves a consciousness of our own relativity (and the discretion associated with this), because it is largely in relation to this that historical consciousness can serve as an antidote to the reign of the immediately useable. The science of history in general, and the science of the history of education in particular, can hardly be reduced to a supplier of academic speeches on the anniversaries of educational institutions (Coss, 2017). Historians of education are certainly not usually the first speakers organisers think of because if they really take their (self-)critical task to heart – we are talking from some experience of our own – they often run the risk of being regarded as a "thorn in one's side". Because an analysis that is divergent from the prevailing opinion, which dares to build a dam against the ever-encroaching category of the past and contradict the opinions of trend-watchers and experience experts that are not always as insightful as they seem, even though these experts increasingly seem to have the last word on everything in our society, will obviously inspire a sense of discomfort. This critical analysis usually does not mesh with the simple story that ordinary citizens wish to hear as "consumers" of this history of the past because of its qualifications and relativisations. As we already mentioned, we do not think it is possible to draw direct lessons from the past for the future, given the variations in contexts and epochs.

But heritage, remembrance, and commemoration can be used alongside research to give people a better understanding of the past, and on that basis to set them thinking, always mindful of the historical contexts. They will undoubtedly offer inspiration to reflect on educational processes without immediately wishing to evaluate or condemn them – or as Spinoza judiciously noted in 1675 in his *Tractatus Politicus*: *"Non ridere, non lugere, neque detestari, sed intelligere"* ("not to ridicule, not to bewail, not to scorn, but to understand"). And this understanding, whether we like it or not, usually starts with "anecdotal" histories, rather than with "great" narratives.

It may well be the case, to paraphrase Hartog (2013, pp. 28–36), that Mnemosyne (the Titaness who was the personification of memory in Greek mythology) has taken the place of her daughter Clio, and that history will ultimately return as a history of the memory, of remembrance. Gaining an understanding of the making of history, of the tensions between present and past, of the use of the past and of interaction, is by no means a superfluous luxury. Instead it is a daily undertaking, that we continue to work on with pleasure with a view to the future. Or as Catherine Hall (2017, pp. 262–263) once expressed it so aptly: "Embracing the possibility of thinking more critically, reflecting dialectically on the relation between past, present and future, probing the silences and absences in the archives, being self-conscious about the limitations imposed on us by the present we inhabit, engaging with politics of changing the course of history by writing about it – that seems a kind of work worth doing" – a sentiment we wholeheartedly hope Paul Smeyers will echo as he commences his retirement.

References

Bantigny, L. (2013). Historicités du 20e siècle. Quelques jalons sur une notion. *Vingtième siècle. Revue d'histoire, 117*(1), 13–25.

Barz, H. (Ed.). (2017). *Handbuch der Reformpädagogik*. Wiesbaden, Germany: Springer.

Brezinka, W. (1972). *Von der Pädagogik zur Erziehungswissenschaft: Eine Einführung in der Metatheorie der Erziehung*. Weinheim, Germany/Basel, Switzerland: Beltz.

Bruter, A. (2012). Teaching the past in the early modern era: Two different ways to make use of history. *Paedagogica Historica, 48*(6), 800–809.

Bürgi, R. (2016). The free world and the cult of expertise: The rise of the OECD's Educationalizing technocracy. *International Journal for the Historiography of Education, 6*(2), 159–175.

Coss, P. (2017). Presentism and the "Myth" of Magna Charta. *Past and Present, 234*, 227–235.

Dekker, J. J. H., & Groenendijk, L. F. (2012). Philippe Ariès's discovery of childhood after fifty years: The impact of a classic study on educational research. *Oxford Review of Education, 38*(2), 133–147.

Dendooven, D. (2017). Het herdenkingsgebeuren in Ieper: "dark tourism"? *VIFF Magazine, 62*, 12–14.

Depaepe, M. (1993). *Zum Wohl des Kindes? Pädologie, pädagogische Psychologie und experimentelle Pädagogik in Europa und den USA, 1890–1940*. Leuven, Belgium/Weinheim, Germany: Leuven University Press/Deutscher Studien Verlag.

Depaepe, M. (2005). Geen ambacht zonder werktuigen. Reflecties over de conceptuele omgang met het pedagogisch verleden. In M. Depaepe, F. Simon, & A. Van Gorp (Eds.), *Paradoxen van pedagogisering. Handboek pedagogische historiografie* (pp. 23–71). Leuven, Belgium/Voorburg, The Netherlands: Acco.

Depaepe, M. (2007). Philosophy and history of education: Time to bridge the gap? *Educational Philosophy and Theory, 39*(1), 28–43.

Depaepe, M. (2010). The ten commandments of good practices in history of education research. *Zeitschrift für Pädagogische Historiographie, 16*(1), 31–34.

Depaepe, M. (2017). On the critical correction of the history of education. *Bildungsgeschichte. International Journal for the Historiography of Education, 7*(2), 249–251.

Depaepe, M., D'hulst, L., & Simon, F. (2013). Crossing the Atlantic to gain knowledge in the field of psycho-pedagogy: The 1922 mission of Ovide Decroly and Raymond Buyse and the travel diary of the latter. In P. Smeyers, M. Depaepe, & E. Keiner (Eds.), *Educational research: The importance and effects of institutional spaces* (pp. 47–60). Dordrecht, The Netherlands: Springer.

Depaepe, M., & Simon, F. (2009). Sources in the making of histories of education: Proofs, arguments, and other reasonings from the historian's workplace. In P. Smeyers & M. Depaepe (Eds.), *Educational research: Proofs, arguments, and other reasonings* (pp. 23–39). Dordrecht, The Netherlands: Springer.

Depaepe, M., & Simon, F. (2016). It's all about interpretation: Discourses at work in education museums. The case of Ypres. In P. Smeyers & M. Depaepe (Eds.), *Educational research: Discourses of change and change of discourse* (pp. 207–222). Dordrecht, The Netherlands: Springer.

Depaepe, M., Simon, F., & Van Gorp, A. (2003). The canonization of Ovide Decroly as a "Saint" of the new education. *History of Education Quarterly, 18*(2), 224–249.

Depaepe, M., Simon, F., Van Gorp, A. (2006). The 'Good Practices' of Jozef Emiel Verheyen – Schoolman and Professor of Education at the Ghent University. A case of using educationally correct discourse at the right place and the right time. In P. Smeyers, M. Depaepe Educational research: Why 'What Works' doesn't work (pp. 17–36). Dordrecht, The Netherlands: Springer.

Depaepe, M., & Smeyers, P. (2008). Educationalization as an ongoing modernization process. *Educational Theory, 58*(4), 379–389.

Depaepe, M., & Smeyers, P. (2016). Educacionalização como um processo de modernização em curso, Perspectiva. *Revista do Centro de Ciências da Educação da Universidade Federal de Santa Catarina, Florianópolis, 34*(3), 753–768.

Fendler, L. (2008). The upside of presentism. *Paedagogica Historica, 44*(6), 677–690.

Gautherin, J. (2002). *Une discipline pour la république. La science de l'éducation en France (1882–1914)*. Bern, Switzerland: Peter Lang.

Ginzburg, C. (1992). *Clues, myths and the historical method*. Baltimore, Maryland: The John Hopkins University Press.

Hall, C. (2017). Thinking reflexively: Opening blind eyes. *Past and Present, 234*, 254–263.

Hartog, F. (2012). *Régimes d'historicité. Présentisme et expérience du temps*. Paris: Editions du Seuil.

Hartog, F. (2013). *Croire en l'histoire*. Paris: Flammarion.

Heinze, C., Witte, E., & Rieger-Ladich, M. (Eds.). (2016). *"… was den Menschen antreibt …". Studien zu Subjektbildung, Regierungspraktiken und Pädagogisierungsformen*. Oberhausen, Germany: Athena.

Jenkins, K. (2009). *At the limits of history. Essays on theory and practice*. London/New York: Routledge.

Jensen, L., Leerssen, J., & Mathijsen, M. (2010). *Free access to the past: Romanticism, cultural heritage and the nation*. Leiden, The Netherlands: Brill.

Kleinberg, E. (2016). Just the facts: The fantasy of a historical science. *History of the Present, 6*(1), 87–103.

Labaree, D. F. (2008). The winning ways of a losing strategy: Educationalizing social problems in the United States. *Educational Theory, 58*(4), 447–460.

Lässig, S. (2016). The history of knowledge and the expansion of the historical research agenda. *Bulletin of the German Historical Institute, 59*(Fall 2016), 29–58.

Latour, B. (2017). *Où atterrir? Comment s'orienter en politique*. Paris: La Découverte.

Masschelein, J., & Simons, M. (2008). Do historians (of education) need philosophy? The enlightening potential of a philosophical ethos. *Paedagogica Historica, 44*(6), 647–660.

Munslow, A. (1997). *Deconstructing history. London*. New York: Routledge.

Németh, A., Stöck, C., & Vincze B., (Eds.). (2017). Survival of Utopias – Weiterlebende Utopien. *Life Reform and Progressive Education in Austria and Hungary – Lebensreform und Reformpädagogik in Österreich und Ungarn*. Frankfurt a.M, Germany: Peter Lang.

Nicolin, F. (1969). *Pädagogik als Wissenschaft*. Darmstadt, The Netherlands: Wissenschaftliche Buchgesellschaft.

Patrimoine, histoire et présentisme. (2018). Entretien avec François Hartog. *Vingtième Siècle. Revue d'histoire, 137*, 22–32.

Phillips, D. C. (2013). *Discussion note on the book edited by Paul Smeyers and Marc Depaepe, "Educational research: The attraction of psychology"*. Unpublished comment given at AERA. San Francisco, March 2013.

Popkewitz, T. S. (2011). Curriculum history, schooling and the history of the present. *History of Education, 40*(1), 1–19.

Popkewitz, T. S. (Ed.). (2013). *Rethinking the history of education: Transnational perspectives on its questions, methods, and knowledge*. New York: Palgrave.

Priem, K., & Fendler, L. (2015). "Rationale Trennung" oder "Marriage d'Amour"? Zum Verhältnis von Geschichte und Philosophie in der Erziehungswissenschaft. *Zeitschrift für Pädagogik, 61*(5), 643–664.

Roland, E. (2017). *Généalogie des dispositifs éducatifs en Belgique du XIVe au XXe siècle. Disciplinarisation et biopolitique de l'enfance: des grands schémas de la pédagogie à la science de l'éducation*. Unpublished doctoral thesis. Brussels, Belgium: ULB, Faculté des Sciences Psychologiques et de l'Education.

Rosa, H. (2005). The speed of global flows and the pace of democratic politics. *New Political Science, 27*(4), 445–459.

Rosenzweig, R., & Thelen, D. (1998). *The presence of the past. Popular uses of history in American life*. New York: Columbia University Press.

Rousso, H. (2012). *La dernière catastrophe. L'histoire, le présent et le contemporain*. Paris: Gallimard.

Rüsen, J. (2017). *Historik. Theorie der Geschichtswissenschaft*. Köln, Germany: Böhlau.

Samuel, R. (1994). *Theatres of memory*. London: Verso.

Smeyers, P. (2008). Qualitative and quantitative research methods: Old wine in new bottles? On understanding and interpreting educational phenomena. *Paedagogica Historica, 44*(6), 691–706.

Smeyers, P., & Depaepe, M. (2008). A method has been found? On educational research and its methodological preoccupations. *Paedagogica Historica, 44*(6), 625–633.

Smeyers, P., & Depaepe, M. (2015). Die Forschungsgemeinschaft "Philosophy and History of the Discipline of Education" – Ein Rückblick. Einleitende Beiträge. *Zeitschrift für Pädagogik, 61*(5), 623–642.

Smith, R., & Keiner, E. (2015). Erziehung und Wissenschaft. Erklären und Verstehen. *Zeitschrift für Pädagogik, 61*(5), 665–682.

Standish, P. (2008). Chroniclers and critics. *Paedagogica Historica, 44*(6), 661–675.

Tenorth, H.-E. (1996). Lob des Handwerks, Kritik der Theorie — Zur Lage der pädagogischen Historiographie in Deutschland. *Paedagogica Historica, 32*(2), 479–508.

Tenorth, H.-E. (2015). Kommunikation über Erziehung und Erziehungswissenschaft – Allgemeine Pädagogik international. Zu den Beiträgen von Paul Smeyers, Marc Depaepe et al. *Zeitschrift für Pädagogik, 61*(5), 683–691.

Tollebeek, J. (2002). De conjunctuur van het historisch besef. In B. Raymaekers & G. Van Riel (Eds.), *De horizonten van weten en kunnen* (pp. 167–193). Leuven, Belgium: Universitaire Pers.

Tröhler, D. (2007). Philosophical arguments, historical contexts, and theory of education. *Educational Philosophy and Theory, 39*(1), 10–19.

Tröhler, D. (2017). Tracking the educationalization of the world: Prospects for an emancipated history of education. *Pedagogika, 67*(3), 211–226.

Van Damme, D., & Simon, F. (1988/1989). De ontdekking van het kind of de verandering van de volwassene. Philippe Ariés en de geschiedenis van kind, school en gezin. *Persoon en Gemeenschap, 41*(9), 326–347.

Van Nieuwenhuyse, K., Simon, F., & Depaepe, M. (2015). The place of history in teacher training and in education. A plea for an educational future with a history, and future teachers with historical consciousness. Bildungsgeschichte. *International Journal for the Historiography of Education, 5*(1), 57–69.

Van Nieuwenhuyse, K., & Wils, K. (2012). Remembrance education between history teaching and citizenship education. *Citizenship Teaching and Learning, 7*(2), 157–171.

Walsham, A. (2017). Viewpoints: Presentism. Introduction: Past and presentism. *Past and Present, 234*, 213–217.

Chapter 3
Seeing the Points of Connection

Richard Smith and Paul Standish

In Lieu of an Abstract

Paul Standish: Some people might expect us to start by explaining why we have written this chapter as a dialogue. Leaving aside the fact that Plato – to whom all philosophy, it has been said, is a series of footnotes – wrote in dialogue form, and never seems to have felt the need to tell us why, we might say that we have written it in this way because it is a dialogue. We push ideas to and fro, question each other, disagree with each other, and so on.

Reader: You say that it is a dialogue. Do you mean that this chapter is a transcription of an actual conversation between you?

Richard Smith: There have been so many conversations among us that these pages are pretty well bound to be true to our spoken words at some time or another. And of course these conversations have involved Paul Smeyers too, and – for many years – Nigel Blake, whose presence can also be detected in these pages.

Reader: So you are saying that there has been something essentially dialogic in your relationship with Paul Smeyers, and you felt that only a dialogue could do justice to that.

Paul: Pretty much so. And while there is something worryingly self-confirming in justifying the dialogue form with a dialogic explanation, it would be odd to cast the justification in some other prose form, as if that were superior to dialogue in respect of clarity or persuasive power or in some other way.

Richard: Then too dialogue is a fine medium for reminiscence, allowing for uncertainty, different perspectives, and debate ("It was in 1993, wasn't it, that you and I and Paul...?") rather than assuming that veridical record is what is at issue here.

R. Smith (✉)
School of Education, University of Durham, Durham, UK
e-mail: r.d.smith@durham.ac.uk

P. Standish
University College London, Institute of Education, London, UK/
e-mail: p.standish@ucl.ac.uk

© Springer International Publishing AG, part of Springer Nature 2018   33
S. Ramaekers, N. Hodgson (eds.), *Past, Present, and Future Possibilities for Philosophy and History of Education*,
https://doi.org/10.1007/978-3-319-94253-7_3

Paul: In any case, reminiscence is largely a way of revisiting philosophical projects and arguments from the past in order to subject their soundness to fresh critique.
Reader: So, if I understand you, this dialogue is both true and fictive, and reminiscence looks forward, as much as back.
Richard: Splendid. I only hope that what follows isn't a disappointment to you.

Paul Wittgenstein. I think that is where I would like to start. I first came to know Paul Smeyers a little in the late 1980s. He regularly attended the Annual Conference of the Philosophy of Education Society of Great Britain. Having spent a year at the London Institute of Education in the early 1980s, he was familiar with the British scene and interested by it. To some extent this reflected his early attraction to anglophone styles of philosophy and, indeed, to analytic philosophy. But, ironically perhaps, this interest manifested itself most clearly in his enthusiasm for Wittgenstein. I was finishing a thesis on Wittgenstein and Heidegger at that time, and so I was interested in what he was doing. I have a recollection of a paper he presented in the Joachim Room at Froebel College in Roehampton, where the conference took place in those years, in a session that I chaired.

Richard I first got to know Paul in 1992, I think: at one of the early meetings of the International Network of Philosophers of Education, in London. I recall sitting with Paul and some other, quite distinguished, philosophers on the terrace of a pub. I was immediately struck by Paul's diffidence and collegiality. Some of our companions were chiefly interested in making it known that they were important people in the field of political or other kinds of philosophy. The contrast with Paul was marked. His instincts were to listen and to make room for other people. I enjoyed his company from the start, whether our conversation was philosophical or on more everyday matters (and these were not always easy to separate: which says something else about Paul, and about philosophy, and of course to his credit). So began a philosophical friendship, involving of course you, Paul, and Nigel Blake, who have your own stories to tell of who met whom and when. I find it rather wonderful that these stories are not the same, and that we seem to have come together in mysterious ways.

Shortly after that meeting in London, Paul invited me to give a paper at the Catholic University of Leuven, Belgium – KU Leuven, as many of us have come affectionately to know it. My paper was titled "Education, the world, and the text". Among other things it recommends the use of forms of rhetoric – dissolving to some extent the traditional and problematic distinction between rhetoric and philosophy – in the face of attempts to relegate philosophy of education in favour of empirical research into education's effectiveness in "the real world". I never published it in the form I took to Belgium: it is not a particularly good paper, though having only now re-read it for the first time in over 20 years I can see clearly themes that I took up again later. I do remember returning from Belgium encouraged by the paper's reception, anglocentric though the paper was. More memorable is my surviving copy of it: produced by a dot matrix printer from a floppy disk. Pre-internet, as I like to tell my students. Imagine! And the journey to Leuven, now so simple by direct flights or Eurostar, involved for me then trains to London, across London from King's Cross to Charing Cross, from there to Dover, a catamaran to Ostend, and a train across Belgium to Leuven. (And, of course, back.) I mention this because it is easy to forget how the survival of philosophy of education from a time when conferences were not well attended, and published work in the discipline was relatively sparse, depended on a handful of educational philosophers, Paul prominent among them, who saw the importance of the internationalisation of our discipline and of encouraging more junior colleagues in their work, and who had the energy and qualities of leadership to put together the structures and organisations to bring this about.

I was at this time, from 1991 to 2001, Editor of the *Journal of Philosophy of Education*. That journal benefited enormously from Paul's hard work in recommending authors, especially young and lesser-known ones, to write papers and submit them to us, and in introducing us to new writers in the field; and from his vision of philosophy of education that he brought to the editorial board of the journal when he joined it later. All this helped philosophy of education to be more welcoming to traditions other than the anglophone, analytic and somewhat parochial, to embrace contexts of education outside conventional institutions such as schools – including parenting and the family, for example – and to notice the technological revolution, with computers and all their gongs and whistles – that was beginning to reshape, or pretend to reshape, education in all its forms. At the same time, Paul was and is steeped in the analytic tradition, partly from his study at the London Institute that you, Paul, have mentioned, and sympathetic to the ways it had been practised since philosophy became a recognised sub-discipline of education in the early 1960s. So he stood as an exemplar of what philosophy of education had been and still is, and of some of the ways in which it might develop.

Paul In the early 1990s Paul invited me to contribute to a collection of essays on Wittgenstein and education that he was preparing with Jim Marshall, and I readily accepted. This was the collection eventually published in 1995 under the title *Accepting Wittgenstein's Challenge*. My paper was entitled "Why we should not speak of an educational science", and I recall that Paul queried the title. With his characteristic shrug and raising of the eye-brows, he pointed out that this might cause a little embarrassment, given that he was working in a Faculty of Educational Sciences. The term in question in *Pedagogische en Psychologische Wetenschappen* does not, of course, translate exactly into "sciences", and perhaps the conversation with Paul at that time was a signal moment in my growing awareness of the difficulties attaching especially to the word in English – especially in international circumstances where English becomes the *lingua franca*. This seems to me doubly problematic. On the one hand, the elision of the dominant meaning of "science" in English with that of *wetenschappen* or *Wissenschaften* allows a broader range of forms of enquiry to be embraced, but, on the other, the English connotations of the term – with the lab-coats and laboratories of the physical sciences – exerts a dragging effect, reinforcing such connections. This means that, in research and policy contexts dominated by English, it is easier for research of an empirical kind to gain credibility, and the current obsession with research methods of empirical kinds perhaps suggests a preoccupation with technical procedure over substance and context. This smacks, I think, of an underlying nihilism – that is, avoidance of the direct addressing of particular questions of value in favour of methodological precision about no-matter-what. The 1990s was the era of the so-called paradigm wars in educational research, between quantitative and qualitative approaches, and there was a kind of narcissism about method at the time that exacerbated this. These quarrels also encouraged the idea that the only way to enquire into education was through empirical research, which carried the objectionable implication that writing about education in the humanities was somehow beside the point. Newcomers to the culture of educational research were schooled to think along these lines. A fine account of the problems all this led to in terms of research methods training was provided by Lynda Stone's "Kuhnian science and education research: Analytics of practice and training", her contribution to the 2005 edition of the Research Community (Stone, 2006), and in fact Naomi Hodgson and I later elaborated on this in "Induction into educational research networks: The striated and the smooth" (Hodgson & Standish, 2006) – both products, direct or indirect, of our wider collaborations that Paul has made possible. Prior to this, however, and back in the '90s, it was in part the assumptions that were apparent in these ways of thinking that prompted the book you and I co-authored with Paul Smeyers and Nigel Blake, *Education in an Age of Nihilism* (2000).

Richard Yes indeed. The dangers to education, and particularly educational research, from scientism – that is, worship of the tropes and images of science, rather than respect for, even admiration of, science itself – strike me as one of the most powerful and enduring themes in Paul's writings. Wittgenstein writes that "a picture held us captive" (Wittgenstein, 1968, § 115): that is, the picture of science especially. Paul's reminders of the significance of Wittgenstein's later writings, in particular, can be traced throughout both his single-authored work and our collaborations with him. Faith in science – what a paradox! – is a dominant aspect of the nihilism in our culture that Nietzsche identified and Paul ensured was a constant theme in our *Education in an Age of Nihilism*. Critique of scientism runs from his earliest work to his recent analysis of neuroscience (Smeyers, 2016) where he incisively rejects the claims – not of neuroscience itself but of those over-impressed by the pseudo-scientific rhetoric it generates – that education can somehow be revolutionalised by over-heated talk of synapses and the hippocampus.

Paul *Education in an Age of Nihilism* in fact came somewhere in the middle of the series of collaborations, concentrated especially within a period of about 10 years, in which three co-authored books stand out. Two years before the *Nihilism* book, we had published *Thinking Again: Education after Postmodernism* (1998). The provenance of this book was rather strange. Wilfred Carr had asked Nigel Blake to organise a workshop on postmodernism for the Oxford Conference in 1995, and Nigel invited us to contribute. The workshop was only, I think, a limited success. People had come in good numbers for a workshop, and of course we talked too much. But it did seem necessary to set out some account of what there was to talk about, and this is what we tried to do. So the ensuing discussion was good (at least, we bene-fited from it!) but not long enough. Afterwards, Eamonn Callan suggested to us that we write a book on the basis of what we had been talking about. Ours was a very sceptical stance towards postmodernism, and it remained so in many respects. But I recall that Paul's own thinking, in particular, changed to some extent in the course of the work we did. We did that work mostly by way of a series of two-day meet-ings, nearly always in central London and often at the Penn Club in Bloomsbury. While we all remained relatively cool about postmodernism – mostly because of the looseness of the term – we were all enthusiastic about poststructuralism in one way or another. Paul had started by thinking that Wittgenstein's later work was at odds with these Continental streams of thought, and he was right about this in terms of the way that postmodernism is so often styled – where a thoroughgoing relativism and scepticism come to the fore, perhaps alongside a denial of truth. (We were all hostile to this.) But his views changed as we did the work – in particular, in the light of the centrality of language to Wittgenstein and to poststructuralism, and the sense that this was to be understood not in a systematic way but in terms of a qualified relativisation to the language game, where human forms of life are realised in cul-turally contingent ways. In our meetings around that time, I recall, in particular, Paul's early interest in Levinas and Lacan, which we discussed one year in a room in the Old Buildings at New College Oxford. I remember in particular Paul's evoca-tion and exploration of the thought that "desire is elsewhere", which is not quite to say that human beings always want something more, but rather that we deceive ourselves about the very nature of our desires, absorbing images of desire and being habitually bound for a kind of disappointment, perhaps an aspect of our *Unheimlichkeit*. Paul's description did not, however, rely on the German or French terms that abound in exegeses of poststructuralist thought. He referred instead to a passage from José Saramago:

> This is the drama, my dear Rei, one has to live somewhere, for there is nowhere that is not somewhere and life cannot be other than life, at long last I am becoming aware of this, the greatest evil of all is that a man can never reach the horizon before his eyes, and the ship in which we do not sail, we would have that be the ship of our voyage, *Ah the entire quay, a memory carved in stone*. And now we have yielded to sentiment and started quoting verses... (Saramago, 1998, p. 129).

The narration here is multi-layered, and the acknowledgement of the role of mem-ory, so captivating and yet tinged with sadness, touch in the most human terms on the paradoxes of desire that Paul was trying to explore.

I think the ability to see the connection here is an important one. It's good to be able to remember things that are apt. But I have also been struck by Paul's abilities of recall in another respect. I personally find it quite difficult to remember the sub-stance of, for example, conference papers I have heard, or for that matter articles I have read. They are live when I am working on them, but then they somehow get filed away and are difficult to find again! Paul, by contrast, will often remind me of a paper and proceed to summarise the argument in it with impressive accuracy. It's good to be able to remember things like that too!

Another thing that comes to mind with this thought is that, again in the mid-1990s, Paul and I and Frank Crawley convened a two-day colloquium, which took place at John Adams Hall, London, on the topic of the university. The colloquium was, as I recall, quite intensive and very good. You participated, as did Nigel Blake, Joe Dunne, Bas Levering, Terry McLaughlin, Sue Mendus, Jorge Vicente Arregui, and Ido Weijers. Some time later, I spent a few days in Leuven working on the editing of the revised papers, and Paul, Frank, and I pondered the best title for the book. Higher Education in Europe was prominent on the agenda at that time, and 1996 was the European Union's Year of Lifelong Learning. Some of our papers had tried to think over the very idea of Europe as part of this discussion, as this was obviously a project that was still in the making, and there was a strong historical dimension to the work we produced. In the end we called the book *Universities Remembering Europe*, intending some of the connotations alluded to just now, but also questioning what it was to be a member of Europe. ... All of which has an irony now that probably did not cross our minds at the time.

Richard I recall this with great pleasure. As you say, it was – to my mind too – intense, demanding, and exhilarating. The book was, among other things, one more marker of the steady shift of philosophy of education away from parochial British (or perhaps I should say English) interests in education to a wider context. And that is reflected in various ways: for example, the programme of the Annual Conference in March this year shows that at least half of those presenting papers are from overseas. This would have been barely imaginable when I first started coming to the Conference in the early 1980s.

Paul Perhaps this is also the point to acknowledge another major contribution Paul has made, which has had a European but then also a wider international dimension. I am thinking of his role in the International Network of Philosophy of Education. INPE had originally been set up in the late 1980s with the intention of opening connections between Eastern and Western Europe, the promise of which was symbolised by the fall of the Berlin Wall. Soon, though, it acquired a more fully international mission. As you said, it was at a meeting of INPE in 1992 that you first remember meeting Paul. In 1994 he hosted INPE's biannual conference in Leuven, and a splendid event it was too. I too met many people at that who have subsequently become colleagues and collaborators around the world. Paul was later the Programme Chair, and he has been an enthusiastic participant ever since. Terry McLaughlin had been a driving force in the establishment of INPE in 1988, and he had been its President from then until the time of his early death, at the age of 56 in 2006. When he died, Paul played a vital role in holding the organisation together, and he was the natural choice as Terry's successor. This is a role that Paul is now relinquishing.

Richard You set me thinking of many things here. One is Paul's ability to see the points of connection in educational and philosophical thinking between Continental European strands, on the one hand, whether that is the work of Wittgenstein or later "poststructuralist" writers, and the anglophone, analytic style and tradition, on the other. A second set of memories surrounds, again, the issue of Paul's tenacious but infinitely collegial and gracious way of philosophising. I recall one day in London when the four of us – Nigel, Paul, you, and I – were involved in a lengthy and quite ferocious discussion of what Wittgenstein meant by "form of life". Some friendships, let alone professional collaborations, might have melted in the furnace of argument. That ours did not then, or at any other time, owes much both to Paul's way of doing philosophy that I mentioned just now and to his instinctive understanding of the importance to philosophy of the idea of "symposium": that if we eat and drink together, we philosophise better together. And Paul's own generosity in making this happen must not go unrecorded and without thanks.

Paul I mentioned earlier that limitations in the ways that educational research methods were being conceived in the 1990s were part of what prompted us to write *Education in an Age of Nihilism*. Paul wrote in that book about Nietzsche, about pain and pleasure, and about aspects of educational relationships. His increasing interest in broadening his writings about education through discussions of literature and film came to the fore a few years later in *The Therapy of Education* (2007), where, for example, he wrote about the David Fincher film, *Fight Club*. Perhaps these interests grew also out of the psychoanalytic themes I mentioned earlier. But he came back to writing more systematically about educational research methods in books you and he began to work on together around that time.

Richard The first of these was *Evidence-based Education Policy: What evidence? What basis? Whose policy?* (2009). There were three editors: David Bridges, Paul, and me. The title of this reprinted special issue of the *Journal of Philosophy of Education* draws attention to the difficulties of using randomised control trials (RCTS) or double-blind, randomised controlled field trials (DBRFTs) – which are rightly taken as the 'gold standard' in medical research – in education.

Paul's own contribution, which has come to be considered a classic critique, looked at the limitations of large-scale population studies in education: the central problem being the need for contextualisation. His central point here is that all kinds of factors may impact on a child's performance in a test, beyond curriculum materials used and the competence of the teacher, which tend to be what RCTs attempt to evaluate. Paul took as an extended example the well-known Tennessee STAR study, which seemed to show significant improvements to student performance from smaller class sizes in the youngest grades. Like some other critics, Paul questioned why this discovery was not followed by the reduction of class sizes in the very youngest grades of all, that is in kindergarten. The strength of Paul's chapter consists in at least three things: his grasp of the technicalities of RCTs and similar methods (in which not many philosophers could match him); his judicious attention to the various contextual factors that may make simple comparison of educational performance invalid; and his cautious suggestion that policy makers find RCTS useful in shifting blame from their own policies. His paper showed neatly the importance of addressing all the three questions that form the title of the book: *What evidence? What basis? Whose policy?*.

In our co-authored 2014 book, *Understanding Education and Educational Research,* Paul and I revisited issues such as these, paying attention to some of the examples of supposedly "scientific" research that had come out in the few years since the 2009 book. But one of our major considerations now was to give what we wrote a more positive slant, showing how and why philosophy itself can constitute excellent educational research. It is neither a business of clearing away confusions so that the "real researchers" can get on with the job (John Locke's "underlabourer" view of philosophy), nor is it some expendable luxury beloved of academics who are not in touch with the real world and prefer not to get their hands dirty. We took some examples, such as self-esteem, parenting, and the well-being and happiness of children, to show how the essential questions are sometimes ontological ones. Is there such a thing as self-esteem, for instance, such that if we try to measure it we can be confident that it is the same kind of thing across time and cultures? And we tried to show how questions about the nature of knowledge cannot be avoided in educational research, where we are often looking not for explanations of a scientific kind but for meaning of an untechnical and everyday nature, the "imponderable evidence" whose importance Wittgenstein reminds us of towards the end of the *Philosophical Investigations* (1968, p. 228). It is a major strength of the book, I think, which appears in many of its chapters, that Paul is so thoroughly at home in both traditions: the one where *Erklärung* or scientific explanation and explanation are at issue, and the *Verstehen* tradition where we want ordinary human understanding: both where we search for causes and where we look for meaning.

It is worth relating this to something that had happened earlier. During my 1993 visit to Leuven I sat in on an undergraduate class Paul was teaching. Around 25 students were grappling with the text of Peter Winch's 1958 book, *The Idea of a Social Science*, in English of course, line by line. I would not have thought to put on a module of this sort with my own students in Durham, not least because I was inclined to think of Winch's claims in that book as overstated. But it was evident that Paul's students were rising to the task and relishing it. I still think Winch overstates things, but I have lately found the contrast between Winch's conception of philosophy and Locke's "underlabourer" view very helpful pedagogically, in a module I teach on the philosophy of social science. Only recently did I remember where the seed of that was sown for me.

Paul One thing we have both benefited from is the rather modestly titled Research Community, which Paul established with Marc Depaepe in the 1990s. This was originally set up with generous funds from the Flemish regional government, and it is extraordinary that Paul and Marc have been able to sustain these annual meetings over nearly two decades. Not only has the community enabled leading scholars around the world in history and philosophy of education to come together: it has now produced an impressive series of books, each targeting a contemporary trend in policy and practice.

Richard The first thing I would like to say about the Research Community is how well it worked to join philosophy with history. Too many of us in the anglophone, analytic tradition were trained (if that isn't too strong a word) to treat philosophy as a series of decontextualised puzzles. As if, say, Descartes' argument for the *cogito* did not make more sense against the background of the Thirty Years' War (from which Descartes is careful to tell us he is enjoying some brief respite). If these started as wars over religious doctrine, how could the combatants be sure that it was really their own ideas they were fighting over, rather than ideas into which they had been indoctrinated? Just which of our ideas could we be sure had not been implanted in us by a malicious demon or, in a more modern way of putting the puzzle, by alien scientists in a distant galaxy experimenting on earthling brains in vats that we like to call "ourselves"? Or as if the leanings of philosophy to be a kind of science or a branch of mathematics or geometry, evident in Descartes himself and still remarkable through most of the twentieth century, were not more understandable in the light of the astonishing achievements of mathematics, geometry, and science from the Age of Scientific Revolutions – around 1600 – during the same period. Of course this does not show philosophy was wrong to emulate physics and so on, but a grasp of the history of ideas here whets one's scepticism, and with luck so too it stimulates the philosophical acumen that even the decontextualised puzzles themselves require.

At any rate, when I look back over the dozen or so books that the Research Community has produced, I am as much struck by the many fine historical and sociological papers there as by those that count as philosophical – and struck too by the difficulty sometimes of distinguishing their different disciplinary perspectives, and the pointlessness of trying to make a distinction. It is also notable how many of the best papers were reprinted elsewhere, for example appearing as journal articles before they were published in the Research Community volumes, most recently as part of a series published by Springer. And for that too the authors owe gratitude to Paul and Marc Depaepe for their efforts to ensure a wider readership and to make the work of the Research Community better known.

Paul It is important to acknowledge also a further contribution that Paul has made on the European scene. The European Educational Research Association was set up in 1994, and Paul has been a strong presence at its conferences from the start. For the last few years, Paul has convened the Network for Philosophy of Education at those conferences, during which time it has thrived. This Network is now happily connected with *Ethics and Education*, the journal that you established and edited for a number of years. Paul took over as Editor some years ago now. In this role, Paul has no doubt drawn on his many years' experience as Editor of the *Pedagogisch Tijdschrift*, the Dutch-language journal in which philosophical approaches to education figured with some prominence.

Richard Paul has made many improvements to *Ethics and Education*. One was working on electronic procedures for receiving, reviewing, and editing papers, not to mention responding to authors, that swept away the dark days of the editor having to keep track of everything that came and went, at every stage of the editing process. Another was to establish *Ethics and Education* as the outlet for papers from the conferences of the International Network of Philosophers of Education. This of course ensured a constant supply of good quality papers and established the international nature of the journal. The founding editor is grateful to Paul for bringing his ugly child to maturity! Those who have never edited journals, who perhaps imagine a commitment supported by their universities, with time allocated for the work, can barely imagine the hours spent and the grey hairs grown and shed in being an editor. You, Paul, will be familiar with this.

Paul In recent years Paul has not shied away from large projects with considerable editorial commitments. As we write, he is in the process of editing the *International Handbook of Philosophy of Education,* published by Springer in June this year (2018).

Richard These projects are often disparaged. It is asked, who will buy them, and who will read them? And how can the chapters they contain contribute to the various research assessment exercises that are mushrooming around the academic globe? Well, as a member of the UK's 2014 Research Excellence Framework Panel 25 (Education), I can report that chapters and entries in the various Handbooks, Compendia, Encyclopedias of Education and the rest were evaluated on their merits without consideration of just where they were published, just like all other "outputs" as they are disgustingly called. And being, in the main, comprehensive overviews of topics, of writers and of themes, by academics who were invited to write them on the basis that they were themselves authorities on those topics, is it surprising that they very often scored highly, especially on the criteria of rigour and significance? Thus the service to academic communities such as the philosophy of education by these volumes, and in particular by their editors, is incalculable. And, as one whose entry on "Wittgenstein, science, and the social sciences" had to survive a lengthy grilling by Paul in the café of the Hotel Metropole in Brussels two years ago, I can report that the editorial process is rigorous.

Preparing a chapter for a book of this kind is also a valuable exercise for the writer, since it calls for an unusually high degree of clarity, from which the writer stands to benefit as well as the reader. It was in the process of working on this chapter during the summer vacation of 2016 that I saw more clearly than I had done before how crucial is Wittgenstein's turn away from science as the paradigm of knowledge and understanding for his later philosophy. I was at the time also reading Anthony Gottlieb's recently published *The Dream of Enlightenment*. In his chapter on Descartes he writes that "falling in love with geometry seems almost to have been an occupational hazard of seventeenth-century philosophy" (2016, p. 138). It was not news to me that Descartes and some of his contemporaries, such as Spinoza, were impressed by geometry as the paradigm of knowledge: Descartes famously wrote that geometry struck him as the most rigorous way of "obtaining clarity in any subject". I was aware too of the lines of influence that run from here through the Enlightenment, on to Bentham and Mill, among others, and culminate in roughly comparable ways in logical positivism, the work of the Vienna Circle, and Wittgenstein's *Tractatus*. But it is possible to know something in a rather sleepy, nodding-along manner, on the one hand, and to be *struck* by it, on the other. At any rate, I now seemed to see the Wittgenstein of the *Tractatus* as another philosopher who fell in love with geometry – and mathematics and science – just as Descartes had done. This, in turn, broke the spell that the *Tractatus,* that awesome and forbidding book, had always had over me; and from there the full force of Wittgenstein's own repudiation of his earlier work was much plainer to me than it had been before. When he wrote "A *picture* held us captive" (Wittgenstein, 1968, § 115), he was writing about language and meaning, and how we cannot see the frame of our discourse because we are looking through it. We try to grasp the essence of something by naming it, which is appropriate in the case of identifying the essence of an element by its position in the Periodic Table and so we imagine it is appropriate everywhere. It is the scientific picture or frame that held the early Wittgenstein captive (science here, again, including mathematics and geometry). There is a vast difference between what counts as good evidence in science – which will be what can be precisely calculated, weighed, and measured – and what the later Wittgenstein calls "imponderable evidence", which may include "subtleties of glance, of gesture or tone" (Wittgenstein, 1968, p. 228).

In my chapter of the *Handbook* (Smith, 2018), I brought this to bear on assumptions about what counts as good evidence in the social sciences, criticising ideas about research, and educational research especially, according to which anything less than a Randomised Control Trial (RCT) hardly counts as research at all. This, I wrote, takes altogether too narrow a view of what can count as a cause so that we cannot say, for instance, that parents' involvement in their children's education is a cause of their success at school unless we have at the least (and impossibly) eliminated all other variables. This is what led to my discussion with Paul in the Metropole Hotel. He felt I was neglecting the account of causes as INUS conditions (insufficient but non-redundant parts of a condition that are themselves unnecessary but sufficient for the occurrence of the effect) associated with J. L. Mackie; I felt that Paul himself was somewhat captured by the picture of science. Neither of us won the argument, of course, and neither of us lost it. One of us, at least, found the discussion taxing and exhilarating: I learned from it, as I had done by writing – and learned further by re-writing – the chapter.

That's a long way of saying that editing a substantial handbook (it contains 95 chapters) is a demanding exercise in academic and organisational terms, and is yet another respect in which philosophers of education are in Paul's debt.

Paul Maybe I should end where I began – that is, with Wittgenstein, who has surely been a sustained presence in Paul's work throughout. Quite recently Paul wrote a piece for Michael Peters and Jeff Stickney's substantial edited collection *A*

Companion to Wittgenstein on Education (Peters & Stickney, forthcoming 2018) with the title "'This is simply what I do'" (quoted from Wittgenstein, 1968, §217). Paul's focus on this phrase from Wittgenstein nicely opens the question of Wittgenstein's conservatism. It was not uncommon at one time for the sentence to be misquoted, in a manner that betrayed the authoritarian prejudice in some interpretations, as "This is simply what we do"! But Paul's discussion relates the alleged conservatism to the problematic remark that philosophy "leaves everything as it is" (§124). In doing so, he criticises a strand in the reception of Wittgenstein in education, which his rather ponderous subtitle spells out: "On the relevance of Wittgenstein's alleged conservatism and the debate about Cavell's legacy for children and grown-ups". He identifies that strand with the work of Naomi Hodgson, Stefan Ramaekers, and myself, as well as, to some extent, Naoko Saito. Michael Peters and Jeff Stickney invited us to respond, and in fact I was the only one who took up the opportunity (Standish, 2018 forthcoming).

The wider context for the remark that Paul takes as his title is the passage: "If I have exhausted the justifications I have reached bedrock, and my spade is turned. Then I am inclined to say: 'This is simply what I do'" (§217). Some readers, on reading these lines, have been struck by the finding of bedrock, and they have paid less attention to the turning of the spade – and this, of course, is to reinforce the sense of conservatism. Here at last is the foundation. My sense is that the twisting of the hand as the spade is turned signifies a kind of frustration or, as Cavell puts it, exasperation. Elsewhere Wittgenstein writes of the riverbed (Wittgenstein, 1969, §§94–98) with its shifting sands. The shifting of the sands can occur naturally and through human intervention, where the river is dredged to make way for the movement of river traffic. Dredging needs to be done continually if the river is to be navigable. The place never quite stays the same, but a way of life is sustained. Paul's worry is that the strand of interpretation that concerns him tends to

> model every relationship between a grown-up and a child along the lines of the way the grown-up is always in a process of attaining a further next self. Ignoring the distinction between the latter process and initiation results in confusions which do neither justice to Cavell or Wittgenstein, moreover, they obfuscate relevant distinctions of the nature of education and child-rearing (Smeyers, 2018a forthcoming, p. 242).

In its own terms this is surely right. There is something wrong with the parent who sees in their relationship with their child merely an opportunity for attaining a "next self", just as there is something disturbing about the parent who does not imagine that, in bringing up a child, they will themselves be changed. But this is to resort to caricature. Of course there are differences between children and adults, and these repay careful attention. My response tried to show that the strands of thought that have provoked Paul's concern offer ways of clarifying and substantiating ideas of cultural initiation.

In the past I have sometimes been struck by what I took to be a degree of sentimentality in the reception of Wittgenstein. That there is hagiography is no surprise, but is there something about education that brings out the sentimental? Paul and I agree about this danger, although our perceptions of how and where it arises are different, and I suppose it is fair to say that we are mutually suspicious in this respect. We do agree in finding interest in questions that Wittgenstein's texts raise, and so it is frustrating to hit an obstacle, to find the spade twisting, over what we disagree about here. But, when the spade is turned, there is always new ground to be dug, a young tree to be replanted, a post to be sunk. Reflection on the significance of cultural initiation for upbringing and education has been a major part of Paul's work, and this in the end is what you and I do too. And it is something we have happily done together, and perhaps the occasional frustration feeds into a stronger relationship!

Richard I should like to end on a Wittgensteinian note too. In his later work, especially the posthumously published *Culture and Value* (1998), Wittgenstein makes a number of points about the importance of slowness in philosophy, and these are connected in interesting ways with the idea that sometimes understanding has to consist in waiting for the penny to drop, and "light dawns gradually over the whole" – a quotation from *On Certainty* (1969) whose significance I think I have heard you, Paul, draw attention to more than once. There is much of relevance to education in this. But what I want to finish with here is his striking remark that in philosophy the winner of the race is the one who can run most slowly and gets to the winning post last (Wittgenstein, 1998, 34e). How appropriate, then, that the theme of the 2018 meeting of the Research Community in Leuven is "Acceleration and Production", prompting reflection on the pressure to produce research faster and publish it almost instantly, in academic repositories and so on, and to arrive at "outcomes", whether of academic research or learning in schools and universities, with maximum efficiency and rapidity. We might think of Wittgenstein as reminding us by contrast of the significance of the journey, as against arriving at the destination that might seem to be its point or outcome. This has been well understood at other times and still is in some other cultures: it is figured as the pilgrimage or *hajj*. Paul has been the best of companions to us all on our philosophical journeys, and has been variously the tireless author, editor, and midwife of the records of those journeys, which some will want to call their outcomes. This would be to miss the point that the journey continues, and we look forward to having Paul on the road beside us for many miles yet.

References

Blake, N., Smeyers, P., & Smith, R. (1998). *Thinking again: Education after postmodernism.* Westport, CN: Bergin & Garvey.

Blake, N., Smeyers, P., Smith, R., & Standish, P. (2000). *Education in an age of nihilism.* London: RoutledgeFalmer.

Bridges, D., Smeyers, P., & Smith, R. (Eds.). (2009). *'Evidence based educational policy': What evidence? What basis? Whose policy?* Oxford, UK: Blackwell.

Gottlieb, A. (2016). *The dream of enlightenment.* London: Allen Lane.

Hodgson, N., & Standish, P. (2006). Induction into educational research networks: The striated and the smooth. *Journal of Philosophy of Education, 40*(4), 563–574.

Peters, M., & Stickney, J. (Eds.) (2018, forthcoming). *A companion to Wittgenstein on education.* Singapore, Singapore: Springer.

Saramago, J. (1998[1984]). *The year of the death of Ricardo Reis* (G. Pontiero, Trans.). London: The Harvill Press.

Smeyers, P. (2016). Neurophilia: Guiding educational research and the educational field. *Journal of Philosophy of Education, 50*(1), 62–75.

Smeyers, P. (2018a, forthcoming). "This is simply what I do." on the relevance of Wittgenstein's alleged conservatism and the debate about Cavell's legacy for children and grown-ups. In M. A. Peters, and J. Stickney (Eds.), *A companion to Wittgenstein on education.* Singapore, Singapore: Springer.

Smeyers, P. (Ed.). (2018b, forthcoming). *International handbook of philosophy of education.* Dordrecht, The Netherlands: Springer.

Smeyers, P., & Marshall, J. (1995). *Philosophy and education: Accepting Wittgenstein's challenge.* Dordrecht, The Netherlands: Springer.

Smeyers, P., & Smith, R. (2014). *Understanding education and educational research.* Cambridge, UK: Cambridge University Press.

Smeyers, P., Smith, R., & Standish, P. (2007). *The therapy of education.* Basingstoke, UK: Palgrave Macmillan.

Smith, R. (2018). Wittgenstein, science, and the social sciences. In P. Smeyers (Ed.), *International handbook of philosophy of education.* Dordrecht: Springer.

Standish, P. (2018, forthcoming). This is simply what I do too: A response to Paul Smeyers. In M. Peters & J. Stickney (Eds.), *A companion to Wittgenstein on education.* Singapore: Springer.

Stone, L. (2006). Kuhnian science and education research: Analytics of practice and training. In P. Smeyers & M. Depaepe (Eds.), *Educational research: Why what works Doesn't work.* Dordrecht, The Netherlands: Springer.

Winch, P. (1958). *The idea of a social science and its relation to philosophy.* London: Routledge & Kegan Paul.

Wittgenstein, L. (1968). *Philosophical investigations.* (3rd ed., G. E. M. Anscombe, Trans.). Oxford, UK: Basil Blackwell.

Wittgenstein, L. (1969). *On certainty.* (P. Denis and G. E. M. Anscombe, Trans.). Oxford, UK: Basil Blackwell.

Wittgenstein, L. (1998). *Culture and value* (Rev. ed., P. Winch, Trans.). Oxford, UK: Blackwell.

Chapter 4
The University as Pedagogical Form: Public Study, Responsibility, Mondialisation

Jan Masschelein and Maarten Simons

Abstract Universities are increasingly mobilised to address societal challenges. We argue that in order to take up their responsibility, universities are confronted first of all with the challenge to maintain themselves as universities, i.e. as forms of public and collective study that are not protecting and facilitating but are complicating and exposing learning and research and, therefore, that constitute a very particular way to deal with the challenges. This requires the invention of and experimentation with new forms, but, as we argue, these are primarily new forms regarding her "pedagogy", i.e. her power to study and think. We first sketch the figure of the researcher and learner today, we then suggest to recall the university as *universitas studii*, and to pay attention to the university's pedagogical form and public aspects. This is the basis to reclaim, in the third section, the university from a pedagogical point of view, that is, as the mondial university.

Introduction

For the past 20 years, governments in Europe and in other world regions have embraced international agendas for university reform (EU, OECD, World Economic Forum, UNESCO, and the World Bank) based on the argument that the future lays in an ideas-driven competitive global knowledge economy. Universities' education, research, organisation, management, and governance were reformed to focus on employability, knowledge transfer, innovation, and entrepreneurialism. More recently, the financial crisis, effects of climate change, accelerating disparities

J. Masschelein (✉)
Laboratory for Education & Society, KU Leuven, Leuven, Belgium
e-mail: jan.masschelein@kuleuven.be

M. Simons
Laboratory for Education & Society, KU Leuven, Leuven, Belgium
e-mail: Maarten.Simons@kuleuven.be

© Springer International Publishing AG, part of Springer Nature 2018   47
S. Ramaekers, N. Hodgson (eds.), *Past, Present, and Future Possibilities for Philosophy and History of Education*,
https://doi.org/10.1007/978-3-319-94253-7_4

between rich and poor, popular discontent, intractable political conflicts, and major population movements in the world have meant that universities are confronted with a diversity of other futures and are increasingly mobilised to address societal challenges (pressing environmental, economic, social, political, and technological problems) that have come under the spotlight. Many policy documents (at international, national, regional, local, and university level) repeat in one way or another that the responsibility for finding inventive responses to these challenges rests – not least – on the shoulders of universities. We will argue that in order to take up their responsibility, universities are confronted first of all with the challenge to maintain themselves *as universities*, i.e. as forms of public and collective study that do not protect and facilitate but that complicate and expose learning and research and, therefore, constitute a very particular way to deal with these challenges, one which is worthwhile to be maintained and sustained.

Today the university has to move in very "toxic" environments (the European Space of Higher Education, EHEA, and the European Research Area, ERA) in which it has to struggle for its very survival. Hence, today, academic responsibility refers crucially to a public engagement in order to ensure the very durability and sustainability of the university itself. This requires, for sure, innovation, invention, and experimentation with new forms, but, as we will argue, what is required primarily are new forms regarding her "pedagogy", i.e. her power to study and think. This echoes, as we will indicate, Bruno Latour's recent "hints for a neo-Humboldtian university", referring to Alexander von Humboldt, a plea for a "radical reorientation: what used to be called extension, outreach or *pedagogy* is no longer the last but the *first frontline* and alongside which all actions of the future university will be evaluated" (Latour, 2016a, p. 10, italics by authors). To arrive at the exploration of this hint, we first sketch the figures of the researcher and learner, the two inhabitants of the contemporary, European university as it is designed today. The second section suggests that we recall the university as *universitas studii*, and pay attention to the university's pedagogical form and public aspects. This is the basis to reclaim, in the third and final section, the university from a pedagogical point of view, that is, the *mondial* university that establishes new fields of (public) study as part of its pedagogy.

The Contemporary University: Protecting Learners and Researchers

The actual learning policies of the EU materialise in two European Areas, the European Higher Education Area (EHEA) and the European Research Area (ERA) (see also Masschelein & Simons, 2015),[1] which call into life the *independent, personalised learner* and the *innovative, creative researcher*. Both figures have to understand themselves as entrepreneurs who invest, calculate, speculate,

---

[1] One could add also the European Area for Lifelong Learning, which is, however, still in the making.

accumulate, and capitalise (produce added value), and who require learning and research environments that *facilitate* and *protect* their individual learning trajectories and research careers (i.e. stimulating, flexible, transparent environments). For them, the university is but one of the possible infrastructures for their proper activity: learning and researching, which they increasingly manage as productive businesses.

A short overview of policy documents and statements is telling in this regard (see EC documents 2000, 2003, 2005, 2006, 2012a, 2012b). In 2006, the European Commission published a *modernisation agenda for universities* based on the diagnosis that "European universities … are behind in the increased international competition for talented academics and students, and miss out on fast changing research agendas and on generating the critical mass, excellence and flexibility necessary to succeed" (European Commission, 2006, p. 4). The Communication of the European Commission, "A Reinforced European Research Area Partnership for Excellence and Growth" (European Commission, 2012a) states: "Knowledge is the currency of the new economy. A world-leading research and innovation capacity, built on a strong public science base, is therefore critical to achieving lasting economic recovery and to securing Europe's position in the emerging global order. … to maximise the return on this investment, Europe must increase the efficiency, effectiveness and excellence of its public research system" (ibid., p. 2). And it defines the ERA as "a unified research area open to the world based on the Internal Market, in which researchers, scientific knowledge and technology circulate freely and through which the Union and its Member States strengthen their scientific and technological bases, their competitiveness and their capacity to collectively address grand challenges" (ibid., p. 3). Modern society faces a number of grand challenges, including climate change, the increasing scarcity of natural resources, public health, food security, and ageing populations. The responsibility for finding inventive responses to these challenges rests on the shoulders of modern universities, and on creative, independent scientists to carry out (in the words of the European Research Council) "investigator-driven research" that will allow "researchers to identify new opportunities" in any field, "rather than being led by pre-set priorities" defined by policy-makers.[2]

In terms of the EHEA, we hear the ministers responsible for higher education in the 46 countries involved in the Bologna Process stating, in 2009, that higher education has to make a vital contribution in realising "a Europe of knowledge that is highly creative and innovative" and that "Europe can only succeed in this endeavour if it maximises and employs the talents and capacities of all its citizens" (Conference, 2009, p. 1). Hence, to improve quality and increase excellence is *the* most important societal aim of the university. Governments have to engage in this permanent struggle and to reemphasise every one's duty to mobilise her competencies and talents and to be employable. A more recent document of the European Commission on "Rethinking Education" (European Commission, 2012b) does not hesitate to put the emphasis from the outset on "delivering the right skills for employment" and on

---

[2] https://erc.europa.eu/sites/default/files/content/pages/pdf/ERC_in_a_nutshell_26022013.pdf

"increasing the efficiency and inclusiveness of our education and training institutions", the starting point being that education is about "boost[ing] growth and competitiveness" (ibid., p. 1). The conclusion, then, is that "Europe will only resume growth through higher productivity and the supply of highly skilled workers, and it is the reform of education and training systems which is essential to achieving this" (ibid., p. 13). It is difficult to state it more clearly than the document itself does. "Rethinking Education" means to conceive of education as the production of learning outcomes. This "fundamental shift", as the document rightly states, implies that educational policy is essentially about "stimulating open and flexible learning" and "improving learning outcomes", i.e. increasing the performance of learning environments (including the performance of institutions, teachers, students) which can be assessed through benchmarking (i.e. comparative performance indicators). The overall aim is a more efficient and effective production process, of which employability (i.e. the competences that are the learning outcomes) is the product.

When we look at these and other documents and declarations which, together with a large variety of instruments (e.g. European Qualification Framework, ECTS, several research funding programs …), circulate within EHEA and ERA, it becomes clear that the orientation towards excellence and employability frame universities within a discourse and strategy that aims at the mobilisation and exploitation of resources (learning force, brain/mind force, learning and creative potential, talents, …) to contribute to the *growth of capital* in all its different forms (individual, collective, social, human, cultural, economic, …). Such a mobilisation and exploitation would be needed for Europe to maintain its position in the global competition of the knowledge economy, in the war on talent and, so it is explicitly argued, in order to deal with the societal challenges of migration, climate change, etc. In this framing, research is defined as the production of knowledge, education as the production of learning outcomes, and public service as the production of impact on social and economic development. And the university is a place of production, a "learning factory" and a "knowledge factory", that attempts to attract and exploit both learners and researchers. Hence, the contribution of the university in relation to societal challenges is understood in terms of the production, transmission, distribution, and application of scientific knowledge.

This installs a hierarchy in the knowledge-oriented university. It is first about scientific research (defined by its method), second, about research-based education (acquiring competences, including research competences, as learning outcomes), and third about impact (application and so-called extension). Hence, the "pedagogy" of the university and her public engagement are secondary and limited to the distribution and application of knowledge in research and extension. This marginalisation of university pedagogy – and all efforts and challenges related to education – complements well a (new) call for the autonomy of research. Research as the production of knowledge is increasingly defined as the core business of the university – in terms of economic value, financial return, and social prestige – and within the university itself research activities are increasingly protected against "teaching efforts" that are framed as risking to distract researchers from their intellectual production. In line with Stengers (2011), we can see here a kind of revival of academic freedom, but one mainly understood in terms of opportunities to take (entrepreneurial) risks and to increase output and in terms of protection from interference and imposed teaching responsibilities that might slow down the knowledge production process. So there is, in fact, an increasing tendency not just to separate research and education, but also to create a hierarchy and to attempt to instrumentalise their relation.[3]

The orientation towards excellence in research and employability in learning that now dominates the university turns her into a habitat that requires and actually fosters the inhabitants of the university to look at themselves in terms of human capital, to become professionals (in their research and learning activities), and to develop a permanently calculating ethos in terms of efficacy and efficiency, investment of time, use of resources and return (Simons & Masschelein, 2009a). The main challenge for the inhabitants of the university is: How can one live up to the virtue of ongoing "competitive self-improvement"? The answer is the development of a professional entrepreneurial ethos, the permanent assessment of yourself (and your research or teaching, as well as your learning) on the basis of quality indicators in terms of productive value or improvement rationales in terms of strengths, weaknesses, opportunities, and threats. Often, the installed mechanism is one of permanent peer comparison and benchmarking; that is, checking ourselves against our closest competitors. Confronted increasingly with the dictate of permanent improvement through permanent comparison, European universities, academics, and students are faced with an additional dictate: the dictate of pro-active self-adaptation and permanent self-mobilisation. It becomes an academic duty to look for opportunities ("niches") to produce something of excellence, which, although indeed an empty concept (Readings, 1996), is the name for a pervasive regime of academic conduct. The space of the university today is a space that permanently and relentlessly *mobilises* researchers, lecturers, and students to orientate themselves to accumulation (e.g. of credits, quotations, projects, publications) and – often ignored in critical commentaries – to the permanent search for (accredited) *recognition* for their learning outcomes or research results. Academic conduct in search of excellence and employability implies indeed a particular mode of visibility. In order to

---

[3] Isabelle Stengers (2011) hints at the revival of two familiar tales. (1) The tale of the goose (*die Ganze*) with the golden eggs: it is in the interest of society and of the industry to keep a distance from academic research. We should leave it to the scientific community, the peers (eventually completed with an ethical commission), to freely define the research questions, since only scientists can define which questions are meaningful and could lead to cumulative development. If society or industry would prescribe its own questions to science it would kill the goose. We get the idea of a science as free source of novelties, which would lead to industrial innovation and contribute to human progress. The official story being that the goose lays her eggs and is happy if some of them transform in to gold in terms of industrial development. And she hopes that some will lead to human progress, but she cannot be held responsible for disabuse. This intentional ivory tower image of academic research can be related (2) to another image of the creative scientist as the sleepwalker i.e. as one who is walking on a small track without fear since she is blind to danger. One should not ask a creative scientist to take into account the consequences of her work, it would be like waking up the sleepwalker. She would doubt and fall, and be lost for science and frontier research.

"exist" as an academic or student, one is required to make oneself (in terms of performance) visible by permanently staging oneself, i.e. by constructing (academic) *profiles* and *managing these profiles*. This branding is not to be considered as an optional extra, but rather is characteristic of academic conduct as it is promoted today; branding or profiling is essential to run one's business as an academic or student.

Today, the figure of the researcher and learner in fact embody the (productive) activities they are named after: research and learning. They inhabit the university as learning and research factories, and are primarily concerned with optimal (personal) working conditions. As inhabitants of these academic factories they are, thus, first of all concerned about recognised and validated excellence and employability, about (managing) their images and profiles, and not about a shared world, or the university itself. Against these developments, and precisely in order to deal with daunting societal challenges (such as sustainability), it is important today to reclaim the university, to ask her back, but also to reinvent and re-cultivate her. This implies, however, that we understand the university as a particular way to deal with societal and existential challenges.

Universitas studii: Re-calling Academic Study

Proper to the university in her originary form is indeed that she deals with societal challenges by turning them into objects/subjects of collective and public study. That is, by gathering, through certain pedagogical practices and material devices, people around these challenges *as students*. This was also the original Latin name for that European invention of the Middle Ages: universitas studii (an association for study). Students were those who devoted themselves to study ("studium") something (a phenomenon, an issue, a problem) and the "scholar" was one of those students (one could call her the "eternal student"). The translation of "studium" entails: to "regard attentively", "to devote to something", "to consider", but also to be respectful, to be concerned, to be thoughtful. Hence, studying is not primarily about producing something but about taking care of something. The notion of "scholar" also clearly indicates that the work of academics and students is essentially (and not accidently) related to the working or practices of a "school": the university, which is bound to "studium". Study is not to be equated with learning. The university marks the difference between learning Spanish, for example, and studying Spanish. The distinction between scholar (academic) and researcher, just like the one between learner and student is no word game; it is important for the way in which research (or learning) happens. At the university as "universitas studii", research always directly relates to practices of making public and gathering a public *around, with, for, and through* that research as study. This means that it is not about scientific research as such, since scientific research can be carried out very well outside the university (as is increasingly the case). Research as study is about a particular kind of scientific research, which we could call academic study and which has nothing to do with retreating into an ivory tower.

As von Humboldt (1810) suggested, research is therefore not so much advanced through contact with "colleagues", but rather through it being part of what could be called "pedagogical forms", as the articulations of *studium*, forms that engage a public of students in a collective movement of thought. Which, in the words of von Humboldt, is operating in and for itself in these forms. Inquiry and thinking not only require public exposition afterwards (as written publication or "report"), but also precisely *in actu*, and this is what *happens* in lectures and seminars (when they actually happen), which in turn makes something happen to (and with) the public. Neither the writing of a text nor its reading can simply replace the working of these pedagogical gatherings (think also about the gatherings around blackboards in mathematics and physics), which constitute forms that turn matter into public matter (bringing it *into company* as part of the collective that is always in the making) and gather a public of students and scholars, that is, of learners and researchers as public figures. This public does not precede the event of gathering, but emerges in it. This gathering articulates, therefore, a movement of de-identification – *we are no disciples (servants of a discipline), no civil servants, no businessmen, no research-ers and no learners, but students and scholars*. It is a movement that also disturbs, questions, or disrupts all kinds of stabilisations, fixations, or crystallisations in insti-tutions and disciplines (Simons & Masschelein, 2009a). The movement has no real beginning and no end, it occurs and "takes place", and implies that students and scholars are moving in a time of suspension (i.e. not simply a time of accumulation or re-production), that is, the particular time of *studium* or of *scholé*.

It is important that the university is dealing with issues and questions, with chal-lenges to which we do not yet have a response, which implies that it is not just about finding solutions or formulating answers, but also always about the "formation" of people and world for a future that we cannot yet imagine. That was what Wilhelm von Humboldt (1810) clearly stated when he inaugurated the modern university, which was, one could say, a reclaiming and reinvention of the university as an inven-tion of the Middle Ages. He claimed that higher education institutions are conceived as starting from problems that do not yet have answers yet, so that they *remain* in the state of investigation, and that higher education is a working through problems (ibid., p. 2) He also writes that "since the intellectual work within humanity flour-ishes only as cooperation, namely not merely in that one fills in what another lacks, but in that the successful work of one inspires the others, and that *the general, origi-nal* power … *becomes visible to all*, the internal organisation of these institutions must bring forth and sustain a collaboration that is uninterrupted, constantly self-renewing, but unforced and *without specific purpose*" (ibid. p. 1, italics are ours). Moreover, according to von Humboldt, the university as gathering with students (which was for him a "kind of study") was at least as important (if not more so) for the advancement of "science" as (or in) the scientific academy (the gathering of col-leagues): "If one declares the university as destined only for the teaching and dis-semination of science, but the academy to its expansion, one clearly does the former an injustice" (ibid., p. 4).

The not-knowing (ignorance) that is at the basis of the university relates not only to things we don't know (and which we know that we don't know), but also to not-knowing what we don't know (Rheinberger, 2007). Moreover, we don't know how and to what extent our necessary abstractions (concepts, theories) and the possible new facts (and "data"), new nature, new things, new ways of doing that our sciences produce or conceive, will have consequences for our common life and common world. And precisely, therefore, we have to be vigilant, attentive, and thoughtful; we have to exercise caution: "il faut faire attention" (Haraway, 2016; Latour, 2017; Stengers, 2013). This also implies that we have to consider that we might be wrong or mistaken. This consideration is not an individual competence or capacity, and is not just a matter of attitude or choice. The exercise of caution is related to the way in which the university organises and arranges (exercises, *makes*) the possibility to object, to be confronted with what we have not yet considered. In this sense, the university refers not to a kind of institution (and embodied idea) but foremost to a practice consisting of material arrangements and technologies that make something possible. What it arranges, in creating possibilities for objection, is making public what one knows and thinks, confronting it with a public, and hence also it arranges the possibility to think in public, with a public, and before a public. Arguably, this was the unique force of that original invention in the Middle ages that is called "university"; it allowed thought to become public, and hence, to turn it into collective study. The academic or scholar within the university is, thus, not the expert or the one who knows, but the one who is looking, searching, the one who is moved by ignorance and ready to think in public and let her knowledge and existing ways of inhabiting the world be put to the test. This is the academic or scholar involved in study practices.

It is precisely the "pedagogy" of the university, i.e. her forms and practices of study, that arrange and embody such collective and public forms of thoughtfulness, cautiousness, vigilance, and attentiveness. And it is these forms and practices that are changed when organising today's research and learning environments, approached in terms of customisation: that is, starting from what they offer for the learner or the researcher in their outcome-defined and outcome-driven business. Those collective and public study practices (including teaching, learning, thinking practices) are first of all interested in something of the world (a phenomenon, a thing, an issue) and what becomes of it. Hence, it is not about what becomes of "me" as learner or researcher, but what becomes of the world. And "interested" in relation to these study practices means: becoming attracted to, attached to, concerned about. It is also these practices that make it possible that, at the same time, people are trained and formed precisely through being interested in the world, by studying something in and of the world, and ultimately by taking care of a common world. It is these practices that extend the world, populate it with more beings and things, and invoke or conjure immediately the question of how to live together with these beings and/or things that emerge and come to life (Simons & Masschelein, 2009b). Again, it is important to stress that study is not a kind of disinterested activity of stepping back as complete detachment, but is motivated by a concern, a form of curiosity (as care), and hence, a stepping back as slowing down exactly in order to relate again, to re-attach and re-compose.

Universities as gatherings of and as students are ways to intensify research, to turn it into a form of collective and public study, but also to produce "vigilance" and "hesitation", which Stengers considers to be part of thinking and consideration, and which becomes manifest in stuttering (not in fast, uninterrupted discourses) (Stengers, 2005). Through such intensified research, students (and scholars) will come to know some things and learn some things, but it cannot be defined in advance what the findings are that they have to attain, who or what could make them change their minds and thoughts during their study process, who or what could object to them, could make them hesitate and ask whether they are not mistaken. In principle it can be everyone and everything. But as students they have something in common, i.e. the issue (thing) that makes them think, imagine, object, co-operate. And university pedagogy that makes study practices possible is exactly about that: to allow that "thing" to obtain the power to make us think (ibid.). This implies that the issue or thing must be made "present", must be presented; just as Alexander von Humboldt, Wilhelm's brother, "discovered" a new common world as object of study (or matter of study) through the large-scale grammatisation (drawing, sketching, mapping, picturing, graphing, collecting of natural life) and composition of a new shared world. The driving force was not just a scientific will to know, but academic curiosity expressed in a deep concern and acceptance that things can make us hesitate and stutter, and force us to think again. Alexander did not discover a hidden world, but carefully composed a world through naming, abstractions, drawings etc.; as scholar, he and his companions made the earth speak in new ways, that is, they transformed the earth into something to relate to, a world to be concerned about.

It is crucial to stress indeed that the academic concern with issues or things is not about avoiding or evading abstractions and addressing the concrete. These abstractions are needed to take a step back in order to re-attach to something, that is, to turn it into a thing of concern. It is here that we find both a slowing down typical for study practices, as well as an effective contribution of the "public" to these practices. Drawing on Dewey's understanding of "the public" (Dewey, 1927/1991) academic research can be defined as studying something in the presence of those who are touched by the consequence of new ideas, new objects, new concepts, new interventions. The public – from the viewpoint of the university and its public study – is not what is located at the end of the production chain of knowledge (users of the produced knowledge, the learners, communities…), but all those in the presence of who we undertake our collective thinking and to whom we are responsible. University study – through its movement of abstraction (e.g. grammatisation of the world) that allows that we, and all others, can relate to something – is a public practice.

This public character makes academic study slow – it cannot decide in advance what it will take in to account and what is a priori defined as irrelevant in order to obtain in predefined outcomes as efficiently as possible. Therefore, as Haraway (2016) formulates it, academic study is perhaps not about accountability (always implying that we know in advance what counts and how to give an account), but about "response-ability". This ability to respond implies "slowness"; however, it should not be confused with what today is often referred to as "slow science". In the plea to slow down science what is often neglected is the university itself, that is, a very specific pedagogic arrangement that allows for public study. In neglecting the university itself, slow science risks reinforcing the hierarchical distinction between scientific research (that is to be protected) and university pedagogy (that somehow interferes with true academic life). Not "slow science" but "academic study" – it is for us indeed pedagogy that is decisive: to gather as students, i.e. to create conditions in which something is given the power to speak, interrupts our common sense and makes us hesitate, and hence, makes us think. Probably, and to draw on a formulation by Nigel Blake, Paul Smeyers, Richard Smith, and Paul Standish (1998), it would be more correct to say: it makes us "think again". At the university it is not about personal or collective flourishing (today often suggested as a way to compensate for one-sided growth models), about who I and we become, want, will, or can become (today often promoted as a way to resist the focus on employability and other economic directives), but about what becomes of the world and about how to inhabit (as future "I" and "we") the world.

Reclaiming the University and its Pedagogy

Our attempt to understand the university as place and time not for research but for public study, and insisting on the importance of university pedagogy, echoes Bruno Latour's "hints for a neo-Humboldtian university" referring to Alexander von Humboldt (Latour, 2016a). Latour criticises the modern university for its "trickle-down epistemology": that is, for taking itself as being "at the vanguard of a teaching and research process" and thereby assuming that "its results – progressively through education and training, then through outreach and … extension" – would trickle down "eventually reaching the general public" and ideally leading to the construction of a shared world view "where everybody would have become scientifically enlightened, at least able to follow, maybe to obey, the expert vanguard in important matters." But such trickling down, so he argued, clearly does not work. We need, therefore, a "radical reorientation: what used to be called extension, outreach or *pedagogy* is no longer the last but the *first frontline* and alongside which all actions of the future university will be evaluated" (ibid., p. 10, italics by authors). This does not imply that we neglect basic research: "quite the contrary", we need "immense advances in scientific inquiry", but it means "that the order, priority and goals have been reversed." According to Latour, we should (re)compose a common world while "rediscovering the old new planet", which "should create as much creative energy as during the period that has been called the 'age of discovery'". For him "*public* engagement" (italics by authors) is no longer something to be "added once basic research has been completed: it is to which basic research is directed" (ibid.). In our understanding, arguing for basic research directed to public engagement is exactly about defending a form of public study, and re-opening a perspective on pedagogical issues.

To reclaim the university as pedagogic form, as form of public study, is to reclaim the right not to be part of the learning factory (being a functionary of the learning robots; Flusser, 1999), which produces learning outcomes or impact and that performs this production in a way that, through feedback loops, adapts itself ever better to exploit ever better the (creative) learning force (instead of labour force). Reclaiming the university is also about the right not to be working in a research fabric with its peer police and surveillance system and its knowledge distribution network. Maybe there is nothing wrong with a sustainable learning or research factory, but to reclaim the university, is to reclaim the right of a place (site) of public and collective study, of exposing and publicly "testing" knowledge. This is not a social right for learners or researchers to have optimal working conditions in the university; it is a right that is reclaimed by the world or in the name of the world. Reclaiming "university" is also about refusing that it refers just to a research institute, a training institution, or learning environment. It is defending its meaning as public movement of thought that articulates in pedagogic forms as particular ways to gather people and other beings and things. The university is a site where learners and researchers can become a public of students, a thinking public that does not exist independently from the issue that brings it into being. In conclusion, it is important to explore in a bit more detail what exactly is at stake in reclaiming the university: what is threatening today, and what could be regarded as an academic responsibility.

Today, it is nearly impossible not to think about academic work in productive terms and as an outcome-driven enterprise. And if we are right, this does mean that what is threatened today is the particular way in which the university could contribute to the formation of people and to dealing with the daunting societal challenges by being "thoughtful" and "regarding" ("studium"). Arguably, it is so difficult to actually engage in public study, as most (basic) mechanisms and policies have another figure of the student and scholar in mind; that is, they address researchers and learners, not academic practices. An obvious case is funding based on output that is aiming at "professional researchers" (and even "professional project writers") managing their research as a business, which succeeds when they emancipate themselves from their institutional bonds (their attachments to the university) and when they ask themselves which research environment offers the best resources for their research (hence: "what can the university do for me?"). Professional researchers don't want to lose time and are actually trained to save time ("to perform better with less") and should consider most if not all university-related obligations as being distracting and to be avoided or delegated.

Together with the way in which both the ERA and the EHEA are being constructed, these ways of financing and shaping research and socialising "professional researchers" also dismantle the university in other ways. As mentioned earlier, there is an increasing tendency to separate education and research, to instrumentalise education in order to protect research productivity and, hence, to undermine and impede the university as the practice of public and collective study. Furthermore, the implication is that both learning and research are framed and organised in terms of an outcome and output orientation. It becomes less evident to work through problems, ill-defined issues, ignorance or "stupidity" (requiring public study), for pre-defined outputs have already decided on what counts and what does not. Finally, it is important to stress the privatisation that is accompanying academic capitalism. The increased concern with "intellectual property", but also the importance of patenting and the protection through licensing and access codes, are clear evidence of this. There is an ambivalence in this commodification of learning and research, however. As Andre Gorz (2008) explains:

> the 'knowledge' (and experience) dimension on which relies the yield of commodities is itself not of the same nature as these commodities: public study (and aspects of thinking, abstraction, conceptualisation, care and curiosity) itself can 'by nature' not be 'owned' or privatised and hence cannot become a true commodity. Knowledge, insights, thoughts (in the broad sense of the French 'savoir') can only be disguised as private property and commodity by reserving *their exclusive use* through juridical or technical artefacts (such as secret access codes, copyrights). But it is really nothing more than a disguisement, for it is not changing anything to its character of common good: it remains a non-commodity which cannot be sold and whose access and free use are 'forbidden' and 'illegal' exactly because this access and free use remain always possible. The researchers and learners, as so-called 'owners', cannot sell their 'knowledge' or 'competences', that is transfer its private property to someone else, they can only sell the right to access or the use 'under license' (Gorz, 2008, p. 37).

The increased regulation and juridification to support and enable privatisation, then, means that it is difficult, if not impossible, to take "the public" out of the university without destroying the university itself.

Academic responsibility concerns in the first place a "responsability" for a world university, or perhaps more accurately termed, a *mondial* university. A university that deals with local and global challenges in a particular way, while she is not interested in globalisation (and "global minds" moving around in a globalised territory or the global surface of the earth) but in "mondialisation" ("globalising").[4] That is,

---

[4] In his inaugural lecture at the Collège de France in 2012 on "The grandeur and misery of the social state", Alain Supiot made an interesting distinction between "globalising" (mondialisation) and globalisation: "The term *globalisation* nevertheless breeds confusion between two types of phenomena which combine in practice but are different in nature. The first are structural phenomena, such as the abolition of physical distances in the circulation of signs between people, or their shared exposure to the health or environmental risks spawned by technological development. These phenomena are irreversible and their impact on the transformations of work and social ties must be envisaged as such. The second is the free movement of capital and goods, which is a contextual phenomenon, the result of reversible political choices that goes hand in hand with the temporary over-exploitation of non-renewable physical resources. The confusion between two phenomena is what causes some to see globalisation as the manifestation of an immanent law, thought to escape all political or legal control. With the distinction it allows between *globalisation* and *mondialisation*, the French language affords the means to bring a little rigour into this debate. In the primary meaning of the word (where *monde* is opposed to *immonde*, just as *cosmos* is opposed to *chaos*), *mondialiser* (to globalise) consists in making a physical realm inhabitable by humans: in making our planet a place that can be inhabited. In other words, globalising consists in mastering the different dimensions of the globalisation process. The command of its technological dimension implies adapting the legacy of legal forms of organisation of labour from the industrial world to the risks and opportunities brought about by the digital revolution. The command of its commercial dimension implies designing an international legal order which prohibits taking

to make and maintain our planet habitable and livable as a shared world. Hence, her central concern is not production, distribution, and application of knowledge, but care for our "worldly" living-together (with people, animals, rivers, things, bacteria, ghosts, ideas …). Her most important concern is what becomes of this shared world (and who and what belongs to it). Hence, a mondial university, a university that is not so much concerned about its added value or the added value it offers for learners and researchers, but about what becomes of a shared world, implies that learning and research are complicated, made harder, and slowed down because these people, animals, rivers, things, bacteria, ghosts, ideas … should have the opportunity to say something and to object. It is about an academic response-ability, which implies also taking up the challenge that they all can raise their voice, that is, they can speak to us, and perhaps foremost, "against" us.

Taking up a responsability for a world university would probably require, first of all, the "revaluation" of our common academic values: not first scientific research and then education (research-based and method-directed) and extension (application, impact), but first public and collective forms of study – forms of academic research – which require public methodologies. The latter implies the further development and elaboration of scientific instruments as "sensing devices for the state of the issue" (cf. Alexander Von Humboldt), for visualisation, for the involvement of publics (and not only "peers" and "experts") in and through study (and not only after research). This response-ability is not to be considered as an abstract ideal. It can be a matter of governing and policy. In her yearly address as rector of University of Amsterdam, entitled "The unconventional future", Karen Maex emphasises first of all education instead of research as the central issue of the university, and hence the reversal of the usual order (Maex, 2016). Not first research (within established disciplines, with known peers) and then education (with students), but education as the way to describe and compose a "field of study" (not a discipline), including the composition of the study-material and the study-object (e.g. future planet studies).

Let us end with subscribing to the slogan used by the German students in their actions against the reforms of higher education: "We are no human capital". Indeed the term "students" has become synonymous with resources to be exploited, talents to be mobilised, the object of investment, the guarantee of a country's competitiveness or, when addressing the possible disobedient component of human capital, the customers to be seduced. Perhaps their de-identification should at once be regarded as an affirmation: "we *are no human capital, we are no learners, we are students*". And allow us to add to this slogan: we don't want to be learners or professional researchers, but scholars, we don't want to be functionaries of the learning or knowledge factory, we don't want to be functionaries of a preprogrammed digital world and preformatted world of competitive research projects and learning environments, we want to (be able to) study. And perhaps we can add as well: we want to reclaim university pedagogy, we need university pedagogues.

---

advantage of the opening of commercial borders to escape the duties of solidarity inherent to the recognition of economic and social rights" (Supiot, 2012, pp. 29–30).

References

Blake, N., Smeyers, P., Smith, R., & Standish, P. (1998). *Thinking again. Education after postmodernism*. Westport, CT/London: Bergin & Garvey.

Conference. (2009). *The Bologna Process 2020 – The European Higher Education Area in the new decade*. Communiqué of the Conference of European Ministers Responsible for Higher Education, Leuven and Louvain-la-Neuve, 28–29 April 2009. Retrieved January 26, 2018, from https://media.ehea.info/file/2009_Leuven_Louvain-la-Neuve/06/1/Leuven_Louvain-la-Neuve_Communique_April_2009_595061.pdf

Dewey, J. (1927/1991). The public and its problems. Athens, OH: Swallow Press/Ohio University Press.

European Commission. (2000). *Towards a European Research Area*. COM (2000) 6, European Commission: Brussels.

European Commission. (2003). *The role of the universities in the Europe of knowledge*. COM (2003) 58, European Commission: Brussels.

European Commission. (2005). *Mobilising the brainpower of Europe: Enabling the Universities to make their full contribution to the Lisbon Strategy*. COM (2005) 152. European Commission: Brussels.

European Commission. (2006). *Delivering on the modernisation agenda for universities: education, research and innovation*. COM (2006) 208, European Commission: Brussels.

European Commission. (2012a). *Communication from the commission to the European Parliament, the Council, the European Economic and Social Committee and the Committee of the Regions*. A Reinforced European Research Area Partnership for Excellence and Growth COM (2012) 392 final. European Commission: Brussels. Retrieved January 22, 2018, from https://ec.europa.eu/research/science-society/document_library/pdf_06/era-communication-partnership-excellence-growth_en.pdf

European Commission. (2012b). *Communication from the Commission to the European Parliament, the Council, the European Economic and Social Committee and the Committee of the Regions*. Rethinking Education: Investing in skills for better socio-economic outcomes. COM/2012/0669 final. Retrieved November 6, 2017, from http://eur-lex.europa.eu/legal-content/EN/ALL/?uri=CELEX:52012DC0669

Flusser, V. (1999). The factory. In *The shape of things: A philosophy of design* (pp. 43–50), A. Mathews, Trans.). London: Reaktion Books. Original edition: Flusser, V. (1993) *Vom Stand der Dinge: Eine Kleine Philosophie des Design*. Gottingen: Steidl.

Gorz, A. (2008). *Écologica*. Paris: Galilée.

Haraway, D. J. (2016). *Staying with the trouble. Making Kin in the Chthulucene*. Durham, NC/London: Duke University Press.

Latour, B. (2016a). *Is Geo-logy the new umbrella for all the sciences? Hints for a neo-Humboldtian university*. Lecture given at Cornell University, USA, 25th October 2016.

Latour, B. (2017). *Où atterir? Comment s'orienter en politique?* Paris: La Découverte.

Maex, K. (2016). *The unconventional future*. Speech on the occasion of the 385th *dies natalis* of the University of Amsterdam, Monday, 9 January 2016. Retrieved January 26, 2018, from file:///C:/Users/u0008954/Downloads/dies-natalis-385-def.pdf

Masschelein, J., & Simons, M. (2015). Lessons of/for Europe. Reclaiming the school and the university. In P. Gielen (Ed.), *No culture, no Europe. On the foundation of politics* (pp. 143–164). Amsterdam: Valis.

Readings, B. (1996). *The university in ruins*. Cambridge, MA: Harvard University Press.

Rheinberger, H. J. (2007, 5 Mai). Man weiss nicht genau, was man nicht weiss. Über die Kunst, das Unbekannte zu erforschen. *Neue Zürcher Zeitung*.

Simons, M., & Masschelein, J. (2009a). The public and its university: Beyond learning for civic employability? *European Educational Research Journal, 8*(2), 204–217.

Simons, M., & Masschelein, J. (2009b). Towards the idea of a world university. *Interchange, 40*(1), 1–23.

Stengers, I. (2005). The cosmopolitical proposal. In B. Latour & P. Weibel (Eds.), *Making things public. Atmospheres of democracy* (pp. 994–1003). London/Cambridge, MA/Karlsruhe, Germany: MIT Press/ZKM.

Stengers, I. (2011). *Another science is possible!. A plea for slow science.* Retrieved from http://we.vub.ac.be/aphy/sites/default/files/stengers2011_pleaslowscience.pdf

Stengers, I. (2013). *Au temps des catastrophes. Résister à la barbarie qui vient.* Paris: La Découverte.

Supiot, A. (2012). *The grandeur and misery of the social state.* Inaugural Lecture at the Collège de France, 29th November 2012. Retrieved January 21, 2018, from http://books.openedition.org/cdf/3093

von Humboldt, W. (1810). *On the internal and external organisation of the higher scientific institutions in Berlin.* Retrieved from http://germanhistorydocs.ghi-dc.org/sub_document.cfm?document_id=3642

Chapter 5
Philosophies of Hospitality: Toward Perpetual Peace and Freedom

Lynn Fendler

Abstract This paper has been inspired by the Research Community: History and Philosophy of Educational Research, of which I have been a member since 2000. Organisers Paul Smeyers and Marc Depaepe have hosted annual face-to-face gatherings of this Research Community for the past 19 years. It is in appreciation of the Research Community as a site of hospitality that this chapter is dedicated. Based on my experiences with this group of philosophers and historians, this chapter celebrates the philosophical themes of *vrede* and *gastvrijheid*.

Introduction

Unlike truth, goodness, freedom, and beauty, hospitality has generally not been regarded as an issue of philosophical gravitas. From most perspectives, hospitality appears trivial: simple practices of good manners or common courtesy. Hospitality can be offered by anyone and received by anyone regardless of wealth, privilege, or brilliance; and so hospitality may be taken for granted as simple, straightforward, and ordinary. Hospitality is not the exclusive property of intellectual or political elites; hospitality is not associated with elite levels of economic, political, cultural, or academic capital. Hospitality is not determined by demography or governed by law; if hospitality is offered, it is an enactment of free will. Hospitality is precisely common and universally available, and so it is not surprising that hospitality would be dismissed as unworthy of philosophical attention. However, some philosophical treatments have recognised hospitality's exceptional philosophical bounty as a fundamental ethic for the prevention of war, the promotion of freedom, and a precondition for all exchanges that might be called educational. Those are abundant yields for acts as simple as the provision of shelter and refreshment! I write with increased appreciation for the hospitality that has been generously offered over many years to

L. Fendler (✉)
Department of Teacher Education, Michigan State University, East Lansing, MI, USA
e-mail: fendler@msu.edu

© Springer International Publishing AG, part of Springer Nature 2018   63
S. Ramaekers, N. Hodgson (eds.), *Past, Present, and Future Possibilities for Philosophy and History of Education*,
https://doi.org/10.1007/978-3-319-94253-7_5

scholars from many foreign countries who gather freely and peacefully to share ideas that may be unfamiliar or strange.

The history of European philosophy includes treatments of hospitality from diverse epistemological standpoints that range from commercial endeavours through Enlightenment moral obligations and postcolonial encounters with others. In his *Practical Philosophy,* Kant addressed hospitality explicitly as a requirement for perpetual peace. Mecksroth (2017) suggests that most commentators have misinterpreted the main purpose of Kant's principled analysis of hospitality, and argues instead that Kant's hospitality is a "comprehensive alternative to a global state of war" (ibid., p. 3). Given that Kant's argument appears in the segment of *Practical Philosophy* titled "Perpetual Peace" [*Zum ewigen Frieden*], Mecksroth's interpretation has merit. As an example of quintessential Enlightenment philosophy, "Perpetual Peace" outlines the necessary and reasonable connections between freedom and the prevention of war. Kant specified that the rights and conditions for peace and freedom differ relative to different scales from universal to continental, national, and individual. This chapter's point of departure is Kant's assertion that hospitality is one of the three definitive articles for the prevention of war and the establishment of perpetual peace in the world.

In the current context of immigration and refugee displacement, the purpose of this chapter is heuretic: to invent a discursive space that welcomes conversations in philosophy of education about hospitality across diverse linguistic and cultural contexts (Ulmer, 1994). Heuretic writing contrasts with expository, didactic, critical, polemical, or advocacy writing in its purpose to be inventive. Jarrett (n.d.) notes that a heuretic approach means: "We can read as artists. In addition to *writing about* texts (oral, printed, and electronic), we can *write with* texts: create inventive or heuretic effects." One dimension of hospitality in educational research is to welcome into the conversation a range of unfamiliar epistemologies and approaches to writing. In this way, I have tried to use language that performs a degree of creative freedom, and that is hospitable to strange ideas.

Across philosophical literatures, hospitality is not associated with legalism, rationality, or economics (Rosello, 2001). Instead, hospitality is construed in terms of ethics as an alternative to a social-contract approach to human relations. As an ethic, hospitality is susceptive to ethical analysis and critique. Pertaining to philosophy of education, Claudia Ruitenberg (2015), for example, theorises education as "the process of introducing newcomers to the world" (ibid., p. 48). Ruitenberg takes the stance that "Education guided by an ethic of hospitality does not aim to cultivate any particular type of moral subject. … Instead, an ethic of hospitality calls on individuals to make space for the other where they dwell" (ibid.). From this perspective, hospitality assumes a place at the ethical heart of philosophy of educational research.

Several commentators have illuminated dimensions of hospitality by focusing on linguistic and etymological features of the word. For example, the French word *hôte* can mean either host or guest. This double meaning allows for a playful and fluid engagement with the word *hospitality*, an ambiguity that comports easily with Derrida's deconstruction. In addition, the Latin *hostis* forms the root of the word *hostile*, which further complicates the semantic scope of hospitality in interesting ways. Germanic languages lend another valence of meanings to the term. In German *Gastfreundschaft* is literally "guest friendship," which connotes kindness and geniality as aspects of hospitality. Most interesting to me is that, in Flemish, hospitality is *gastvrijheid*, literally "guest freedom," and, in a poetic way, this delightfully connects hospitality with freedom. The etymology and languages of hospitality are conducive to heuretic readings.

I continue by travelling around to summarise various discourses of hospitality including religious, gendered, postcolonial, and New Materialist approaches. I then highlight felicitous dimensions of philosophies of hospitality. In an effort to welcome more diverse theories of hospitality to the conversation along the way, the summaries also historicise hospitality by inviting dimensions of scale to the theoretical frames, which opens spaces for epistemological diversity. The chapter concludes by reassessing the value of hospitality as an ethic for research in philosophy of education.

Philosophies of Hospitality Around the World

Some philosophical treatments of hospitality begin with examples from Homer's *Odyssey*, but most begin with a discussion of "Perpetual Peace" from Kant's (1795) *Practical Philosophy*. Kant argued that cosmopolitan hospitality is a universal human right: "Hospitality means the *right* of a visiting foreigner not to be treated as an enemy" (italics in original). Writing from an Enlightenment ethos, Kant argued that hospitality is an article of peace insofar as a visitor has the reasonable human right to set foot on foreign soil without being attacked: "The law of world citizenship is to be united to conditions of universal hospitality" (ibid., p. 11). However, Kant's philosophy of hospitality does not specify that the visitor must be *accepted* into the foreign society; the right of hospitality is a feature of civilisation to prevent war, but does not obligate nations to accommodate nations. Individuals (as citizens of the world) are to be welcomed unconditionally, while relations between nation-states are not subject to the same ethical obligations of unconditional hospitality. In this way, Kant's philosophy introduces dimensions of scale into a philosophy of hospitality.

After gesturing to Kant's "Perpetual Peace", philosophical studies of hospitality typically take up Derrida's (2000) interview [*De l'hospitalite*] with Dufourmantelle (2011). Predictably, in Derrida's theoretical hands, hospitality deconstructs as both possible and impossible: "The perversion and pervertibility of this law... of hospitality... is that one can become virtually xenophobic in order to protect or claim to protect one's own hospitality, the own home that makes possible one's own hospitality" (ibid., p. 53). Critchley (1999) extends the deconstructive frame by welcoming Levinas (1969) to the conversation: "Derrida rightly argues that Levinas's *Totality and Infinity* can be read as 'an immense treatise on hospitality', where ethics is defined as a welcome to the other, as an unconditional hospitality" (ibid. p. 274). As in Kant's philosophy, Derrida also argues that hospitality is a philosophical issue of paramount importance for the prevention of war and establishment of perpetual peace.

It is generative to historicise the philosophy of hospitality by including elements of scale, namely, the specifics of time and place that contextualise lived experiences of hospitality. Following Kant, Matei Candea (2012) explicitly addresses the issue of scale as pertinent to the theorisation of hospitality: "Hospitality as a social practice is grounded in specific objects, sites, and boundaries—houses, thresholds, coffeepots, televisions, tables, and chairs—and its form is thus profoundly modified by attempts to scale it up" (ibid., p. S44). This chapter suggests that dimensions of scale, in relation to frames, may serve as mechanisms for welcoming and including more diverse epistemological perspectives. This section attempts to be broadly inclusive by offering brief summaries of a wide range of philosophical treatments of hospitality, arranged roughly from a large world-wide scale to a small individual scale. I have clustered various treatments under seven themes that illustrate the extent of hospitality offerings across various cultural contexts and epistemological commitments.

Mediterranean Hospitality

I was intrigued to find how much philosophical literature on hospitality has been written from and about Mediterranean regions. Even Kant's "Perpetual Peace" includes mention of the Barbary Coast (northern Africa), which is described as a particularly inhospitable place. Perhaps hospitality became a prominent issue when early sea traders went on voyages that landed them in unfamiliar places where they were dependent on local hosts for safety and provisions. In any case, several accounts of Mediterranean hospitality have survived to document encounters with strangers from faraway. Some of these accounts have been incorporated into narratives about hospitality in literature, history, and philosophy. These early accounts have recently taken on new meanings in relation to current refugee and immigrant conditions, also primarily located in Mediterranean regions. One example of an early reference to hospitality in the Mediterranean is related in Homer's *Odyssey*: "Stranger, it would be wrong for me to turn a guest away, even one in a worse state than you, since every beggar and stranger is from Zeus, and a gift, though small, from such folk as us is welcome" (2004, Book 14, lines 53–58). This passage has been cited by philosophers to document the long history of hospitality as an ethic, and to illustrate that hospitality can be offered freely by anyone, regardless of how rich or poor, as a way of sustaining peaceful relations among strangers.

In another example from the Mediterranean, Visser (1992) cites a Bedouin tenet of hospitality as "People who had eaten salt together would not fight each other," a premise that also underwrites the argument in Kant's (1795) "Perpetual Peace." *Besa* is an Albanian term that means both "keep the faith" and "hospitality"; *besa* is celebrated today as a cultural commitment pertaining to the hospitality of Albanians who sheltered Jews during World War II. Moroccan writer Tahar Ben Jelloun (1999) also focuses on French hospitality in Mediterranean countries of North Africa. Ben Jelloun defines hospitality as "a reciprocal right to protection and shelter" (ibid., p. 1). His postcolonial analysis argues that we can understand racism as an effect of the disintegration of an ethic of hospitality. Ben Jelloun's philosophical narrative illustrates grounded connections between hospitality, peace, and freedom.

Julian Pitt-Rivers' (1977/2012) anthropological study of the Mediterranean includes a chapter called "The Law of Hospitality". He writes: "The status of guest... stands midway between that of hostile stranger and that of community member. He is incorporated practically rather than morally" (ibid., p. 504). In this account, hospitality gestures to the problem of how to deal with strangers. Using anthropological stories and allusions to Homer's *Odyssey*, Pitt-Rivers recognises the importance of rituals of hospitality as mechanisms for maintaining peace, justice, and order when strangers from different cultures meet one another.

Radical Religious Hospitality

Pitt-Rivers (1977/2012) analysed religious dimensions of the ethic of hospitality in the Mediterranean region, noting that there is an association "between divinity and the unknown" (ibid., p. 507). In this cultural context, hospitality became a sacred obligation deriving from the possibility that any stranger may be a god in disguise.

In religious literature, especially early Jesuit writings, hospitality is generally defined in universal terms as radical and unconditional (see, e.g., Boothroyd, 2013; Gani, 2017). Religious frames connect hospitality in education to Freire's dialogical teaching (from Catholic Liberation Theology) where, at a broad scale, both parties are positioned to learn something from the encounter. Religious frames for hospitality often appeal to universal moral commitments to caring for the Other (Jacobs, 2008; Pohl, 1999), and some make connections to the term "host" as a synonym for eucharistic bread offered at the communion table. For example, Canadian English scholar Dale Jacobs (2008) writes: "The idea that any guest is welcome is a key feature of monastic hospitality; unlike the kind of hospitality we might offer in our homes, monastic hospitality is radical in its acceptance of all, including those who might be hostile to us" (ibid., p. 566). In this view, monastic hospitality is unconditional, which aligns with Kant's ethic of hospitality at the person-to-person scale, and contrasts with Kant's ethic of hospitality at the nation-to-nation scale.

Postcolonial Hospitality

Postcolonial philosophers often consider hospitality side-by-side with cosmopolitanism. Postcolonialism generally positions hospitality in relation to the complicated role of global wealth distribution (see, e.g., Rosello, 2001; Yuval-Davis, 2011). Ben Jelloun (1999), for example, argued that any lack of hospitality can be attributed to relatively wealthy industrialised countries' unwillingness to provide because hospitality does not fit easily into a neoliberal-productivity efficiency lifestyle: "Hospitality has gradually given way to cold calculation" (ibid., p. 38). Again, we can see that Ben Jelloun's is an example of philosophy that illustrates real-world connections between hospitality, peace, and freedom.

Postcolonial studies suggest that there are two different relations of power in relations of hospitality: others as strangers, and the socioeconomic privilege of having the wherewithal to offer hospitality in the first place (Claviez, 2013; Gauthier, 2007; Nikiforova, 2016; Rosello, 2001). Ben Jelloun (1999) remembers with great fondness the examples of hospitality he witnessed as a child in Morocco, and his book is devoted to the aim of converting hospitality as an ethic into hospitality as a policy and a right. Along similar lines, Rosello (2001) considers hospitality in relation to refugees and questions of asylum, raising the question of scale as an alternative to universal notions:

> The question may not be whether states or cities are more or less hostile or hospitable entities, whether or not one of them is better structured, better equipped either to welcome or exclude strangers. Instead, we may want to ask under which specific conditions freedom and cities go together or are mutually exclusive... Consequently, I propose to think about the different possible patterns that would turn the city into a hospitable environment. (ibid., p. 151)

These postcolonial accounts of hospitality reiterate Levinas' philosophy of hospitality at the scale of person-to-person, face-to-face relationships between strangers as a mechanism for preventing war and establishing perpetual peace.

Gendered Hospitality

Several philosophical treatments of hospitality consider gender, especially the maternal, as a pivotal facet of hospitality (Derrida, 2000; Ruitenberg, 2015; Still, 2010a, 2010b, 2011, 2012). Aristarkhova (2012) and McNulty (2007) highlight gendered dimensions of hospitality by calling our attention to the maternal provisions of hospitable conditions to welcome visitors. Ethico-political analyses often debate the problems of assimilation and inequality that might be signalled in theorisations of hospitality. Describing the Bedouin of Egypt, Pitt-Rivers (1977/2012), for example, wrote: "The notion of hospitality derives in this instance from the sacredness of the womenfolk of the household" (ibid., p. 507). Stretching the concept somewhat, Still (2012) includes harems and adoption as gendered examples of Enlightenment hospitality.

McNulty's (2007) psychoanalytical feminist treatise on "The Hostess" addresses the possibility that a precondition for hospitality is the possession of property, that is, having the wherewithal to offer anything to a visitor. The critical implication of this observation is that efforts to provide hospitality could lead to a patronising attitude. Drawing primarily on Lacan, McNulty argues against the idea that hospitality must be an example of ego-driven masculinity:

the hostess's function both illuminates and gives new resonance to the subjective logic delineated in Lacan's reading of Freud's *Wo es war, soll Ich werden*. ... she is that 'stranger within' whose irreducibility to the identity of the host defines hospitality as something other than a confirmation of the ego's mastery. (ibid., p. 235)

In McNulty's analysis, an ethic of hospitality does not presuppose the possession of property. Her philosophy of hospitality also pertains between egos and can operate as a reflection of feminine psychic endowments.

Ruitenberg (2015) devotes a chapter of her book to the gender and culture of hospitality, specifically in the context of educational philosophy. Ruitenberg disagrees that hospitality is inherently gendered because, she argues, hospitality is not an essence but rather an ethos. Nevertheless, recognising that hospitality is enacted in space and time, Ruitenberg acknowledges that the "contextual particularity" of hospitality may entail gender elements. She also argues against the stance that maternal-type teaching is therefore ethically careful.

Face-to-Face with the Other

The most widely referenced philosophical resource on hospitality is perhaps Levinas' *Totality and Infinity: An Essay on Exteriority* (1969). Derrida has famously described Levinas' entire book as an extended meditation on hospitality. Abi Doukhan (2010) emphasises the importance of the concept of "exile" to Levinas' philosophy of hospitality, which renders Levinas' philosophy timely for current conditions of immigrants and refugees. Levinas (1969) explores the relationship between strangers in terms of "exteriority," and philosophises the possibility of knowing the Other face-to-face: "in the welcoming of the face ... equality is founded" (ibid., p. 214). When the self is introduced to the other, the closed loop of totality is opened to—hospitable to—altered relations between the self and the other. For Levinas, hospitable relations are understandable not as *totality*, but as *infinity,* consisting of love, eros, fecundity, filiality, and fraternity.

Similarly, Derrida's (2000) interview with Dufourmantelle approaches hospitality by elaborating on the concept of the stranger [*étranger*] and contrasting unconditional hospitality with conditional or legalistic hospitality:

absolute hospitality requires that I open up my home and that I give not only to the foreigner, ... but to the absolute, unknown, anonymous other, and that *give place* to them, that I let them, that I let them come, that I let them arrive and take the place in the place I offer them, without asking of them either reciprocity (entering into a pact) or even their names. (ibid., p. 25)

Face-to-face hospitality does not presume assimilation between the guest and host. Rather, hospitality presupposes that both guest and host will change in response to one another under a specific set of circumstances. Again illustrating *gastvrijheid,* Levinas characterises hospitality as a freely chosen moral act designed to forestall violence between strangers and thereby to prevent war.

Literacy as Hospitality

For some academic scholars (e.g., Davis, 2001), the university Writing Centre serves as an exemplary site of hospitality that welcomes reading and writing. Ruitenberg (2015) draws on a similar vision to construct her metaphor of education as hospitality. Further developing this theme, Richard Haswell and Janis Haswell (2015) theorise literacy and authoring as acts of hospitality:

> Hospitality is a social and ethical relationship not only between host and guest but also between writer and reader or teacher and student. Hospitality initiates acts of authoring, … As an ageless social custom that eases two strangers into deep conversation, hospitality is the necessary companionable gesture to every genuine act of literacy. (ibid., p. 3)

Insofar as literacy is central to education, the theorisation of literacy as hospitality is intimately connected with philosophy of education. Alluding to a poem by Roethke, Haswell and Haswell write: "Hospitality can start taking place where hand is shaken, greeting exchanged, book opened, syllabus handed out, tutor space broached—any place or time where knock is open wide" (ibid., p. 6). Following Kant and Levinas, Haswell and Haswell also illustrate how hospitality provides us with an alternative to war: "The opposite and enemy of hospitality is war" (ibid., p. 32). Even at the person-to-person scale, philosophers offer hospitality as an article of peace and freedom.

In literary approaches to hospitality, acceptance of strangeness can occur when we read and when we write. When we read hospitably, we accept the strangeness of the other's presence, language, and ways of coming to the world. When we write, we invite strangers to come into our thoughts, sometimes intimately. Haswell and Haswell (2015) appreciate the hospitality of educational relationships by noting that we cannot learn by repeatedly encountering the same; education is possible only in the encounter with the Other:

> Only the absolutely foreign—the students different in age, gender, cultural background, experience, politics, religion, ethnicity to the teacher, and the teacher different in age, gender, cultural background, experience, politics, religion, ethnicity to the student—can instruct. And hospitality is one of the few intuitive social practices that fully accepts the absolutely foreign. (ibid., p. 46)

The Haswell's theorisation of literacy as hospitality also exemplifies the possibility of heuretic engagement: free, creative, and peaceful engagement with strange ideas as an ethos to prevent hostilities.

New Materialist Hospitality

Candea (2012) highlights material dimensions of hospitality: "concrete objects and situations of interpersonal hospitality (a door to knock on, a threshold to cross) are precisely what enables actual hosts and guests to distinguish in each concrete instance 'welcome' from 'trespass'" (ibid., p. S44). Nikiforova (2016) draws on

Derrida and New Materialism to examine European border conditions. Nikiforova suggests that New Materialisms make it possible to change the past in a way that helps to prevent war:

> In the new materialists' view, the 'past' is open to change …. There is no inherently determinate relationship between past, present, and future on the border. History suggests that borders and borderlands are territories where the possibility to 'repair' the 'now' situation exists. (ibid., p. 152)

New Materialist frames of hospitality invite us to consider sensual dimensions of hospitality at the person-to-person scale. Affect is a core concept in New Materialism, and Michalinos Zembylas (2009), for example, posits that affect is the central component of peace education in the divided Mediterranean island of Cyprus. Zembylas explains that peace education projects had previously been framed in terms of psychology and/or politics. However, Zembylas (2006) argues that peace education has actual impact on affective dimensions instead because of the ungovernability of affect: "the 'virtual' dimension of affect is based on the fact that the space of embodiment is extended by a fleeting moment in which activities and relations take place before they are registered by conscious thought" (ibid., p. 311). Similarly, Yuval-Davis (2011) theorises belonging as an affective attachment of "feeling at home" (ibid., p. 10). New Materialist philosophies of hospitality illuminate possibilities for peace and freedom at intimate and affective dimensions at micro person-to-person scales.

Diversification of Scale to Extend Hospitality

Some philosophical treatments of hospitality construct oppositions (such as conditional versus unconditional), and then promote the benefits of one stance over others. However, I have tried to suggest a more hospitable approach to epistemological diversity by pointing out how these very diverse frames may be accommodated comfortably at different scales, which is what Kant's analysis in "Perpetual Peace" endorsed more than 200 years ago. For example, hospitality at large-scale global studies may serve as an article of peace and freedom, without necessarily implying unconditional welcome for all strangers at all times. Similarly, small, unique case-studies may be amenable to New Materialist or literacy-level analyses of hospitality and subscribe to more unconditional views of hospitality as a universal human right. Singularity has been discouraged by some educational research entities, and it is true that educational research includes many examples of inappropriate generalisations from case studies. Nevertheless, Haswell and Haswell (2015) helpfully describe how an individual ("singular") case study can be educationally generative—heuretic—without being generalisable: "at any moment any writer has the potential to produce singular text. As the singular reader receives the singular text offered by the singular writer, potentiality will actualize" (ibid., p. 5).

Finally, by inviting scale into the frame for considering diverse theorisations of hospitality, we are provided with accommodation for exploring social media and virtual connections as potential sites for hospitality. We are welcome to consider academic conferences as sites of hospitality for educational research and we are invited to examine research methodologies in terms of hospitality:

> an act of generosity and charity, yes, but … also an act of courage, transgression, disruption, resistance, or rebellion. And it is always a site for learning. One essential motivation for genuine hospitality … is gaining new experience and new knowledge. (Haswell & Haswell, 2015, p. 6)

In all of these cases, at all of these different scales, hospitality functions as an ethic for the exercise of freedom and the prevention of war.

Felicitous Hospitality

As an ethic, hospitality has much to recommend it. Many philosophers, notably Derrida, argue that hospitality must be conditional, and its offering can be only partial or imperfect; nevertheless, even those thinkers stipulate several happy features of hospitality as an ethic. Hospitality can be understood in terms of fulfillment: of an ethical obligation, of human connection, and of mutual needs. Pitt-Rivers (1977/2012), for example, elaborates that an ethic of hospitality can provide a model of relations with the other that does not essentialise identities of people or groups of people. A hospitality ethos aligns with Kant's end principle in which we treat other people with respect for their inalienable rights of dignity and freedom. Hospitality is a set of actions that can be performed by anyone toward anyone, and so it is not necessary to stipulate that "hosts" are one kind of people and "guests" are some other kind of people. Hospitality is not adjudicated by quantity or quality; poor people can be as hospitable as rich people. "Hospitable" describes a disposition, the tendency to behave in a particular way; as such, to be hospitable does not imply that we provide exactly the same accommodations to all travellers under all circumstances at all times. The ethic of hospitality does not dichotomise host and guest, or friend and stranger. Pitt-Rivers points out a logical necessity implied by the definition of hospitality: "strangeness is logically reciprocal" (ibid., p. 509). In these ways, an ethic of hospitality manages to avoid affixing labels, hierarchies, or predetermined responses in human relations.

For the most part, hospitality avoids commodification (the so-called "hospitality industry" notwithstanding) because there is no expectation of payment, exchange, or quid pro quo between guest and host. Hospitality is by definition a gracious, and not an economic, transaction. Hospitality in philosophy implies universal entitlement; hospitality is not needs-tested (i.e., if eligibility is needs tested, then it's not hospitality). In an ethic of hospitality, there is no expectation of reciprocity. Haswell and Haswell (2015) write: "The attributes of traditional hospitality are not balancing the ledger, evening the social score, or harvesting souls. They are goodwill, generosity, welcome, opening to the other, trust, mutual respect, privacy, talk, ease, gift exchange, elbow room, risk, marginality, social retreat, and embrace of change" (ibid., p. 6).

Hospitality brings people closer together by cultivating a non-violent and non-impositional intimacy between strangers. Following Kant and Levinas, Pitt-Rivers (1977/2012) also takes the position that hospitality is an alternative to war; it "does not eliminate the conflict altogether but places it in abeyance and prohibits its expression" (ibid., p. 513).

Hospitality is different from the discourse of inclusion in a felicitous way. Writing specifically about education, Ruitenberg (2015) argues that inclusion seeks to incorporate the guest into a preexisting culture, while hospitality is anti-colonialist and anti-assimilationist. Therefore, in Ruitenberg's view, inclusion—which restricts freedom and narrows possibilities—is incompatible with hospitality, which is freeing and expands possibilities for ways of being in the world.

Another felicitous feature is that an ethos of hospitality interrupts determinism. There can be no fatalistic encounter. Especially in Levinas' philosophy, hospitable relations cannot be imagined before the self meets the unknown and unknowable other. For Ruitenberg (2015), the central tension of hospitality is that between freedom and constraint. An ethos of hospitality pertains to encounters with the unfamiliar; therefore, it is impossible to know in advance what will happen in an encounter between strangers. Hospitality is that which transforms all parties from their previous designations as strangers into guests and hosts. Hospitality is a relation that is entered into freely, as an alternative to hostility that can prevent war.

Rancière (2009) argues that Derrida's conceptualisation of hospitality is incompatible with democracy. Rancière analyses Derrida's "Democracy to Come" and "Politics of Friendship" in order to characterise Derrida's conceptualisation of hospitality as a conflict between two oppositional demands: the unconditional ethical imperative to welcome all strangers, and the political impossibility of welcoming all strangers unconditionally: "Derrida emphasizes the difference between conditional and unconditional hospitality. For him there is a duty of unconditional hospitality toward any newcomer, no matter who. But that unconditional hospitality cannot be political" (ibid., p. 281). For Rancière, Derrida's ethical stance inserts a sovereign law—a Kantian regulative idea—that supersedes the negotiations that constitute democratic decision-making. For Rancière, Derrida's stance is incompatible with democracy because "the justice that is inherent in the idea of democracy to come is the justice of the unforeseeable event or the unforeseeable coming of the other" (ibid., p. 283). Rancière seems to suggest that democracy rests on an ethic of hospitality because participants welcome each other's ideas, and offer a place for strange voices.

Conclusion

In its colloquial use, hospitality is an ordinary word that describes what ordinary people enact by ordinary means in ordinary times. However, when brought into the realm of philosophy of education, it becomes possible to appreciate that hospitality is far more dynamic: hospitality provides an alternative to hostilities. John Bennett (2000; online, no pagination) writes explicitly about the importance of hospitality in the academy: "Being intellectually hospitable means being open to the different voices and idioms of others as potential agents for mutual enhancement, not just oppositional conflict." Even in the academy, hospitality can be appreciated as an alternative to conflict.

Like Derrida, Haswell and Haswell interpret Levinas' book as an extended treatise on hospitality, and the stakes for an ethic of hospitality could not be higher:

> the process of hospitality is a radical relation with the Other, a face-to-face encounter—creative, uncontrollable, and therefore understandable only as *infinity*. In the hospitable encounter lies the root of ethics, whereas war pursues winning by any means and thus stands outside of morality … Within hospitality war is always a possibility, but only hospitality can prevent war. (Haswell & Haswell, 2015, pp. 32–33)

"*Only hospitality can prevent war.*" That is a remarkable thought that endows our experiences in the face-to-face meetings of the Research Community with an entirely new *raison d'etre*.

References

Aristarkhova, I. (2012). Hospitality and the maternal. *Hypatia, 27*(1), 163–181. https://doi.org/10.1111/j.1527-2001.2010.01147.x

Ben Jelloun, T. (1999). *French hospitality: Racism and North African immigrants*. New York: Columbia University Press.

Bennett, J. B. (2000, Spring/Summer). The academy and hospitality. *Cross Currents, 50*(1–2). Available: http://www.crosscurrents.org/Bennett.htm

Boothroyd, D. (2013). *Hospitality, friendship and justice*. Edinburgh, UK: Edinburgh University Press. https://doi.org/10.3366/edinburgh/9780748640096.003.0009

Candea, M. (2012). Derrida en corse? Hospitality as scale-free abstraction. *Journal of the Royal Anthropological Institute, 18*, S34–S48. https://doi.org/10.1111/j.1467-9655.2012.01759.x

Claviez, T. (2013). *The conditions of hospitality: Ethics, politics, and aesthetics on the threshold of the possible*. New York: Fordham University Press.

Critchley, S. (1999). *Ethics, politics, subjectivity: Essays on Derrida, Levinas and contemporary French thought*. London: Verso.

Davis, J. C. (2001). Pitching a tent, welcoming a traveler, and moving on: Toward a nomadic view of the writing center. *Writing Lab Newsletter, 25*(10), 12–15.

Derrida, J., & Dufourmantelle, A. (2000). *Of hospitality* (R. Bowlby, Trans.). Stanford, CA: Stanford University Press.

Doukhan, A. (2010). From exile to hospitality: A key to the philosophy of Emmanuel Levinas. *Philosophy Today, 54*(3), 235–246. https://www.questia.com/library/journal/1P3-2146445641/from-exile-to-hospitality-a-key-to-the-philosophy

Dufourmantelle, A. (2011). *Philosophy of hospitality*. European Graduate School Lecture. Available: https://www.youtube.com/embed/vWWRpMu_l3E

Gani, J. K. (2017). The erasure of race: Cosmopolitanism and the illusion of Kantian hospitality. *Millennium: Journal of International Studies, 45*(3), 425–446. https://doi.org/10.1177/0305829817714064

Gauthier, D. (2007). Levinas and the politics of hospitality. *History of Political Thought, 28*(1), 158–180.

Haswell, R., & Haswell, J. (2015). *Hospitality and authoring: An essay for the English profession*. Logan, UT: Utah State University Press.

Homer. (2004). *The odyssey* (A. S. Kline, Trans.). Available online: https://www.poetryintranslation.com/PITBR/Greek/Odhome.php

Jacobs, D. (2008). The audacity of hospitality. *Journal of Advanced Composition, 38*(3/4), 563–580.

Jarrett, M. (n.d.). *Heuretics*. Penn State York Blog. Available: http://www2.york.psu.edu/~jmj3/elheuret.htm

Kant, I. (1795). *Toward perpetual peace: A philosophical sketch*. Available: http://www.earlymoderntexts.com/assets/pdfs/kant1795.pdf

Levinas, I. (1969). *Totality and infinity: An essay on exteriority* (A. Lingis, Trans.). Pittsburgh, PA: Duquesne University Press.

McNulty, T. (2007). *The hostess: Hospitality, femininity, and the expropriation of identity*. Minneapolis, MN: University of Minnesota Press. https://doi.org/10.5749/j.ctttxt7

Meckstroth, C. (2017). Hospitality, of Kant's critique of cosmopolitanism and human rights. *Political Theory*, online first.

Nikiforova, B. (2016). European borders and identity from the new materialist approach. *Pogranicze Studia Społeczne, 27*(1), 151–162.

Pitt-Rivers, J. (1977/2012, Spring). The law of hospitality. *HAU: Journal of Ethnographic Theory, 2*(1), 510–517. Available. http://www.journals.uchicago.edu/doi/full/10.14318/hau2.1.022

Pohl, C. (1999). *Making room: Recovering hospitality as a Christian tradition*. Grand Rapids, MI: Eerdmans Publishing.

Rancière, J. (2009). Derrida and the time of the political. In P. Cheah & S. Guerlac (Eds.), *Should democracy come? Ethics and politics in Derrida* (pp. 275–290). Durham, NC: Duke University Press.

Rosello, M. (2001). *Postcolonial hospitality: The immigrant as guest*. Stanford, CA: Stanford University Press.

Ruitenberg, C. (2015). *Unlocking the world: Education in an ethic of hospitality*. New York: Routledge.

Still, J. (2010a). *The dangers of hospitality: The French state, cultural difference and gods*. Edinburgh, UK: Edinburgh University Press. https://doi.org/10.3366/edinburgh/9780748640270.003.0005

Still, J. (2010b). *Introduction to the question of hospitality: Ethics and politics*. Edinburgh, UK: Edinburgh University Press. https://doi.org/10.3366/edinburgh/9780748640270.003.0001

Still, J. (2011). *Enlightenment hospitality: Cannibals, harems and adoption*. Oxford, UK: Voltaire Foundation.

Still, J. (2012). *Derrida and hospitality: Theory and practice* (1st ed.). Edinburgh, UK: Edinburgh University Press. https://doi.org/10.3366/j.ctt1r20fq

Ulmer, G. L. (1994). *Heuretics: The logic of invention*. Baltimore, MD: Johns Hopkins Press.

Visser, M. (1992). *The rituals of dinner*. New York: Penguin Books.

Yuval-Davis, N. (2011). *Politics of belonging: Intersectional contestations*. New York: Sage.

Zembylas, M. (2006). Witnessing in the classroom: The ethics and politics of affect. *Educational Theory, 56*(3), 305–324.

Zembylas, M. (2009). Affect, citizenship, politics: Implications for education. *Pedagogy, Culture and Society, 17*(3), 369–383.

Chapter 6
Why, Perhaps, Philosophers of Education (and Other Educational Researchers) "Leave Everything as It Is"

David Bridges

Abstract It has long been a complaint of philosophers of education and other educational researchers that, in particular policy makers pay little heed to their arguments and evidence. Equally, policy makers complain that too much educational research is irrelevant or uninformative or fails to dress their concerns. Despite the almost exponential growth in the quantity of educational research, this seems to have little impact, to "leave everything as it is".

This paper will explore this problem through four lines of thought:

(i) by looking at the role of the communicative and social practices that take philosophy and other forms of educational inquiry into practice and policy;
(ii) by looking at the logic of arguments that might take us from philosophical work (in particular) to convincing prescriptions for educational policy and practice;
(iii) by looking at the controversy and uncertainty that is intrinsic to research endeavour as a barrier to its impact on policy and practice;
(iv) by looking at philosophical interest as something detached from engagement with policy or practice.

It will conclude that there are a number of compelling reasons why we should have low expectations of the impact on policy or practice of philosophical and other work characterised and communicated in the ways set out here.

The philosophers have only interpreted the world in various ways. The point, however, is to change it.
Karl Marx in *Eleven theses on Feuerbach* – and also inscribed on his gravestone.

D. Bridges (✉)
University of East Anglia, Norwich, UK

St Edmund's College, Cambridge, UK

Homerton College, Cambridge, UK
e-mail: db347@cam.ac.uk

© Springer International Publishing AG, part of Springer Nature 2018   77
S. Ramaekers, N. Hodgson (eds.), *Past, Present, and Future Possibilities for Philosophy and History of Education*,
https://doi.org/10.1007/978-3-319-94253-7_6

Introduction

In their invitation to contribute to this *liber amicorum* Stefan Ramaekers and Naomi Hodgson expressed a key concern about what appear to be the limitations of both philosophy and history as forms of educational research: that "they leave everything as it is". This concern was related specifically to what might be seen as the failure of 15 years of scholarship by members of the "Leuven" "research community" to have any discernible impact on the developments in the practice of educational research that have been the focus of their critique over this time,

This is, of course, a concern that we can share with many in the educational research community. There is a good deal of interesting and important research that investigates what sources policy-makers do in fact draw on to inform their policy decisions, and which suggests that they rely primarily on commissions, trusted experts, and think-tanks for ideas, and that academic research on social issues, including education, sits at the bottom of the list of resources drawn upon, below the media, constituents, and consumers (see, for example, Edwards, Sebba, & Rickinson, 2007). Whitty's account of New Labour's relationship with educational research in the UK supports these observations and concludes that "in reality, policy is driven by all sorts of considerations, of which the findings of educational research are likely on some occasions to be pretty low down" (Whitty, 2006, p. 168).

This disappointment (if that is what it is) reflects, perhaps, a wider question as to whether philosophy, history, or indeed any other forms of educational inquiry *can* sensibly be expected to have any particular "impact" (to borrow from the contemporary discourse on research assessment) on society – or even, contrary to the expectations of both Marx and rather more conservative and neo-liberal political administrations, *should* be expected to have such impact.

This paper will explore this problem through four lines of thought:

 (i) by looking at the role of the communicative and social practices that take philosophy and other forms of educational inquiry into practice and policy;
 (ii) by looking at the logic of arguments that might take us from philosophical work (in particular) to convincing prescriptions for educational policy and practice;
(iii) by looking at the controversy and uncertainty that is intrinsic to research endeavor as a barrier to its impact on policy and practice;
(iv) by looking at philosophical interest as something detached from engagement with policy or practice.

These are indeed themes that the Research Community, convened over the last 15 years by Paul Smeyers and Marc Depaepe, have addressed, almost in anticipation of the questions raised by the editors of this volume, and I draw in this chapter on some of the work that I produced in this context, acknowledging in particular the enormous support I have received over this time from my esteemed philosophical colleague and friend, Paul Smeyers, to whom this volume is a tribute much deserved.

On the Communication of Research

I shall not labour this point, because it is fairly obvious and has been for some time. Most philosophical work and indeed most educational research in all forms, is communicated, made public, "published" via academic journals and books. The incentive structure that dominates the academy values and rewards above all else the academic's success in getting papers published, in particular, in highly rated "international" journals. In some cases, for example in the Belgian system, the *number* of such publications is rewarded; in other cases, as in the UK, it is the peer-assessed *quality* of a restricted number of such publications (see www.ref.ac.uk). One consequence of this requirement has been the enormous proliferation of such journals, driven by the ready supply of papers and by the anxiety of scholars to access, and in particular university libraries to supply, a comprehensive range of published material. The result is an exponential increase in the volume of material inviting attention on a scale that defeats most scholars, let alone anyone whose primary commitment is to educational practice in the classroom or in educational administration. One study of publishing in the field of higher education alone calculated that there are now 86 English language journals focussed on higher education (a 40% increase since 2000) and that these published in 2016 more than 40,000 pages of text – an annual output of some 16 million words and growing! (Tight, 2017). No wonder that the author of this study reported to the *Times Higher Education* that "We know how to do things better, but these findings are not always being communicated or packaged up for the people who might benefit" (*Times Higher Education*, 2017, p. 10). The indications are that much of such material is actually read by only a handful of people. There are repeated claims (on a somewhat obscure evidential base) that some 50% of journal articles are read by only the editors and the reviewers and that the average readership of research in the arts is 7, though more recent evidence from downloads (perhaps not an entirely reliable proxy for reading) suggests that things are not quite as bad as this (Ware & Mabe, 2012, para. 2.7).

Not only this, but the criteria against which papers are assessed as suitable for publication are primarily shaped by academic requirements to do with its rigour, its located-ness within an appropriate literature, its theoretical framing, its conceptual sophistication etc., all of which drives it into a rather technical language and in some forms an impersonal, unengaging style.[1] It is hardly surprising, then, that work com-

---

[1] There are exceptions: how refreshing to read writers of case studies being urged to achieve the narrative vitality of a best-selling novel!

municated in this manner has little impact on the wider educational community, which was never the intended audience.

Of course, one option for researchers, including philosophers, is to contribute to wider debate through other channels: by writing pieces for popular or professional newspapers and magazines; through blogs; through contributions to professional conferences and public events; through radio interviews or briefings for policy makers. None of these carry any guarantee of "impact", however; nor do they count for much credit in academic circles.

Such alternative modes of reporting also provide considerable challenges to researchers in terms of the risk of over-simplification of what they have to say. I recall some years ago, at the end of a project on school accountability on which five of us had worked for 18 months, we were delighted to be asked for an interview by a BBC reporter. Our project director took nearly 20 min to answer, thoughtfully, the interviewer's first question. At the end of the response the reporter turned off his tape recorder and sighed, "I don't know how to put this to you", he said, "but I will probably get 45 sec on air for this piece. Shall we start again?" 18 months of carefully nuanced research by five people – and you have 45 seconds to explain what you have found: what do you say? It was not a lot easier to encapsulate my report on a 12 month inquiry into school reform in Kazakhstan by an even larger team in the form required by the then Deputy Prime Minister – "no more than six bullet points" –though in fairness he did allow us to expand on one or two points he found especially interesting. "He who generalises" wrote G.K. Chesterton, "generally lies: he who simplifies, simply lies".

If the movement from the academic journal to more popular (and cursory) forms of communication carries certain risks (and uncertain effects), so also does an even more radical strategy for joining research to policy or practice. In a different context – that of the application of scientific research to business innovation and development – it is often argued that "knowledge transfers best on two legs" i.e. by academic researchers moving directly into the business environment and taking their research with them. By analogy, might not researchers move personally into the domains of practice or policy? The first offers perhaps the opportunity for the most intense application of whatever one has learned (in so far as it lends itself to applicability!); the second offers a broader scope, but at the price of a multitude of interferences and compromises, for the simple reason that policy is framed not just by research but also by politics and a wide range of considerations (including, as I will explain more fully below, cost, opportunity cost, and the gaining or loss of political capital) that educational research will rarely have taken into account.

Once the philosopher/researcher moves into the policy/political sphere, with all the compromises that this requires, he or she becomes exposed to a different set of risks – of selling out, hypocrisy (because he or she is now associated with policies or interests unaligned with previously declared beliefs) – and claims from the sanctuary of the ivory tower that (s)he should not be there at all (see Bridges, 2015). Perhaps philosopher/researchers will have some impact on policy through this sort of engagement or should at least try to do so, but it is easy to see why, as Plato observed:

A philosopher is like a man coming among violent beasts unwilling to take part in their ill-doings and unable by himself to make head against these. (Plato, trans. Richards, 1966, p. 110).

It is so much easier simply to content oneself with one's conference paper.

In any case, as William Sutherland et al. argue in the context of the translation of scientific knowledge through the movement of scientists into the political sphere:

Although laudable, it is unrealistic to expect substantially increased political involvement from scientists. Another proposal is to expand the role of chief scientific advisers, increasing their number, availability and participation in political processes. Neither approach deals with the core problem of scientific ignorance among many who vote in parliaments (Sutherland, Spiegelhalter, & Burgman, 2013, p. 335).

From Philosophical Work to Convincing Prescriptions for Educational Policy and Practice

Thus far I have treated the problem (that we leave things unchanged) as essentially a problem of communication reinforced by structures that tend to favour one form of communication (directed at an academic audience) over others that might more plausibly channel researchers' work to educational practitioners and policymakers. The problem, conceived of in these terms, is an essentially *practical* one, amenable to empirical investigation that asks questions about the consequences or effects of employing different approaches to the communication of the insights of philosophy or other forms of research, the lessons or recommendations these may suggest, and hence changing policy or practice.

I suggest, however, that the problem is more deep-seated than this approach suggests, and that there is indeed a *logical* gap between what philosophy or research can contribute and arriving at a rational prescription for educational policy and practice (see, more fully with respect to empirical research, Bridges & Watts, 2008).

To begin with, a substantial body of philosophical work does not even attempt to prescribe what should be done: rather it questions and examines critically what others inside and outside the philosophical community have proposed; it unpicks and challenges assumptions; it provides alternative ways of seeing things; and, as Marx suggests offers endless interpretations and re-interpretations of our experience – all of which *may* eventually go to inform thinking about educational policy or practice, but not, in any very direct way, to generate specific changes in either.

Some philosophical work may come closer to prescription. John White's work for example, made a case for a compulsory curriculum in schools and later for an aims based curriculum, and both prescriptions were eventually adopted in England and Wales (1973, 2007, 2008), though perhaps not necessarily in the form or for the reasons that White advanced. Both the ethical and social/political branches of philosophy, of course, provide the resources for recommendations about the good life, about the good person, and about the good society, from which implications can be drawn, more or less systematically, for education.

Such work can point to directions for policy and practice or, like Peters' "process model" of education (Peters, 1967), can advance principles that such practice should satisfy, but this still leaves a big gap between the philosophical work and action. There are a number of significant considerations that have to be taken into account before one can move from high-level philosophical prescription to action in the social and political sphere.

First, we need to define what are often rather high-level aspirational terms into operational terms. We may be persuaded by philosophers that education should help children to become "autonomous", but what, more precisely does this mean in practice? What would it look like in the classroom? What knowledge, understanding, skills, attitudes, dispositions etc. would together constitute such autonomy? Similarly, few can be opposed to a "just" society or a "fair" education system; the problems arise out of rival conceptions of what this means and enormously complex decisions about how to operationalise any of them in a way that does not offend the same principle or another principle (personal freedom or excellence perhaps) that competes for our attention.

Secondly, we need a lot of empirical evidence as to the conditions that have in the past supported the development of the qualities we are looking for, of what are the actual consequences of doing this rather than that, and of what we might reasonably expect to lead to what we are looking for in the future. It was precisely this requirement that led Lawrence Stenhouse, who explicitly embraced Peter's "process model" against the prevailing orthodoxy of an objectives led curriculum, to demand that teachers become researchers in their own classrooms. A curriculum was, in Stenhouse's view, merely a hypothesis – a theory about what practice might lead to what achievement – that had to be tested by teachers in the contextually specific conditions of their own classrooms (Stenhouse, 1975). The roads from educational policy to practice are paved with good intentions (as well as some not so good), which have foundered because things did not work out as they were intended.

However, as I have already noted, empirical evidence does not necessarily take you to practice either. In terms of what I call the logical gap, and this is my third point, this is partly because of the circumscribed scope of most educational research. It may be able to show that better paid and better qualified teachers raise student attainment: but this evidence then faces the competition for resources both within the government department responsible for education and between this department and others. The research does not assess either the financial or political cost implied by its recommendations and the reality of overcoming both sources of resistance, so its power as an enactable set of recommendations is curtailed. Education as a field of policy and practice is especially vulnerable to these considerations – budgetary and political. It is vulnerable to budgetary considerations because of the sheer scale of the system and, hence, the cost implications of even relatively minor changes. It is vulnerable to political considerations both because it is high in the priorities of the voting public, all of whom have some first-hand experience of the system, and also because the normative character of the judgements that underpin policy and practice render it exposed to ideological considerations that often over-ride considerations of evidence or carefully considered argument. Philosophy has, of course, the intellectual resources to enable it to engage with ideology, and the pages of philosophical journals and the publications of the Research Community are full of such critical engagement, but it is of the nature of ideology and its supporting infrastructure of power and influence that it is generally impervious to such critical engagement.

So my first observation is that there is, inevitably I would say, a logical gap between what philosophy can do even in combination with empirical research and possible prescriptions for actionable educational policy or practice. This is not a matter of the human frailty or failing; it is a matter of the difference between the sort of knowledge and understanding which philosophical or empirical work as such *can* generate and the admixture of knowledge and understanding that is required if one is to know what to do – in general as a matter of policy or in one's own setting as a matter of practice.

This conclusion carries the interesting consequence that researchers – including philosophers – would be wise to resist the pressure they are often under to come up with "recommendations", since any such recommendations would almost certainly rely on considerations that went beyond the scope of the research. They can provide insights, understanding, challenges to established ways of seeing things that might and perhaps should inform the decision making of policy-makers and practitioners, but that is as far as the researcher/philosopher *as such* can go. Of course, as an individual citizen, equipped too with experience, political nouse, financial acumen, normative and ideological commitment and wisdom, the researcher philosopher may have a good deal more to say, but if (s)he is to do that s(he) must avoid claiming validation from the research for recommendations that rely on a good deal more and that has, perhaps, less rigorous foundations.

Uncertainty, Post Truth, and the Discrediting of Academic Work

This third set of considerations begins with the observation of a logical limitation of any research, but perhaps of philosophy in particular, that then renders it vulnerable to disempowerment in the domains of policy and practice.

Academics of all kinds are schooled in humility – a quality that frequently appears in accounts of academic virtue (see, for example, MacFarlane, 2009; Pring, 2001). Their academic functioning *requires* them to think critically, to be sceptical of any opinion – to the extent that, as Karl Popper advised: "in searching for the truth, it may be our best plan to start by criticising our most cherished beliefs" (Popper, 1963, p. 6). For philosophers, of course, there are no boundaries to such speculative doubting – does the material world exist when I am not observing it? Am I alone in the world? Can I actually know anything? – though such scepticism sometimes provides (as with Descartes, for example) the foundation for the restoration of belief.

In other fields too, reviewers of academic papers will be quick to observe claims made in a conclusion that go beyond what is supported by the evidence from the research. Researchers are expected to acknowledge the limitations of their research, to advance and treat seriously the counter-hypothesis; to acknowledge and describe their "positionality" and its possible influence on their work. The result is that any conclusions are, or should be, offered cautiously, acknowledging uncertainty or alternative readings of the evidence. And of course the debates that the researcher has with himself or herself become externalised in the often bitterly fought contests within the larger academic community, so that, almost whatever opinion is offered by one academic, another can be found who will advance a contrary one.

But such equivocation, scepticism, and uncertainty (or so it might appear) does not help to carry much conviction in the public sphere. It was US President Harry Truman who famously demanded that someone should send him a one-armed econ- omist, because he was fed up with hearing "on the one hand … on the other hand" from his expert economic advisors. A more contemporary US president exploits such debates to discredit any expert opinion (for which he says there are always "alternative facts") in favour of his own authoritative pronouncements. "Trust me", he urges the world and the American people, "the experts are in disarray and the rest is 'false news'".

Kai Horsthemke argues that sections of the academic community (including cer- tain constructivists, postmodernists, and postcolonial theorists, even some femi- nists) are themselves at least partly responsible for "the current climate in which truth, facts and rationality are treated with disdain" (Horsthemke, 2017, p. 274). "In the post truth era", wrote Ralph Keyes, who coined this term in his book of the same name, "borders blur between truth and lies, honesty and dishonesty, fiction and nonfiction. Deceiving others becomes a challenge, a game, and ultimately a habit" (Keyes, 2004, p. 1). Why, in such a world, should anyone seek to ground either policy or practice in the outcomes of research?

Such argument is correct in one respect, even if it leads to the wrong conclusion. It is correct in making a connection between the truth claims of research and its entitlement to inform (if not to determine) policy or practice. If research does not deliver understanding that it is better informed and interpreted than some other claims, if it does not provide "warranted belief", if it does not provide "good grounds" for doing this rather than that (to draw on a number of expressions from traditional epistemology), then of course it is not deserving of attention. But on the whole – I say this cautiously – I think we have to believe that it does: this is what all the attention to care, rigour, thoroughness, responsibility, questioning, "systematic and sustained" inquiry, peer and public scrutiny provide. What research does not provide, however, is *certainty* and hence absolute confidence, and this is an issue that has to be addressed.

A November 2017 conference of the University of Cambridge Centre for Science and Policy treated the question as a problem of communication (The University does after all have, in the person of Sir David Spiegelhalter, the Winton Professor of the Public Understanding of Risk), and the conference asked: "How can we com- municate uncertainty without endangering trust and credibility?"

The answers given were couched in terms of less confusing presentation of data, greater use of graphic images, fuller explanation of terms such as "usually". These might usefully mitigate some sources of misunderstanding and fear. But they do not really address the underlying problem – the logical problem about the validity and reliability of beliefs that are advanced out of research, the possibility of error, and the availability of alternative interpretations of the same evidence.

A second approach to the problem of public or at least political understanding of the strengths and limitations of (in this case) scientific research is outlined in the article by Sutherland, Spiegelhalter, and Burgman, "Twenty tips for interpreting scientific claims", referred to above. The authors argue that:

> The immediate priority is to improve policy-makers' understanding of the imperfect nature of science. The essential skills are to be able to intelligently interrogate experts and advisers, and to understand the quality, limitations and biases of evidence (Sutherland, Spiegelhalter, & Burgman, 2013, p. 335).

The "tips" that follow are interesting in this context, because they point to basic requirements that any researcher (or at least any scientific researcher in this case) or the reviewer of such research would recognise as conditions of the rigour of the work and hence the dependability of what it is claimed to show. The authors urge readers of research to consider, for example: whether results are presented with a precision that is appropriate for the associated error and whether the sample size is fit for purpose and sufficiently randomised; they warn against implying an unjustified degree of accuracy, against assuming causation on the basis of evidence of a correlation, against extrapolation of significance beyond the data, against generalisations from e.g. laboratory experiments on animals to human beings and against the cherry picking of evidence to support one's point of view.

Whether policy makers or practitioners will have the time or motivation to engage in this kind of scrutiny of research is another question, but the approach recommended here does offer some tools for coping with the conflicting voices of research and the uncertainty that surrounds it. It acknowledges uncertainty but suggests (which is after all a fairly common sense response) that some propositions may be more reliable, more deserving of belief than others and, further, some tools for determining which are which.

> Till philosophers become kings or those now named kings and rulers give themselves truly and rightly, and these two things — political power and philosophic thought — come together ... states will have no rest from their troubles, dear Glaucon, and if I am right, man will have none. (Plato trans. Richards, 1966, p. 97)

In terms of the argument in this section, I have suggested that neither of Plato's alternatives is very realistic: too few "philosophers" are ready to move across into the political or policy arena; and too few kings or policy makers have the time to give themselves "truly and rightly" to philosophy. We can offer Plato a third possibility, however: that kings or policy makers might at least be equipped to recognise when the philosophers, historians or the wider educational research community are talking rubbish!

We should hope so: the political consequences of a collapse of faith in all reason, argument and evidence and public as well as academic's capacity to deploy all these effectively was not lost on Karl Popper, who experienced it at first hand:

> Disbelief in the power of human reason, in man's power to discern the truth is almost invariably linked with distrust of man [sic]. This epistemological pessimism is linked historically with a doctrine of human depravity, and it tends to lead to the demand for the establishment of powerful traditions and *the entrenchment of a powerful authority that would save man from his folly and wickedness'* (Popper, 1963, p. 6 my italics).

In contemporary disdain for reason and evidence, in populism and in the actions of those who exploit these for their own political advantage, there are disturbing echoes of the conditions that nurtured the rise of dictatorships of the right and left in the 1920s and 1930s. Popper espoused a form of epistemological fallibilism and made it the task of science to challenge and test beliefs in order to identify their fragility, inadequacy, or weakness. But here, as in other applications of scientific and philosophical scepticism, such testing was precisely what could render some beliefs more deserving of our confidence (provisionally and pending their capacity to survive further challenges) than others and a more reliable source than others for intelligent policy or practice.

"Leaving Everything as It Is": Does It Matter?

This whole discussion has so far been based on an assumption that producing academic work that "leaves everything as it is" is some kind of failing. In Marx's terms, after all, the point is not just to interpret the world but to change it.

The thrust of my argument is that our responsibility *qua* philosophers, historians, or any other kind of educational researcher is properly and indeed necessarily limited to such an interpretative role, albeit that our insights and interpretations *may* go on to inform those engaged in change in policy or practice – and I fully accept that we could do better, despite the problems, in communicating the outcomes of our work so that a wider public has at least the option of ignoring it or taking it into account. Nor, as I indicated earlier, does this position exclude other obligations for example towards creating a fairer society or exercising our trusteeship of the natural world that we may carry *qua* citizens, parents, workers, or members of our community, but the fact that we are philosophers or researchers does not in itself impose on us any greater duty than that which applies to any other citizen or entitle us to a privileged position in the exercise of these responsibilities, even if it helps to sharpen our contributions to public debate. In this sense, perhaps we should not lie awake at night worrying too much if others, *having had chance to take our work into account*, choose not to take much notice of what we have to say.

There is perhaps an even more chilled response rooted in the academic's romance with what is sometimes referred to as curiosity-led research. In my own case, for example, participation in the KU Leuven-based research community has been a rare opportunity and stimulus to follow lines of thought into unfamiliar and unpredict-able territory as I have dutifully grappled with the topics set each year – in many cases without a clue as to how I might respond to them. It has expanded my horizons and been *interesting* (and, I confess, especially enjoyable, when extended through dinner and a late night beer and conversation in one of Leuven's historic squares). I write now in retirement and with no need to continue with any kind of academic work, but I do so not because I expect to change anything, nor because I expect some form of credit (which those in employment may require), but because it teases my *curiosity*.

I can see that those, including taxpayers, who support academic institutions financially may feel that they want rather more in return for their money than the provision of quiet, harmless and inconsequential entertainment for academic staff, and perhaps this entertainment has to be found around and after paid work, except that, as I have found over and over again, the curiosity driven work keeps connect-ing back to and informing the more applied tasks of sponsored educational research and development, and keeps enriching the contributions I have been able to make there. So perhaps we need to sustain academic work which does not *aim* to change the world – and may not in any very obvious way do so – but which might neverthe-less enrich it through untracked and circuitous routes with unpredictable destina-tions? *If* this is indeed the way "impact" works, dare we acknowledge this in a higher education discourse that demands to know not only where it is going but also how it can measure whether it has got there? It would be more honest than participa-tion in the sometimes fanciful narratives that the educational community now feels compelled to construct about its work in order to justify a place at the table of research funding, but perhaps that is a dare too far.

References

Bridges, D. (2015). Working without shame in international education: From consequentialism to casuistry? *Ethics and Education, 10*(3), 271–284.

Bridges, D., & Watts, M. (2008). Educational research and policy: Epistemological considerations. *Journal of Philosophy of Education, 42*(Supplement1), 41–62.

Edwards, A., Sebba, J., & Rickinson, M. (2007). Working with users: Some implications for edu-cational research. *British Educational Research Journal, 35*(5), 647–661.

Horsthemke, K. (2017). #Facts MustFall–Education in a post-truth, post-truthful world. *Ethics and Education, 12*(3), 273–289.

Keyes, R. (2004). *The post-truth era: Dishonesty and deception in contemporary life*. New York: St Martins.

MacFarlane, B. (2009). *Researching with integrity: The ethics of academic inquiry*. New York/London: Routledge.

Peters, R. S. (1967). What is an educational process? In R. S. Peters (Ed.), *The concept of educa-tion*. London: Routledge & Kegan Paul.

Popper, K. (1963). *Conjectures and refutations: The growth of scientific knowledge*. London: Routledge and Kegan Paul.

Pring, R. (2001). The virtues and vices of an educational researcher. *Journal of Philosophy of Education, 35*(3), 407–422.

Richards, I. A. (Ed.). (1966). *Plato's republic*. Cambridge, UK: Cambridge University Press.
Stenhouse, L. (1975). *An introduction to curriculum research and development*. London: Heinemann.
Sutherland, W. J., Spiegelhalter, D., & Burgman, M. A. (2013). Twenty tips for interpreting scientific claims. *Nature, 503*, 335–337.
Tight, M. (2017). *Higher education journals: Their characteristics and contribution*. Higher Education Research and Development. Downloaded as a pre-publication e-print at http://www.research.lancs.ac.uk/portal/en/publications/higher-education-journals(e174a909-2219-4b70-a3ea-103e3dde7e7b)/export.html 30th November 2017
Times Higher Education. (2017, November 16). Too many higher education journals – Here are the best ones. pp. 9–10.
Ware, M., & Mabe, M. (2012). *An overview of scientific and scholarly journal publishing*. The Hague, The Netherlands: International Association of Scientific, Technical and Medical Publishers.
White, J. P. (1973). *Towards a compulsory curriculum*. London: Routledge and Kegan Paul.
White, J. P. (2007). *What schools are for and why?* (IMPACT Paper No 14). Oxford, UK: Wiley/Philosophy of Education Society of Great Britain.
White, J. P. (2008). Aims as policy in primary education. Research Survey 1/1. In R. Alexander (Ed.), *The primary review*. Cambridge, UK: University of Cambridge.
Whitty, G. (2006). Education(al) research and education policy making: Is conflict inevitable? *British Educational Research Journal, 32*(2), 159–176.

Chapter 7
Truth "After Postmodernism": Wittgenstein and Postfoundationalism in Philosophy of Education

Michael A. Peters

Abstract In a range of path-breaking publications that shaped his engagement with educational theory Paul Smeyers sympathetically investigated the claims and 'atmosphere' of postmodernism. In this chapter I investigate the backlash against postmodernism that holds it responsible for 'post-truth politics,' and of promoting a cynical attitude to truth and facts. I argue for an intellectual history of truth in which it is contested, not only in Continental tradition and in what some have called postmodernism, but also in the analytic tradition. I explore these issues through a reading of Wittgenstein's place and role in the history of analytic philosophy and by investigating how he moves away from a notion of truth grounded in a form foundationalism in the Tractatus to embrace a form of anti-foundationalism in the Investigations and On Certainty.

Introduction

In a range of path-breaking publications that shaped his engagement with educational theory Paul Smeyers sympathetically investigated the claims and "atmosphere" of postmodernism. In *Thinking again: Education after postmodernism*, Smeyers (with Blake, Smith, and Standish) tries to demonstrate how postmodern thinkers "illuminate puzzling aspects of education." Writing in 1998 Smeyers and his colleagues suggest "Postmodernism is not new but we are not satisfied with the way is has been received in education. In another sense, however, we also want to advance ideas *after the style* of postmodernism to see how education looks after we have worked through some of the writings of postmodernism" (Blake, Smeyers, Smith, & Standish, 1998, p. 186). The authors want to encourage us to "think again"- a trajectory that led to *Education in an Age of Nihilism* (Blake, Smeyers, Smith, & Standish, 2000) and *The Therapy of Education* (Smeyers, Smith, & Standish, 2007).

M. A. Peters (✉)
University of Waikato, Hamilton, New Zealand
e-mail: mpeters@waikato.ac.nz

© Springer International Publishing AG, part of Springer Nature 2018   89
S. Ramaekers, N. Hodgson (eds.), *Past, Present, and Future Possibilities for Philosophy and History of Education*,
https://doi.org/10.1007/978-3-319-94253-7_7

In this chapter I investigate the backlash against postmodernism that holds it responsible for "post-truth politics," and of promoting a cynical attitude to truth and facts (Dennett cited in Cadwalladr, 2017; see also Chen, 2017; *The Post-Truth Issue*, 2017). Jennifer Delton (2017) in a Letter to the Editor of the *Chronicle* succinctly puts it in response to Andrew Perrin's (2017) "Stop blaming postmodernism for post-truth politics": "Its main idea was that 'truth' was unstable, contingent, contested. We were told this would make us feel uncomfortable, but that recognizing it was a first step toward liberation from the cultural hegemony that prevented positive social change." Delton (2017) goes on to write: "It turns out that that cultural hegemony also prevented what might be seen as negative social change, such as the alt-right and Trump's unexpected election."

I argue for an intellectual history of truth in which it is contested, not only in Continental tradition and in what some have called postmodernism, but also in the analytic tradition. Critics like Dennett and Delton mistakenly claim that postmodernism is responsible for post-truth politics – a kind of category mistake – while conveniently ignoring the troublesome recent history of analytic truth on which there is still little consensus with multiple theories such as correspondence, coherence, semantic, pragmatic, redundancy. I explore these issues through a reading of Wittgenstein's place and role in the history of analytic philosophy and by investigating how he moves away from a notion of truth grounded in a form foundationalism in the *Tractatus* (1986) to embrace a form of anti-foundationalism in the *Philosophical Investigations* (1968) and *On Certainty* (1969). In the *Tractatus* Wittgenstein argues for a pictorial theory of representation: "a sentence is true if and only if it depicts a possible fact that obtains"; while in the *Investigations*, Wittgenstein replaces this "with a *deflationary* view of truth" on the basis of "meaning qua use" (Horwich, 2016, p. 95).

In tune with Smeyers, I claim that "after postmodernism" we are in a better position to understand and critique the emergence of "post-truth" regimes both as an expression of "alt-right politics" and as a reflection of the changing political economy of social media that has the power to disrupt liberal politics. The very same critics of postmodernism on grounds to do with truth, often aimed at Foucault in the popular press, seem to be generally unaware of the distinction that Foucault introduces between the analytic theory of truth and the history of truth-telling.

The accusation of epistemic treason made against Foucault needs to recognise that he is interested in a *history of truth-telling* (*parrhesia*) rather than a notion of conceptual or factual truth. Indeed, when he draws the distinction between an analytic account of truth and a history of truth-telling (Foucault, 2001), he writes: "My intention was not to deal with the problem of truth, but with the problem of truth-teller or truth-telling as an activity" (ibid., p. 169). He continues: "What I wanted to analyze was how the truth-teller's role was variously problematized in Greek philosophy. And what I wanted to show you was that if Greek philosophy has raised the question of truth from the point of view of the criteria for true statements and sound reasoning, this same Greek philosophy has also raised the problem of truth from the point of view of truth-telling as an activity" (ibid.). In sum, the questions Foucault was raising were not the same ones as those discussed in analytic philosophy. He was not "post-truth" in the sense that he was denying or making assertions about truth or truth conditions; he was not part of *that* discussion at all.

Similarly, Derrida also sees himself as a philosopher very much concerned with the truth: "The value of truth (and all those values associated with it) is never contested or destroyed in my writings, but only re-inscribed in more powerful, larger, more stratified contexts" (Derrida, 1988, p. 146). Elsewhere he contrasts two inter-related notions of truth in the Western tradition: truth as presence and truth as agreement:

'Truth' has always meant two different things, the history of the essence of truth – the truth of truth – being only the gap and the articulation between the two interpretations or processes … The process of truth is *on the one hand* the unveiling of what lies concealed in oblivion … *On the other hand* … truth is agreement (*homoiôsis* or *adaequatio*), a relation of resemblance or equality between a re-presentation and a thing (unveiled, present), even in the eventuality of a statement of judgment. (Derrida, 1981, pp. 192–3)

As Christopher Norris puts it in *A Companion to Derrida*, "[far] from rejecting or denouncing the notion of truth, Derrida can be found insisting on its absolute indispensability to philosophical enquiry in general and – more specifically – its crucial pertinence to the project of deconstruction" (Norris, 2014, p. 23).

These questions concerning truth can be taken up within analytic philosophy by reference to Wittgenstein and the issue of foundationalism. In this essay first I discuss Wittgenstein on truth and foundations based on the picture theory of meaning that he outlines in the *Tractatus* as an early episode in the history of the analytic theory of truth.

In what follows I will consider Paul Smeyers as a Wittgensteinian who is strongly influenced by the later Wittgenstein and by an account of language based on the role of cultural practices. As a scholar who teaches philosophy of education and methodology of the *Geisteswissenschaften,* Smeyers is heavily influenced by Wittgenstein's conception of philosophy that takes "form of life" as a bedrock concept of our "language games"—the "given" so to speak, which as a whole must be accepted as grounding our activities. As Smeyers argues: "A shared 'form of life' is a prerequisite for objectivity itself and the existence of a common world is its logical presupposition" (Smeyers & Marshall, 1995, p. 7). For Smeyers, following Wittgenstein and R.S. Peters, education is an initiation into a "form of life" and philosophy of education is a clarification of the "grammar" of educational language and concepts. It is a view he comes to early in his career, in the late 1980s, and consolidates it in the early to mid-1990s (Smeyers, 1991, 1993; Smeyers & Marshall, 1995). It guides his work on the threat of nihilism (Smeyers, 1998, 1999) and his concept of education as therapy that follows (Smeyers, Smith, & Standish, 2007).

Truth is indispensable for (educational) theory. In the strict "scientific" sense, truth is the means by which the status of competing theories can be judged. Realists hold that truth as correspondence to reality is what scientists try to achieve. Anti-realists and some of those who embrace a form of coherence as truth, like some pragmatists including James and Peirce, hold that researchers aim only for "usefulness" in predicting outcomes in experiments or for accounting for the best "fit" of current data with the world. Dowden and Swartz (n.d.), following Giere (2004), suggest:

> science aims for the best available "representation", in the same sense that maps are representations of the landscape. Maps aren't true; rather, they fit to a better or worse degree. Similarly, scientific theories are designed to fit the world. Scientists should not aim to create true theories; they should aim to construct theories whose models are representations of the world (Dowden & Swarts, n.d., http://www.iep.utm.edu/truth/#SH8e).

There are accounts of truth in relation to representation and models that argue for both realist and non-realist accounts (Cartwright, 1999). Anti-realists seek to replace the correspondence theory of truth, and any methodology that relies on truth-conditions, with a theory of meaning that defines truth on the basis of justifiable assertibility conditions.

Wittgenstein, Truth, and Foundations

Foundationalism is the philosophical doctrine that holds that there is a privileged class of fundamental beliefs that are self-evident, infallible, or indubitable that serve as the ground, basis, or foundations for all knowledge, inquiry, and morality. It is from these "first principles" or indubitable foundations that the rest of the edifice of knowledge can be inferred or derived. The doctrine is sometimes conceived in terms of a number of interrelated elements: the *structure* of knowledge, a theory of the justification, the nature of reasoning, and a theory of experience. Richard Fumerton (2010) provides the following description of foundationalism:

> Foundationalism is a view about the structure of justification or knowledge. The foundationalist's thesis in short is that all knowledge and justified belief rest ultimately on a foundation of noninferential knowledge or justified belief (ibid., https://plato.stanford.edu/archives/sum2010/entries/justep-foundational/).

The foundationalist, then, must find a special kind of truth that can be known without inference. The search for what this class of statement or sentences might consist has been a defining feature of modern philosophy since Descartes, and one that both Dewey and Wittgenstein characterise as the search for certainty. Both Dewey's (1929, 1960) *The quest for certainty* and Wittgenstein's *On certainty* (1969) are, some would say, odd bedfellows, yet they hold similar kinds of contextualist views about knowledge that emphasise "the primacy of the pragmatic over the epistemic" (Hobbs, 2008). Rather than the certainty of epistemic foundations, Wittgenstein indicates in *On certainty* that our "acting" lies "at the bottom of the language-game" (1969, § 204). He provides a picture of language-use where any possible meaning is grounded in public human ways of acting, what he calls language-games. For Wittgenstein, sentences only have meaning as they appear contextually as parts of a "form of life". He remarks: "Our knowledge forms an enormous system. And only within this system has a particular bit the value we give it" (ibid., §410, §432). While some beliefs stand firm for us they stand in a special position in that they escape doubt and act as *foundations* (ibid., §89, §415, §449, §512), *axes, hinges,* and even *axioms* (ibid., §152, §341, §551) in that they serve as entry points for truth in the belief system (ibid., §83) and constitute "the inherited background against which I distinguish between true and false" (ibid., §94).

The argument for foundationalism is often stated in the following form: if we don't have firm foundations—that is, inviolable or *indubitable* foundations—then the rest of knowledge is open to question. Foundations are supposed to provide a secure platform for certainty, where doubt is logically excluded. Descartes is perhaps the best known modern philosopher whose search for indubitable foundations lead him to find the alleged basis in the fact of his own existence. The commonly quoted "*Cogito ergo sum*" ("I think therefore I exist") is the essence of Descartes' foundationalism, along with "clear and distinct ideas". With this statement Descartes begins the modern preoccupation with the search for firm foundations of knowledge that characterises modern epistemology.

The so-called "search for certainty" is a motif or metaphor that many philosophers of different persuasions have called into question, including, not only Dewey and Wittgenstein, but also Peirce, Neurath, Quine, Sellars, Popper, Rorty, Derrida, and Foucault.

Sung Kyu Park (2010) offers a useful summary:

> Epistemologically, foundationalism at all times implies the holding of a position in an inflexible and infallible manner; invoking ultimate foundations on which to construct the evidential support system of various convictional beliefs. Foundationalism is the 'thesis that all our beliefs can be justified by appealing to some item of knowledge that is self-evident or indubitable' (Van Huyssteen, 1997, pp. 2–3). Schrag and Peters (2006, p. 21) state, 'Foundationalism finds its mission in a quest for certainty. Unimpeachable knowledge-claims is what it is after'. These foundational systems of knowledge are called 'first principles' (Thiel 1994, p. 2) or 'aristocratic beliefs' (Rescher 1992, p. 161), which are intrinsically credible. Such basic givens can be anything from sense data to universals, essences, and experiences, including religious experiences. (Park, 2010, p. 1)

In epistemology, "postmodernism" is another name for anti-foundationalism, non-foundationalism, or post-foundationalism, movements that reject the idea that there is a class of fundamental beliefs that are self-evident and serve as the ground, anchor point, or building block foundations for all knowledge and inquiry. Foundations are supposed to provide a secure platform for certainty.

Lurking in Smeyers' work is a Wittgenstein that offers a conception of truth, and while Smeyers does not address this issue directly to my knowledge, he might advert to something like the following account. In *Notebooks 1914–1916* Wittgenstein (1979) makes the remark "'p' is true says nothing else than p". This advances a deflationary view of truth (often referred to as a "disquotationalist" view of truth)—"true" is simply what is asserted, yet this remark must be placed within the context of a truth-conditional theory of meaning, and the *Tractatus,* which argues for a picture view of truth in terms of its agreement or correspondence with reality. In section §136 of the *Investigations*, as Kripke famously points out, Wittgenstein makes the transition from the truth-conditional model of propositional meaning to a model based on communally accepted assertibility conditions, that is, "a philosophically appropriate description of assertoric practice" (Frascolla, 2017, p. 211), which does not require appeal to an abstract notion of truth. Frascolla argues that "Wittgenstein ends up recognising that the concept of truth has no additional normative content beyond that which the notion of warranted assertibility, or justifiability according to socially accepted standards, has of its own." In other words, Wittgenstein "dispenses with the notion of truth in favour of the notion of warranted assertibility" (ibid., p. 214). The same argument essentially is put forth in *On Certainty,* as noted by Frascolla:

> Since the ascription of truth to a proposition 'p' adds nothing to the mere assertion of 'p', any discourse on truth is to be reframed in terms of warranted assertibility, and the implications realistic philosophers usually associate with the attribution of a descriptive role to empirical propositions can thus be watered down (ibid., p. 217).

What does this demonstrate, if anything? First, it might be taken to suggest that Wittgenstein in the contemporary history of analytic truth has good reason in terms of his position to move away from an abstract notion of truth and his earlier Tractarian concept of truth as agreement with reality. Second, in ascribing something like this view to Smeyers, we can also suggest how we might respond to philosophers like Dennett and Delton who blame postmodernists for post-truth and, also presumably, for post-truth politics. Philosophers and other commentators who fly off the handle to blame "postmodernism" in some sense for undermining truth and causing "post-truth politics" need to bear this little piece of history in mind. It is weird to hold postmodernists responsible for a situation that is based in a kind of politics that promotes the alt-right and relies on new social media, and Twitter in particular, to broadcast a welter of palpably false claims. Part of the response to these critics is to tell them the story of the contested nature of truth – to explain that Wittgenstein once held a classic correspondence notion of truth and for good philosophical reasons jettisoned it. This historical strategy also helps to curtail the rhetoric around postmodernism and truth by sensitising us to the uneven historical patchwork of the modern analytic concern for truth.

Wittgenstein and the History of Analytic Truth[1]

Wittgenstein was instrumental in both the rise and fall of logicism. The doctrine of logicism – that mathematics can be reduced to logic – was inherited from Richard Dedekind and Gottlob Frege, and developed by Bertrand Russell and Alfred Whitehead. The idea that set theory was the means to reduce the theory of real numbers to rational number theory was a key development in analytic philosophy, in that the truths of logic were held to be analytic truths. Logicism is a foundationalist project that holds (at least in the strong version) that all mathematical truths are

---

[1] This section draws on "Afterword: Viral Modernity. From Postmodernism to Post-Truth", Besley, Peters, and Rider (2018).

forms of logical truth: they are true by virtue of the meanings of the terms themselves. Mathematical certainty, then, is seen to be a product of the certainty of logical truth, a position challenged both by Gödel's incompleteness theorem and the ascendancy of Zermelo-Fraenkel set theory.

In the *Tractatus* Wittgenstein holds that mathematical propositions are pseudo-propositions – a consequence of his picture theory of meaning and his idea that the only meaningful propositions are contingent propositions that are regarded as true if they accurately describe reality. Mathematical propositions thus do not describe the world; they are purely syntactical. Russell falsely attributes to Wittgenstein the view that propositions, in order to belong to mathematics, must be tautologies. In "Wittgenstein reads Russell", Gregory Landini (2012, p. 47) argues that Wittgenstein embraced a form of logicism although his doctrine of showing, which rejects logical objects, distanced him from both Russell's and Frege's forms of logicism: "Wittgenstein came to hold more radically an eliminativistic form of logicism than *Principia*" (p. 50). As Victor Rodych (2011) puts it:

> Perhaps the most important constant in Wittgenstein's Philosophy of Mathematics, middle and late, is that he consistently maintains that mathematics is our, human invention, and that, indeed, everything in mathematics is invented. Just as the middle Wittgenstein says that '[w]e *make* mathematics,' the later Wittgenstein says that we 'invent' mathematics (*RFM* I, §168; II, §38; V, §§5, 9 and 11; *PG* 469–70) and that 'the mathematician is not a discoverer: he is an inventor' (*RFM*, Appendix II, §2; (*LFM* 22, 82). Nothing *exists* mathematically unless and until we have invented it. (https://plato.stanford.edu/archives/sum2011/entries/wittgenstein-mathematics/)

Much of the apparatus for Wittgenstein's mature views on the foundations of mathematics comes from the development of views first gathered together in the *Investigations*. In one sense, Wittgenstein traverses the modern history of foundations and truth in mathematics and logic of analytic philosophy.

Wouter H. Slob (2002, p. 33) in "A Short History of Truth and Related Matters", Chapter Two of *Dialogical Logic*, maintains: "All theories of truth share a remarkable feature: they are all relatively young." Following George Pitcher, he suggests that the great philosophers in fact had little to say about truth; rather they were, he [Pitcher] claims, more interested in truths (in the plural) until the Absolute Idealist in the nineteenth century sparked an interest in theories of truth that called for a philosophical account. Slob draws the conclusion: "The relatively late attention given to theories of truth may indicate that *truth has only quite recently become problematical*" (ibid., my italics).

The history of analytic philosophy is rather the history of a specific kind of engagement with a historically specific set of questions concerning truth, language, and meaning.[2] But the work emanating out of those questions today is largely based on the application of formal methods to arrive at formal definitions, which is to say that the "truth" of professional epistemologists does no real work outside of the seminar room and journal articles. Already in 1967, in his famous paper "Truth and Meaning" (1967), Donald Davidson concludes that natural languages are not ame-

---

[2] See also *The Journal of the History of Analytic Philosophy* https://jhaponline.org/

nable to the direct application of formal methods to construct a correct definition of the expression "true sentence" in harmony with the logic and spirit of everyday language use, which is where the question of truth actually gets interesting.

Conclusion: Postfoundationalism, Wittgenstein, and Philosophy of Education

In our contribution to *The Cambridge History of Philosophy 1945–2010*, Jeff Stickney and I (Peters & Stickney, forthcoming) provide an account of post-foundational approaches through Dewey, Wittgenstein, and Foucault, pitting them against Harvey Siegel's and Denis Phillips' shared viewed of education as the embrace of universal standards of rationality that makes critical thinking the funda-mental aim of education – a version of epistemological foundationalism concerning justified belief. Finding our way "after postmodernism" (Blake et al., 1998) we tell a genealogical story about attempts to disentangle "reason" from the legacy of liberal-Enlightenment traditions that privilege a universalist account of reason. By contrast, we feature philosophers of education who are influenced by Dewey, Wittgenstein, and Foucault in providing non-foundationalist accounts:

> different thinkers who together and in remarkably similar ways advanced non-foundationalist accounts of knowledge, ultimately paving the way for forms of post-foundationalism (Smeyers & Peters, 2006) based on 'the primacy of practice' (Smeyers & Burbules, 2005). (Peters & Stickney, forthcoming)

One of the post-foundationalist themes was to view Wittgenstein as a pedagogi-cal philosopher, an interpretation that admitted "contextualist" aspects of Wittgenstein's biography to read him as a philosopher of the Austrian counter-Enlightenment, against the background of Viennese modernism (Peters & Marshall, 1999). This reading emphasised its sympathy with many of the main concerns of European formalism in linguistics and the humanities, drawing on French poststruc-turalist thinkers such as Foucault, Lyotard, and Derrida. This reading was developed as an expressed intention to deconstruct the appropriation of his "method" by R.S. Peters and the London School who had extracted a foundationalist reading of Wittgenstein based in conceptual analysis.

Smeyers collaborated with Jim Marshall on a landmark collection entitled *Philosophy and education: Accepting Wittgenstein's challenge* (Smeyers & Marshall, 1995) that provided a framework for philosophy of education that had, until that time, represented a "superficial" engagement with Wittgenstein. It included a range of Wittgenstein scholars working in education. In the introduction "The Wittgensteinian Frame of Reference and Philosophy of Education at the End of the Twentieth Century", Smeyers and Marshall (1995) provide the necessary back-ground to concepts of "meaning" and "action" focusing on "form of life" and "lan-guage game" analysis to support a non-foundationalist reading of the *Investigations,* where consistency of meaning rests on the community of language users where meaning and understanding are socially determined. There is an account of doubt in *On Certainty* and a clear view that education cannot be reduced to a science – understanding human action cannot be based on the natural sciences – a view that Smeyers pursues in later work. Smeyers and Marshall comment: "Far from being an advocate for nihilism, Wittgenstein holds a subtle balance between the Enlightenment and a full-blown post-modernist position" (ibid., p. 12) and they spend considerable effort to unpack the meaning of this claim. They take issue with the foundationalist reading of analytic philosophy of education, suggesting that its "appeal to 'language games' and conceptual clarity, distorted and subverted the force of the intellectual challenge" of Wittgenstein to educational theories (ibid., p. 24).

Smeyers and Marshall (1995) offered a nonfoundationalist account of Wittgenstein based on an interpretation of the *Investigations* that countered the foundationalist reading of the London School, and so undertook a serious engagement with Wittgenstein's work that at one and the same time recuperates the work of C. J. B. Macmillan on learning, while opening up the challenge to scholars such as Paul Standish on "Why we should not speak of an educational science" (Standish, 1995), and Marshall and Peters on bringing Wittgenstein into conversation with Foucault and Lyotard (Marshall, 1995; Peters, 1995). Smeyers and Peters (2006) coedited a special issue of *Educational Philosophy and Theory,* a *festschrift* for Jim Marshall, later produced as a monograph entitled *Postfoundationalist Themes in Philosophy of Education*, and they collaborated again with Nick Burbules on *Showing and Doing: Wittgenstein as a Pedagogical Philosopher* (2008), which includes Burbules' investigation of tacit teaching, and a further development of Smeyers and Burbules' (2005) thinking in terms of education as "initiation into practices". Peters and Stickney (forthcoming) survey the collaborations that feature Smeyers in developing the notion of Wittgenstein as a pedagogical philosopher:

> Following Macmillan, the 2008 collaboration [*Showing and Doing*] also traced the 'pedagogical turn' of Wittgenstein's thinking during the period from 1920 to 1926 (see Medina 2002) and suggested learning and initiation into practices are fundamental to understanding his philosophy. Wittgenstein was cast as a 'pedagogical philosopher', building from a broader approach called 'philosophy-as-pedagogy' that was influenced by Janik and Toulmin, Cavell, and the postmodern reading developed in Peters and Marshall (1999) that focuses on anti-representational and post-foundational rejections of truth as correspondence to reality. This move was accompanied by a general suspicion of transcendental viewpoints and arguments (what Lyotard referred to as meta-narratives), and clearer focus on questions of subjectivity going back to Kierkegaard and taken up afresh by Foucault.

This is not to say that Smeyers, Burbules, and I share exactly the same non-foundational account of Wittgenstein – *Showing and Doing* was a book of individually written and sometimes different collaboratively written chapters, although it would be fair to say there was some agreement on Wittgenstein as a pedagogical philosopher. While we agreed on a view of Wittgenstein as a "therapeutic" philosopher, a position strongly influenced by the work of Cavell, and while we might also agree on Wittgenstein as someone who offers the grounds for a critique of liberal education as Enlightenment Reason, I suspect that how we might interpret Wittgenstein's anti-foundationalism may differ considerably. For my part I wanted to interpret Wittgenstein's anti-foundationalism as a critique of the liberal philosophy of the subject, and as a starting point to engage in the kind of subjectivity studies that characterise Foucault's work.[3] As I put it in the chapter with Jeff Stickney:

> Our purpose in surveying post-war PoE, offering a critique of liberal Reason through a Foucauldian 'critical history of the present', is not to illumine the correct way of escaping enthrallment in liberal-Enlightenment images of the autonomous self and of absolute truth, but rather to unsettle established ground in order to open spaces of possibility for alternatives (Peters & Stickney, forthcoming).

Our argument is that Dewey, Wittgenstein, and Foucault are different thinkers who together but in different ways advanced non-foundationalist accounts of knowledge that paved the way for new and viable forms of post-foundationalism. All three thinkers emphasise contingency and the primacy of practice. Post-foundationalism is the common ground for five very different intellectual movements that still dominate early twenty-first century thought —*postpositivism, postmodernism, poststructuralism, postcolonialism, and posthumanism*—which indicates there are different forms and expressions of postfoundationalism that have been opened up by these three philosophers.

Where Dewey puts his faith in progress in empirical science and "warranted assertability", following a Peircean fallabilism, both Wittgenstein and Foucault, more radically and in different ways, want to question this faith in Enlightenment rationality, science, and its inheritance. Wittgenstein does so in terms of his spiritual distaste for the results of "American scientific civilisation" that accompanies the disappearance of culture. Foucault raises the question of power in terms of the concept of "power-knowledge" and the genealogy of truth, truth regimes, and truth-telling. Each philosopher provides a distinctively different postfoundational answer and way of doing philosophy. In terms of the five "post-" traditions above, Dewey can be most easily associated with postpositivism, and Foucault with postcolonialism (via Edward Said) and posthumanism (after Heidegger). The movement known as poststructuralism, of course, is also an American label associated with the broader movement to which Foucault belonged and shaped. (He naïvely suggested he didn't know what "postmodernism" meant). In so far as postmodernism expressed a cultural movement, in poetry, architecture, literature, literary theory, and the performing arts (and only later applied to philosophy and the social sciences), it could be argued that the later Wittgenstein strongly exhibited *avant la lettre* stylistic and philosophical features of postmodernism (Peters & Marshall, 1999).

---

[3] See e.g., http://explore.tandfonline.com/page/ed/education-expert-panel/education-philosophy-expert-michael-peters/education-philosophy-expert-michael-peters-full-introduction

References

Besley, T., Peters, M., & Rider, S. (2018). Afterword: Viral modernity. From postmodernism to post-truth. In M. A. Peters, S. Rider, M. Hyvönen, & T. Besley (Eds.), *Post-truth, fake news, viral modernity & higher education*. Singapore, Singapore: Springer.

Blake, N., Smeyers, P., Smith, R., & Standish, P. (1998). *Thinking again: Education after postmodernism*. New York: Bergin & Garvey.

Blake, N., Smeyers, P., Smith, R., & Standish, P. (2000). *Education in an age of nihilism*. London: Falmer Press.

Cadwalladr, C. (2017). Interview with Daniel Dennett. *The Guardian*. https://www.theguardian.com/science/2017/feb/12/daniel-dennett-politics-bacteria-bach-back-dawkins-trump-interview

Cartwright, N. (1999). *The dappled world: A study of the boundaries of science*. Cambridge, UK: Cambridge University Press.

Chen, T. (2017). Is postmodernism to blame for post-truth? *Philosophy Talk*. https://www.philosophytalk.org/blog/postmodernism-blame-post-truth

Davidson, D. (1967). Truth and meaning. *Synthese, 17*, 304–323.

Delton, J. (2017, January 15). Don't absolve postmodernism so quickly. Letter to the Editor. *The Chronicle of Higher Education*. http://www.chronicle.com/blogs/letters/dont-absolve-postmodernism-so-quickly/

Derrida, J. (1981). *Dissemination*. London: Athlone Press.

Derrida, J. (1988). *Limited, Inc.* Evanston, IL: Northwestern University Press.

Dewey, J. (1929/1960). *The quest for certainty*. New York: Capricorn Books.

Dowden, B., & Swartz, N. (n.d.). Truth. *Internet Encyclopedia of Philosophy*. http://www.iep.utm.edu/truth/#SH8e

Foucault, M. (2001). *Fearless speech*. Los Angeles: Semiotext(e) Available also at https://foucault.info/parrhesia/

Frascolla, P. (2017). The role of the disquotational schema in Wittgenstein's reflections on truth. *Philosophical Investigations, 40*(3), 205–222.

Fumerton, R. (2010). Foundationalist theories of epistemic justification. In E. N. Zalta (Ed.), *The Stanford encyclopedia of philosophy* (Summer 2010 edition). http://plato.stanford.edu/archives/sum2010/entries/justep-foundational/

Giere, R. (2004, December). How models are used to represent reality. *Philosophy of Science, 71*(5), 742–752. https://doi.org/10.1086/425063

Hobbs, C. (2008). Dewey, Wittgenstein, and contextualist epistemology. *Southwest Philosophy Review, 24*(2), 71–85.

Horwich, P. (2016). Wittgenstein on truth. *Argumentation, 2*(1), 95–105.

Landini, G. (2012). Wittgenstein reads Russell. In O. Kuusela & M. McGinn (Eds.), *The Oxford handbook of Wittgenstein*. Oxford, UK: Oxford University Press.

Marshall, J. (1995). Wittgenstein and Foucault: Resolving philosophical puzzles. In P. Smeyers & J. Marshall (Eds.), *Philosophy and education: Accepting Wittgenstein's challenge* (pp. 205–220). Dordrecht, The Netherlands: Kluwer Academic Publishers.

Norris, C. (2014). Truth in Derrida. In Z. Dyrek (Ed.), *A companion to Derrida* (pp. 23–41). Oxford, UK: Wiley.

Park, S.-K. (2010). A postfoundationalist research paradigm of practical theology. *HTS Teologiese Studies/Theological Studies, 66*(2). Art. #849, 6 pages. https://doi.org/10.4102/hts.v66i2.849

Perrin, A. (2017, August 4). Stop blaming postmodernism for post-truth politics. *The Chronicle of Higher Education*. https://www.chronicle.com/article/Stop-Blaming-Postmodernism-for/240845

Peters, M. A. (1995). Philosophy and education: 'After' Wittgenstein. In P. Smeyers & J. Marhsall (Eds.), *Philosophy and education: Accepting Wittgenstein's challenge* (pp. 189–204). Dordrecht, The Netherlands: Kluwer Academic Publishers.

Peters, M., Burbules, N., & Smeyers, P. (2008). *Showing and doing: Wittgenstein as a pedagogical philosopher*. Boulder, CO: Paradigm Publishers.

Peters, M. A., & Marshall, J. (1999). *Wittgenstein: Philosophy, postmodernism, pedagogy*. Westport, CT: Bergin and Garvey.

Peters, M. A., & Stickney, J. (forthcoming). Philosophy of education 1945–2010 and the 'education of reason': Post-foundational approaches through Dewey, Wittgenstein, and Foucault. In *Cambridge history of philosophy, 1945–2010*. Cambridge, UK: Cambridge University Press.

Rodych, V. (2011). Wittgenstein's philosophy of mathematics. *The Stanford Encyclopedia of Philosophy* (Summer 2011 Edition). E. N. Zalta (Ed.). https://plato.stanford.edu/archives/sum2011/entries/wittgenstein-mathematics/

Slob, W. H. (2002). A short history of truth and related matters. Dialogical rhetoric. *Argumentation Library, 7*, 33–65.

Smeyers, P. (1991). Educational research from a Wittgensteinian point of view. *Proceedings of the Tenth Conference of the International Human Science Research Association* (pp. 1–10). Göteborg, 18–22 August 1991. Göteborg: International Human Science Research Association.

Smeyers, P. (1993). Some radical consequences for educational research from a Wittgensteinian point of view or does almost anything go? In *Philosophy of Education Society yearbook 1993* (pp. 139–147). Urbana, IL: Philosophy of Education Society.

Smeyers, P. (1998). The threat of nihilism: New educational opportunities. Paideia: Philosophy educating humanity. Twentieth World Congress of Philosophy. Boston, MA, 10–15 August 1998.

Smeyers, P. (1999). Four versions of nihilism. *Papers of the Annual Conference of the Philosophy of Education Society of Great Britain* (pp. 110–135). Oxford: Philosophy of Education Society of Great Britain.

Smeyers, P., & Burbules, N. (2005). "Practice": A central educational concept. In K. R. Howe (Ed.), *Philosophy of education 2005* (pp. 336–343). Urbana, IL: Philosophy of Education Society.

Smeyers, P., & Marshall, J. (Eds.). (1995). *Philosophy and education: Accepting Wittgenstein's challenge*. Dordrecht, The Netherlands: Springer.

Smeyers, P., & Peters, M. (Eds.). (2006). *Postfoundationalist themes in the philosophy of education*. Oxford, UK: Basil Blackwell.

Smeyers, P., Smith, R., & Standish, P. (2007). *The therapy of education*. London: Palgrave.

Standish, P. (1995). Why we should not speak of an educational science. In P. Smeyers & J. Marshall (Eds.), *Philosophy and education: Accepting Wittgenstein's challenge* (pp. 143–158). Dordrecht, The Netherlands: Kluwer Academic Publishers.

The Post-Truth Issue. (2017, January 11). *The Chronicle of Higher Education*. https://www.chronicle.com/specialreport/The-Post-Truth-Issue/84

Wittgenstein, L. (1968). *Philosophical investigations* (3rd ed., G. E. M. Anscombe, Trans.). Oxford: Basil Blackwell.

Wittgenstein, L. (1969). *On certainty* (D. Paul & G. E. M. Anscombe, Trans.). Oxford: Basil Blackwell.

Wittgenstein, L. (1979). *Notebooks 1914–1916* (G. E. M. Anscombe, Trans.). Oxford: Blackwell.

Wittgenstein, L. (1986). *Tractatus logico-philosophicus* (C. K. Ogden, Trans.). London: Routledge and Kegan Paul.

Chapter 8
"Plowden" at 50—R.S. Peters' Response to Educational Progressivism

Stefaan E. Cuypers

Abstract In this chapter, I reconstruct the basic structure of Peters' analytic response to educational progressivism as politically expressed in the 1967 Plowden Report. The report expressed a particular line of thought in educational theory, namely that of educational progressivism or child-centred education. In the 1960s, Peters introduced the analytic paradigm into the philosophy of education in Great Britain. In the socio-economic context of the 1960s, this new paradigm had some institutional as well as political effects. In particular, Peters' theoretical response to the Plowden Report in *Perspectives on Plowden* had a practical influence. The chapter proceeds as follows. After a short historical note and a brief rehearsal of the contrast between progressivism and traditionalism, I detail Peters' fundamental presuppositions in the light of which his critique of child-centred education can be elucidated. These two main presuppositions are, first, the primacy of the social or the public and, second, the ideal of liberal education. Next, I organise his critique around two central themes: first, education and its aims, and, second, the curriculum and the teacher.

Introduction

As the fiftieth anniversary of the publication of the so-called "Plowden Report" has arrived this year (2017), it seems fitting to pay attention to the reaction of mainstream philosophy of education in Great Britain at the time of the report's release in 1967. This immediately leads us to the figure of R.S. Peters.

In the 1960s, Peters introduced the analytic paradigm into the philosophy of education in Great Britain. This report expresses a particular line of thought in educational theory, namely that of educational progressivism or child-centred education. In the socio-economic context of the 1960s this new paradigm had some

S. E. Cuypers (✉)
Centre for Logic and Philosophy of Science, KU Leuven, Leuven, Belgium
e-mail: Stefaan.Cuypers@kuleuven.be

© Springer International Publishing AG, part of Springer Nature 2018
S. Ramaekers, N. Hodgson (eds.), *Past, Present, and Future Possibilities for Philosophy and History of Education*,
https://doi.org/10.1007/978-3-319-94253-7_8

101

institutional as well as political effects. In particular, Peters' theoretical response to the Plowden Report in *Perspectives on Plowden* (1969a) had a practical influence. In this chapter, I reconstruct the basic structure of Peters' analytic response to educational progressivism as politically expressed in the 1967 Plowden Report. After a short historical note and a brief rehearsal of the contrast between progressivism and traditionalism, I detail Peters' fundamental presuppositions in the light of which his critique of child-centred education can be elucidated. Next, I organise this critique around two central themes: first, education and its aims, and, second, the curriculum and the teacher.

The Historical Context of the Plowden Report

In the UK, during the Second World War (1939–1945), Winston Churchill was Prime Minister with a cabinet including Conservative, Labour, and Liberal Members of Parliament.[1] Immediately after the war, partly because of people's desire for a fairer society, the Labour Party came to power under Clement Attlee (1945–1951). After the elections of 1951 the Conservatives held office, under successively Churchill (1951–1955), Anthony Eden (1955–1957), and Harold Macmillan (1957–1964), and remained in power until 1964. After this thirteen-year period of Conservative government, Labour came to power in 1964 under a new leader, Harold Wilson (1964–1970). It was under the first Wilson government that the Plowden Report appeared.

Towards the end of the war, the Norwood Report (1943) correlated the so-called three kinds of mind—abstract, mechanical, and concrete—with a tripartite structure of secondary education: the grammar, the technical, and the modern school. Shortly afterwards, the Butler Education Act (1944), known as the Butler Act, made free, state-funded, secondary education (age 11–15) a right for all children. The war had inspired plans for post-war social renewal and aspirations for a better society. However, in post-war Britain, under the Labour government, the tripartite system of education was criticised as unfair and socially discriminatory. The alternative, comprehensive model, combining elements from the grammar, technical, and modern curricula but with no divisions into separate compartments, gained popularity and was passionately promoted by Anthony Crosland, Secretary of State for Education and Science in Wilson's Labour government (1965–1967). As a theorist of the left, Crosland had already published *The Future of Socialism* in 1956, arguing for egalitarianism through comprehensive education. It is in this progressive context with Labour in power that the appearance of Plowden Report has to be situated.

From the process of the comprehensivisation of secondary education ensued plans for the modernisation of *primary* education. The blueprint for the future reform of primary education was precisely the 1967 Plowden Report on *Children*

---

[1] My sketch of the historical context is based on Black (2010), part two, especially pp. 200–204.

and their Primary Schools.[2] The document, named after the chairperson of the then responsible Central Advisory Council of Education (England), Lady Bridget Plowden, embodies "a recognisable philosophy of education, and … a view of society" (§504), which goes by the name of educational progressivism.

Against the Plowden vision and the progressive conception of (primary) education, Peters launched an attack that had a significant impact on the world of education, which he himself describes as follows:

> There is no doubt that, during the progressive hey-day of the 1960s, culminating in the Plowden Report, it [analytic philosophy of education] made an impact, if an adverse one, in many quarters. For the analytic approach was brought to bear on some of the slogans of progressivism such as 'growth', 'the needs and interests' of the child, and 'learning by discovery'. *Perspectives on Plowden*, which I edited, created quite a furore … (Peters, 1983, pp. 35–6).

The Progressive-Traditional Contrast

To get a better idea of the Plowden vision, let me briefly contrast its educational progressivism—(P) for short—with traditionalism, (T) for short. (P) has its roots in the theories of philosophers of education such as Jean-Jacques Rousseau, Johann Heinrich Pestalozzi, Friedrich Froebel, and John Dewey. In contrast to (T), which is school subject-orientated and teacher-directed, (P) is child-centred. (P) differs sharply from (T) as regards the conceptions of childhood, the curriculum, and the teacher. I remind you of the basic contrasts.[3]

According to (P), childhood is a self-contained phase of life or a state of its own, and the child's self is an intrinsic package of individual talents, personal needs, and interests. As for (T), childhood is a preparatory phase of life or a stage on the way to adulthood, and the child's mind is a blank slate (*tabula rasa*) to be written on by the environment. The basic metaphor of (P) is an acorn growing into an oak, whereas that of (T) is a lump of clay to be moulded. This contrast is connected with other ones: natural growth versus cultural imprint, autonomy (identity from within) versus heteronomy (identity from without), *Wachsenlassen* versus *Führen*, and *vom Kinde aus* versus *vom Lehrer aus*.

The disagreement in opinion about childhood is complemented by a disagreement about the curriculum and the teacher. According to (T), after instructing the three Rs—reading, writing, and arithmetic—pupils should be taught a compartmentalised, school subject-based curriculum that introduces and transmits the body of knowledge accumulated in western civilisation. As for (P), with the exception of radical de-schoolers, a curriculum should holistically integrate units of a topic or

---

[2] For the report's full text on line, see http://www.educationengland.org.uk/documents/plowden/. For assessments of "Plowdenism" twenty years later, see Halsey and Sylva (1987) and Dearden (1987).

[3] For a more extensive account of the (P)-(T) contrast, see Cuypers and Martin (2013), pp. 214–15.

project type that are geared to the children's individual talents, personal needs, and interests.

Correspondingly, according to (T), the teacher is the authoritative master or instructor imparting a body of knowledge: the teacher *teaches* and the pupil learns by *being taught*. As for (P), in contrast, the teacher's role is restricted to that of a facilitator or coach: the learning progresses by the child's own enquiry and discovery in a friendly environment that facilitates the exploration of the world at his own pace.

Roughly speaking, the progressive-traditional contrast mirrors the nature-nurture contrast. The implied naturalism and anti-culturalism of (P) is a complex issue. Ponder the following remarks. Progressive naturalism cannot be identified with scientific, Darwinian evolution theory. As stated by Darwinism, nature is indifferent to man's predicament. Evolution is impersonally regulated by the survival of the fittest in the struggle for life, that is, by the mechanism of natural selection. Progressive naturalism, by contrast, considers nature as intrinsically good. Nature is an immanent principle, a sublime power, or a creative force, with which one wants to make contact in order to discover one's own authenticity. Accordingly, progressive naturalism is a kind of literary, romantic biologism. Its conception of nature remains, however, ambivalent. On the one hand, nature is modelled after the wilderness, the jungle, or the rainforest, but on the other, it is modelled after the (botanical) garden or the park. Note, for example, that the German word for the nursery school is *Kindergarten*. The basic model of (P) is ambiguous between pristine nature and cultivated nature, between Victor d'Aveyron, a feral child, and Émile, Rousseau's hero (or, perhaps, Kipling's Mowgli). On balance, it is fair to say, I think, that progressive naturalism as an educational theory cannot escape from a minimal culturalism and, consequently, that the cultivated garden is more apt as its basic model than the uncultivated wilderness. Consider, for example, Émile's first and only book prior to early adulthood, introduced after the age of 12: Daniel Defoe's *Robinson Crusoe*, about a shipwrecked person who domesticates a deserted island to his own needs and interests.

Peters' Fundamental Presuppositions

In order to understand Peters' critique of the progressive philosophy of education that the Plowden Report contains, it is vital to uncover the presuppositions of his criticism. The two main presuppositions are:

1. the primacy of the social or the public, (S) for short, and
2. the ideal of liberal education, (L) for short.

Peters *presupposes* these doctrines as the bedrock of his critique without explicitly arguing for their validity. Yet, elsewhere in his work some material can be found in partial support of both underlying principles. I assemble this evidence to back up both assumptions. In addition, I explicitly construct arguments to fortify these basic assumptions of Peters' thinking. So, arguably, although these fundamental presuppositions are controversial, they are perfectly well defensible.

Sociality

As to the development of the child's mind and the content of the child's education, the social takes priority over the individual as the basic constitutive factor. In Chapter II of *Ethics and Education* (1966), Peters is critical of the classical emphasis on private individual experience and the inner world of consciousness as constitutive of mind and reason. According to him, the social or public has precedence over the individual or private in the development of mind and the differentiation of conscious awareness. He writes:

> The ideas and expectations of an individual centre of consciousness, however, do not develop as deposits out of an atomic individual experience. This is one of the misleading features of the … [classical] account. On the contrary they are the product of the initiation of an individual into public traditions enshrined in the language, concepts, beliefs, and rules of a society. … The objects of consciousness are first and foremost objects in a public world that are marked out and differentiated by a public language into which the individual is initiated. … His [the child's] consciousness, as well as his individuality, is neither intelligible nor genetically explicable without the public world of which he is conscious, in relation to which he develops … (Peters, 1966, pp. 48–9, 50).

Peters himself does not give any argument for (S). I surmise that, in writing the above passage, he implicitly relies on a pillar of Wittgenstein's philosophy, namely the private language argument in the *Philosophical Investigations* (1953). Whether Peters had it in mind or not, this argument against the possibility of a private language can certainly be appealed to in support of (S). Although it is (only) an argument about language, it has far reaching consequences for the way in which the experiences, concepts, beliefs, and rules are structured in the child's mind. According to Peters, language is the gate to a view of the world or "a form of life": "To live at ease he has to get on the inside of it [the social world], to incorporate it in his own mental structure. This he does mainly by learning a language; for a people's language is the key to the form of life which they enjoy. By means of it [language] they pick out and create the public world peculiar to them" (Peters, 1966, p. 52).

To make the private language argument explicit, consider the following version of it.

(1) Language-use is meaningful.
(2) If language-use is meaningful, then there are criteria of correctness (for using words and sentences).
(3) If language-use is private, then there are no criteria of correctness.
(4) If there are criteria of correctness, then language-use is not private.
(5) If language-use is meaningful, then language-use is not private
(∴) Language-use is not private, or
No language-use is private.

Premises (1) to (3) are the substantial ones. Premise (4) formally follows from premise (3) by contraposition. Premise (5) is the result of a hypothetical syllogism on premises (2) and (4). And the conclusion—the denial of private language—is deduced from premises (5) and (1) by modus ponens.

Premises (1) and (2) are substantial, but uncontroversial. Premise (1) uncontroversially states that the (correct) syntactic, semantic, and pragmatic use of words and sentences is meaningful. Premise (2) formulates the equally uncontroversial thesis of the normativity of meaning. Meaningful language-use implies rule-following. We have to follow linguistic rules (or norms) in order to correctly use words and sentences. Linguistic rules provide the criteria to distinguish correct from incorrect language-use. So, language-use can only be meaningful, if the distinction between the right and wrong use of words and sentences can be made.

Yet, the substantial premise (3) is (highly) controversial. Wittgenstein supports this key premise of the private language argument by the following consideration.

> Let us imagine the following case. I want to keep a diary about the recurrence of a certain [private] sensation. To this end I associate it with the sign "S" and write this sign in a calendar for every day on which I have the sensation. … that is done precisely by the concentration of my attention; for in this way I impress on myself the connection between the sign and the sensation.—But "I impress it on myself" can only mean: this process brings it about that I remember the connection *right* in the future. But in the present case I have no criterion of correctness. One would like to say: whatever is going to seem right to me is right. And that only means that here we can't talk about 'right'. (Wittgenstein, 1953, I, §258)

The private language argument is complex (see Candlish & Wrisley, 2014). There are several problems here: (i) the problem of memory; (ii) that of (inner) ostensive definition; and (iii) that of (correct) rule-following. For simplicity's sake, I limit myself here to the third problem, that of the normativity of meaning.

Suppose hypothetically that someone uses a private language. Call the purported private language-user, Privatus. Consider his diary of three consecutive days.

Day 1	Day 2	Day 3	
'S'	'S'	'S'	sign 'S'
⋮	⋮	⋮	connection
ps_1	ps_2	ps_3	tokens of the same type
	ps'	ps"	tokens of different types

On day 1 Privatus impresses on himself the connection (or reference-rule) between sign "S" and private sensation ps_1 for future use. But immediately there is the following problem when on day 2 he writes "S" in his diary.

The problem is this. Is Privatus remembering and applying his reference-rule of day 1 correctly? Does "S" really refer to a private sensation ps_2 of the same type? Is he remembering the *same* connection as on day 1, or does he on day 2 connect "S" with another private sensation, ps', of a different type? Does "S" perhaps refer to ps'? So, the question is whether Privatus on day 2 is following the *same* reference-rule as on day 1, or another reference-rule.

Now, given that in the hypothetical private language case one has only recourse to one's own inner life, Privatus on day 2 cannot make the distinction between the *right* (or correct) reference-rule linking sign "S" to private sensation ps_1 and the *wrong* (or incorrect) reference-rule linking sign "S" to private sensation ps'. Making such a distinction would imply that he could appeal to a norm which was independent of his own inner life and that is *ex hypothesi* impossible. The difficulty only gets worse on day 3, for it is then possible that all the private sensations ps", ps', and ps_1 belong to different types. Privatus cannot make the distinction between the right and wrong use of sign "S" because whatever is going to *seem* right to him, from the perspective of his own inner life, is right. In the private case, there is no possibility of an independent check of one's use of the sign "S". Hence, Privatus has no possibility on day 2 or 3 to know that he is wrong and, therefore, no possibility to correct himself. But if there is no way in which he can correct himself, then the distinction between the right and wrong use of sign "S" collapses. That is to say, Privatus cannot establish any criterion of correctness from the perspective of his own inner life. Yet, as stated in premise (2) of the above version of the private language argument, correctness-criteria are necessary conditions for meaningful language-use. Consequently, private language-use is pointless or meaningless. So, according to Wittgenstein, private rule-following would undermine the normativity of meaning: "... to *think* one is obeying a rule is not to obey a rule. Hence it is not possible to obey a rule 'privately': otherwise thinking one was obeying a rule would be the same thing as obeying it" (Wittgenstein, 1953, I, §202).

If the private language argument is sound, then all language-use is public. The linguistic community and the possibility of public checkability establishes and guarantees the normative distinction between correct and incorrect language-use. Whether or not Peters had this argument in mind, it unquestionably supports (S).

Liberal Education

The driving force behind Peters' philosophy of education as a whole is (L) (Peters, 1966, pp. 43–45). In all his writings, Peters explicitly or implicitly works from the principle that all education, properly speaking, is *liberal* education. At times, he has weakened this principle, but he has never abandoned it. Let me briefly explain what Peters means by "liberal education".

Peters' basic metaphor to capture the essence of education is "education *as initiation*". He circumscribes education as an initiation into "public traditions enshrined in a public language" or a "public form of life" (Peters, 1963, pp. 102–3, 104). Notice that he here presupposes (S). Two questions come to mind right away: Which form of life? And which initiation?

As to the first, Peters answers, most of the time implicitly: the western way of life, or culture, or civilisation.[4] Two things follow from this. First, the western way of life

---

[4] Peters assumes that something like a *western* civilisation exists. The very idea of western civilisation might, however, be contested; see, for example, Appiah (2016).

is *worthwhile* because parents and teachers cannot possibly educate their children and pupils in a way of life they themselves deem worthless or despicable. And second, western culture is a *knowledge* culture because it is founded on philosophy and science. Western civilisation originates in Greek philosophy and the Copernican scientific revolution, as against religion, superstition, myth, and ideology.

As to the second question, Peters answers: after an unavoidable causal training in the beginning, as soon as possible, an initiation on the basis of *reasons*. Education, strictly speaking, excludes coercion, indoctrination, training, drill, conditioning, and other illegitimate forms of causal control. Education should minimally respect the "liberty" of the child or pupil.

Peters likens education to initiation as follows.

'Initiation', ..., even when connected with various ceremonies or rites, suggests an avenue of access to *a body of belief* [knowledge], ... Furthermore, 'initiation' ... [does] convey the ... suggestion of being placed on the inside of a form of thought or awareness by a wide variety of processes which at least involve some kind of *consciousness and consent* [liberty] on the part of the initiate. (Peters, 1966, p. 54; my italics)

So, liberal education respects the minimal requirements of wittingness and voluntariness on the part of the child or pupil. In addition, liberal education is closely connected to the western knowledge culture.

The subsequent question that comes to mind is, of course: which body of knowledge is, or "forms of thought and awareness" are involved in liberal education? According to Paul H. Hirst, Peters' closest collaborator, the "vast inheritance" of the western knowledge culture is not an undifferentiated, homogeneous unity, like religion, mythology, or ideology. As stated by his so-called "forms of knowledge" thesis, the domain of knowledge differentiates into fundamentally different modes of knowledge (and experience) on the basis of the principle that "all our concepts seem to belong to one of a number of distinct, if related, categories which philosophical analysis is concerned to clarify. ... It is these categoreal concepts that provide the form of experience in the different modes" (Hirst & Peters, 1970, p. 64). Among these foundational categories are the following: "number" and "plane"; "space", "time" and "cause; "person" and "intention"; "God" or "the transcendent". These categoreal lines partition the knowledge domain in radically different fields which can neither be equated nor be reduced to each other.

Hirst (1965) listed seven (or eight) basic forms of knowledge or disciplines—mathematics, physical sciences, human sciences, history, religion, literature and the fine arts, and philosophy (as well as moral knowledge, which does not constitute a separate discipline)—for the range of liberal education. This amounts to identifying liberal education with *general* education.[5]

Peters later had doubts about this all-round interpretation of Hirst. In view of the existential significance of a *specific* "human heritage", he narrowed down the scope

---

[5] Besides this conception of liberal education, there are at least two other ones: liberal education as (i) knowledge for its own sake and as (ii) nonauthoritarian education. See Cuypers and Martin (2013), pp. 108–116.

to "a sphere of knowledge, sometimes referred to loosely as 'the humanities', which is of central importance in any attempt to determine the type of knowledge which should form the content of liberal education" (Peters, 1977, p. 66). Bearing in mind that Peters adheres to a purposive, rule-following model of human action as against a causal, covering-law model in the social sciences (Peters, 1958, pp. 1–26), he also incorporates the "humanistic", hermeneutic subdisciplines of this knowledge field—in particular Freudian psychoanalysis and Weberian sociology—into the humanities. As a consequence, the field of the human sciences, in Peters' sense, is composed of a subset of Hirst's original set of basic (sub)disciplines: *literature and the fine arts, history, philosophy, religion, (moral knowledge), "humanistic" psychology and sociology.* This amounts to identifying liberal education with *humanistic* education.

Peters does not explicitly give an argument for (L) as the ideal of humanistic education, (L*) for short. In his "The justification of education" (1973) he takes up the question "Why is education intrinsically good?" and gives a transcendental argument for the thesis that knowledge and understanding are intrinsically valuable (in a non-hedonistic sense).[6] Yet, this is a very abstract argument for the value of education *simpliciter* and not for humanistic education in particular. Although Peters himself does not explicitly give an argument for (L*), I submit that an explicit argument can be constructed for the value or importance of liberal education as education into the humanities from the material in his "Subjectivity and standards" (1974). It is noteworthy that he republished the same article under the slightly but significantly changed title "Subjectivity and standards *in the humanities*" (1975; my italics).

To make this, what I call, justificatory argument from *existential concern* explicit, consider the following loose version of it (Cuypers & Martin, 2013, pp. 124–25):

A. Every human being is (a) confronted with the predicaments of life, (b) emotion- and reason-responsive to them, and (c) concerned about the quality of life.
B. Only the humanities rationally articulate (a′) the meaning of the human condition, (b′) emotional and reasonable attitudes to human life, and (c′) standards for the search of life-quality.
(∴) Therefore, the humanities are existentially important or relevant for every human being, given that each one wants to make something out of him- or herself (i.e. self-concern).

Consider, next, the formalised version of this argument to inspect its validity. Its domain is the set of human beings—$D = \{x \mid x$ is a human being$\}$.

(1) For all x, x is concerned about him- or herself (self-concerned).
(2) For all x, if x is self-concerned, then x has an existential concern.
(3) For all x, if x has an existential concern, then the humanities are important for x.
(4) For all x, if x is self-concerned, then the humanities are important for x.
(∴) For all *x*, the humanities are important for *x*.

---

[6] For a critical account of this argument, see Cuypers (2012).

Under the scope of the universal quantifier, premise (4) is the formal result of a hypothetical syllogism on premises (2) and (3). The conclusion follows from premise (1) and (4) by modus ponens.

Premise (1) is a very plausible assumption. Take, for example, the foundational ideas that human beings possess a *conatus* (principle of self-conservation) or that they are motivated by *l'amour-propre* (self-love). Premise (2) is self-evident. Think, for instance, about Martin Heidegger's *Dasein ist Sorge* (Being-in-the-World is Care). Self-concern implies existential concern. If one wants to make something out of one's life, then one is concerned about the quality of one's life in confrontation with the predicaments of life to which one responds emotionally and rationally. Premise (3) is the crucial one. In support of this key premise take the following into account. Only the humanities speak to the existential concern of human beings: they hypothetically offer the rational articulations (a'), (b'), and (c') to try to cope with (a), (b), and (c). The humanities have a unique and distinctive character in that they "study the meaning-making practices of human culture, past and present, focusing on interpretation and critical evaluation" (Small, 2013, p. 23).

The argument from existential concern is, I submit, not only valid but also sound. It justifies (L*) because the humanities constitute a body of knowledge with a *specific* and *unique* role in relation to man's place in the universe. And it constitutes a justification precisely because of the universality of its basic premise, namely the fact that *every* human being is placed in the *same* existential situation.[7]

Peters' (and Dearden's) Critique of the Plowden Report

According to Peters, (P), as expressed in the Plowden Report, "is theoretically not satisfactory and is far from appropriate to the practical needs of our time" (Peters, 1969a, p. ix). The target of his critique is not the report's list of concrete recommendations but "the implicit ideology of the Report" (Peters, 1969b, p. 3)—"the little vade-mecum of educational theory" or "recognizable philosophy of education" (p. 2)—that it contains. I organise his critique around two central themes: first, education and its aims, and, second, the curriculum and the teacher. Peters' criticism directly flows from his fundamental presuppositions: (S) and (L) (or (L*)).

Although I focus here on Peters' response to (P) in general, it was Robert F. Dearden who extensively and thoroughly analysed the progressive philosophy of *primary* education in his *The Philosophy of Primary Education* (1968) and its sequel *Problems in Primary Education* (1976). Here I only pay attention to his contribution to *Perspectives on Plowden*, in addition to Peters'.

---

[7] For a further elaboration of this argument, see Cuypers (2018). One could further ask: What then about the justification of Science, Technology, Engineering and Mathematics (STEM), the other segment of Hirst's forms of knowledge thesis? Arguably, in our present day technological culture STEM does not stand in need of any *intrinsic* justification because its self-evident instrumental justification amply suffices. In this sense, STEM is on a par with the three Rs.

Development and the Aims of Education

The Plowden Report begs the nature-nurture question from the start:

> At the heart of the educational process lies *the child*. No advances in policy, no acquisitions
> of new equipment, have their desired effect unless [i] they are in harmony with *the nature
> of the child*, unless [ii] they are *fundamentally acceptable* to him. (§9; my italics)

Dearden (1969, p. 24) critically observes that this statement "assumes: (i) that the child has a 'nature', which is a dubious metaphysical assertion; (ii) that we ought to adopt the principle of always starting from and being acceptable to this 'nature', which is an unargued ethical recommendation." The child's nature or self is the basis of the Plowden ideology: it is (a) an innate package for further (psychological) development, like the power of a bud for unfolding into a flower, and (b) an inalienable (ethical) principle of personal autonomy or authenticity. Let me take these points in turn and look at Peters' (and Dearden's) critique of them.

In view of (S) and (L), the key progressive notions—"development", "growth", "unfolding", "maturation", and "ripening"—as (P) construes them, are devoid of meaning. In Peters' (and Hirst's as well as Dearden's) educational theory, the concepts of *development* and *growth* taken separately and independently of the concept of education (as social initiation into forms of knowledge) are empty. (P) pretends to work with a concept of development/education that is descriptive and scientific. The trajectory of child development is statistically divided into successive stages of ripening, at the end of each of which the child is "ready" to go to the next one. (P) takes the basic aims of education—self-development and self-actualisation—as given facts of human nature. However, in the light of (S) and (L), development inevitably implies a *norm* that differentiates between good and bad development. Additionally, education as directed towards a valuable form of life—the western knowledge culture—is inescapably *evaluative*. Aims of education cannot be determined scientifically on a statistical basis. Even the notions of "need" and "interest" presuppose value-judgements about what man should be. (P) cannot avoid the discussion on the cultural (or social) justification of educational aims.

According to Peters, "[t]he plea for the development of selves is always to be understood within a framework of shared valuations" (Peters, 1969b, p. 8) In view of the fact that development is inextricably bound up with education, he doubts "whether there is any field of study called 'child development' which can be clearly distinguished from 'education'. Of course there is the physical and physiological side of 'development' ... But is mental development distinguishable from 'education'?" (p. 8). These considerations tip the nature-nurture scale in favour of the latter. (S) and (L) imply that mental development *necessarily* depends upon education by others and learning a body of knowledge. Child development and growth cannot proceed independently and in isolation from education as social initiation.

Peters summarises his main point of critique as follows:

> Most of what is wrong with it [(P)] can be summed up by saying that it systematically
> ignores the *inescapably social character* of thought and language, of processes of transmission, and of motivation. The notion that children can peel concepts off the world without

sensitization to selected aspects of it incorporated in a *public* language, that most of their interests are self-originated rather than caught from *others*, that children become 'ready' by some kind of internal ripening without imitation, identification, and instruction—all such notions are highly suspect. (Peters, 1969b, p. 16; my italics)

(P) intrinsically connects the basic goals of self-development and self-actualisation to other, more specific educational aims, such as those of critical thinking (as against indoctrination), individual autonomy (as against paternalism), and creativity (as against conformism). Dearden explicates the key value of personal autonomy or authenticity as follows.

There are two aspects to such an autonomy, one negative and one positive. The negative aspect is that of *independence of authorities* who dictate what we are to believe, or direct us in what we are to do. The complementary positive aspect is, first, that of *testing the truth of things for ourselves*, whether by experience or by a critical estimate of the testimony of others, and secondly, that of *deliberating, forming intentions, and choosing* what we shall do, according to *a scale of values which we can ourselves appreciate*. (Dearden, 1969, p. 31; my italics)

In the light of (S) and (L), autonomy or authenticity as the central progressive value, "like any other value, must surely be asserted not absolutely but with an 'other things being equal' clause" (Peters, 1969b, p. 10). If there exists a bedrock or overarching aim of education, then it can only be the social initiation into different forms of knowledge and understanding, especially into those of the humanities. Since this aim can be thought of as foundational or, at least, the "first among equals", Peters' view on the aims of education can be expressed by the following Asymmetrical Dependency Thesis.

(ADT) All other educational aims *asymmetrically depend upon* the basic aim of initiation into different modes of knowledge and understanding, especially of the human condition.

According to (ADT), critical thinking, individual autonomy, and creativity asymmetrically depend upon social initiation in a (humanistic) body of knowledge. We can only test the truth of things for ourselves if we can rely on test procedures that belong to our shared scientific inheritance. We can only rationally form intentions and deliberately choose according to our own value scales, if we know "what is worth understanding, and what deserves to be chosen" (Dearden, 1969, p. 32), and such goals and values belong to our common way of life.

So, autonomy or authenticity is incomprehensible except against the background of an inherited form of life. First-hand experience and self-governance must be informed and empowered by the heirlooms of our cultural inheritance. And against the backdrop of (L*) and (ADT), the humanities in particular are needed to make something out of one's own life:

if we accept that there are many ways in which an individual can strike out on his own in a pluralist type of society, and if we think that children should be encouraged to stand on their own feet and find their own way, then we must think seriously about equipping them to do this effectively. ... It is not enough, therefore, to say that children should learn to be themselves at school; we must give them the equipment to find out properly what sort of selves they want to be. In my view the forms of awareness grouped roughly together under the title of 'the humanities' are particularly important in this. (Peter, 1969b, pp. 11–12)

Curriculum and the Teacher

Both Peters (1969b, pp. 13–14) and Dearden (1969, pp. 34–37) subscribe, generally speaking, to Hirst's forms of knowledge thesis, the centrepiece of (L). They both have their own emphases and qualifications (such as (L*)), but by and large they are in agreement with Hirst that apart from teaching the basic skills of reading, writing, and arithmetic—the three Rs—the curriculum should be differentiated and include slots for teaching (humanistic) science, history, and the arts (and literature). Dearden summarises the claim that the curriculum—at least the central school subjects—should be based on the forms of knowledge as follows:

> First, these forms of understanding are structural of what have historically turned out to be very wide-ranging modes of experience, ... Secondly, as such they are relevant to very many, and probably to all of the more important, choices that we have to make, both in our work and in our leisure. And thirdly, their consequent essential connection with the exercise of personal autonomy, together with the requirement of a systematic schooling for their development, make them obviously central candidates for education in the curriculum of our primary schools. (Dearden, 1969, p. 37)

As against the forms of knowledge thesis, the key feature of (L), the Plowden Report maintains "that knowledge does not fall into neatly separate compartments" (§505). Against the compartmentalised, school subject-centred curriculum, it favours an integrated curriculum structure with units of a topic or project type. The primary aim of such an integrated curriculum is emphatically not that of systematically initiating children into the different structures of the several forms of knowledge separately. In opposition to the traditional atomistic method, the Plowden Report promotes a progressive holistic method of learning and teaching.

In view of (L)/(L*), Peters critically asks what exactly the point of integration could be. Does it imply a return to "knowledge" as a single, monolithic, and undifferentiated whole—a return to religion or mythology? Is the topic or project approach more stimulating and more motivating than the subject-centred approach? Is the real purpose of holism perhaps moral education or education for citizenship? How can a unifying topic or project (for example, environment, transport, or multiculturalism) in which many different disciplines come together (mathematics, science, psychology, sociology, the arts, etc.) be mastered without a systematic and detailed knowledge of the several component disciplines?

Yet, for Peters the issue is not so much conceptual as empirical. Sticking rigidly to the traditional subject-centred curriculum is just as short-sighted as substituting it for an integrated, topic or project-based curriculum. He does not reject progressive curriculum integration as such. What he rejects is the myopic elevation of *a* curriculum structure to *the* curriculum structure. What has to be abandoned on both sides is educational ideology. Instead of proclaiming educational dogmas, Peters pleads for an empirical investigation of the merits of both alternatives in different learning and teaching situations:

> My contention is that no such overall recipe is possible. What is needed is a down-to-earth, clear-headed, experimental approach which takes due account not only of general criteria but of the differences in what is taught and the children to whom it is taught. (Peters, 1969b, p. 15)

The Plowden image of the teacher is that "of a child-grower who stands back and manipulates the environment so that children will proceed from discovery to discovery when they are 'ready'" (Peters, 1969b, pp. 15–6). In the light of (S) and (L), this progressive notion of the teacher-facilitator or teacher-coach is hardly intelligible, balancing on the verge of a contradiction in terms. If all educational learning is social learning, then learning by individual discovery simply cannot get started. If all education is initiation, then education without an initiator is nonsense. The Plowden Report has much to say about learning by first-hand discovery and experience, but almost nothing about teaching. It is significant that Peters chose a quote from B.F. Skinner for the frontispiece of *Perspectives on Plowden*: "The school of experience is no school at all, not because no one learns in it but because no one teaches. Teaching is the expedition of learning; a person who is taught learns more quickly than one who is not" (Skinner, 1968, cited in Peters, 1969a, p. iii). By being taught, a great number of pupils can be brought to, for instance, the intellectual level of Isaac Newton by the end of their secondary education. How many of them would have learned mathematical calculus by sheer discovery and experience, even when they were "ready" for mastering it? Not only the speed but also the range of learning is multiplied exponentially by being taught.

Against the backdrop of (S) and (L), the role of the teacher cannot be reduced to that of a facilitating bystander. If the social or the public precedes the individual, and if education is initiation into public traditions enshrined in a public language and a public form of life, then the educational process inevitably stands in need of an *initiator* or *master* already speaking that language and living according to that form of life. Education is, therefore, a process of authoritative transmission of a shared heritage from teachers to pupils. Far from being passive bystanders, teachers are active agents of civilisation with a sacred mission.

On this central point, Peters is in full agreement with Michael Oakeshott's glorifying picture of the teacher:

> Every human being is born an heir to an inheritance to which he can succeed only in a process of learning. … What every man is born an heir to is an inheritance of human achievements; an inheritance of feelings, emotions, images, visions, thoughts, beliefs, ideas, understanding, intellectual and practical enterprises, languages, relationships, organizations, canons and maxims of conduct, procedures, rituals, skills, works of art, books, musical compositions, tools, artifacts and utensils—in short, what Dilthey called a *geistige Welt*. … This world can be entered, possessed and enjoyed only in a process of learning. … It is into this *geistige Welt* that the child, even in its earliest adventures in awareness, initiates itself; and to initiate his pupils into it is the business of the teacher. Not only may it be entered only by learning, but there is nothing else for a pupil to learn. … initiation into the *geistige Welt* of human achievement is owed to the Sage, the teacher: and this debt is to be acknowledged with the profoundest reverence—for to whom can a man be more deeply indebted than to the one to whom he owes, not his mere existence, but his participation in human life? It is the Sage, the teacher, who is the agent of civilization. (Oakeshott, 1965, pp. 37–39)

In view of this pivotal role of the teacher-sage, one can now readily understand why the Plowden philosophy is not only "theoretically not satisfactory", but also why it is "far from appropriate to the practical needs of our time" (Peters, 1969b, p. ix):

does not the Plowden image of the teacher tend to down-grade the role of the teacher at a time when the teacher should be occupying an increasingly important role? For in a pluralistic society, when there is no unified ideal that can be handed on by *the priests*, who else is there to stand between the generations and to initiate others into the various aspects of a culture within which the individual has eventually to determine where he stands? (Peters, 1969b, pp. 16–7; my italics)

In a pluralist, modern society with no overarching religious or political ideals anymore, the teacher is our last resort for the intergenerational transmission of those cultural aspects that individuals need to make something of themselves.

Conclusion

In the light of Peters' (and Dearden's) critique of the 1967 Plowden Report, let me briefly conclude. To my mind, Peters' particular position is still highly significant even in the contemporary debate because it offers a counterbalance against too radical versions of child-centred progressivism, of (P), and individualism in general. His insistence on initiation into public modes of experience, knowledge, and understanding of the human predicament in order to become an educated and morally responsible person remains particularly important for present-day educational theory. Peters' view against the backdrop of his fundamental presuppositions (S) and (L)/(L*) is, therefore, an everlasting contribution to the philosophy of education and a permanent source of inspiration for its future advancement.

Tribute

I am honored to be included in this *Festschrift* for Paul Smeyers. He introduced me to the philosophy of education, and especially to the work of Peters, in the autumn of 1985. From that time onwards, Paul has been extremely kind to me, offering me opportunities, support, and advice. I am very much indebted to him, and I would like to thank him sincerely for his kindness, wisdom, and generosity.

References

Appiah, K. A. (2016). There is no such thing as western civilisation. Retrieved March 28, 2017, from https://www.theguardian.com/world/2016/nov/09/western-civilisation-appiah-reith-lecture

Black, J. (2010). *A brief history of Britain 1851–2010*. London: Robinson.

Candlish, S., & Wrisley, G. (2014). Private language. In E. N. Zalta (Ed.), *The stanford encyclopedia of philosophy* (Fall 2014 ed.). Available at https://plato.stanford.edu/archives/fall2014/entries/private-language/

Crosland, C. A. R. (1956). *The future of socialism*. London: Cape.

Cuypers, S. E. (2012). R.S. Peters' "The justification of education" revisited. *Ethics and Education, 7*(1), 3–17.

Cuypers, S. E. (2018). The existential concern of the humanities. R.S. Peters' justification of liberal education. *Educational Philosophy and Theory, 50*(6/7), 702–711.

Cuypers, S. E., & Martin, C. (2013). *R.S. Peters*. London: Bloomsbury.

Dearden, R. F. (1968). *The philosophy of primary education*. London: Routledge and Kegan Paul.

Dearden, R. F. (1969). The aims of primary education. In R. S. Peters (1969a) (Ed.), *Perspectives on Plowden* (pp. 21–41). London: Routledge and Kegan Paul.

Dearden, R. F. (1976). *Problems in primary education*. London: Routledge and Kegan Paul.

Dearden, R. F. (1987). The Plowden philosophy in retrospect. In R. Lowe (Ed.), *The changing primary school* (pp. 68–85). London: The Falmer Press.

Education Act. (1944). Available at http://www.legislation.gov.uk/ukpga/Geo6/7-8/31/enacted

Halsey, A. H., & Sylva, K. D. (Eds.). (1987). Special issue: Plowden twenty years on. *Oxford Review of Education, 13*(1), 3–11.

Hirst, P. H. (1965). Liberal education and the nature of knowledge. In P. H. Hirst. (1974). *Knowledge and the curriculum* (pp. 30–53). London: Routledge and Kegan Paul.

Hirst, P. H., & Peters, R. S. (1970). *The logic of education*. London: Routledge and Kegan Paul.

Norwood Report. (1943). *Curriculum and examinations in secondary schools. Report of the committee of the secondary school examinations council appointed by the President of the Board of Education in 1941*. London: HM Stationery Office Available at: http://www.educationengland.org.uk/documents/norwood/norwood1943.html

Oakeshott, M. (1965). Learning and teaching. In M. Oakeshott. (2001). *The voice of liberal learning*. Indianapolis, IN: Liberty Fund.

Peters, R. S. (1958). *The concept of motivation*. London: Routledge and Kegan Paul.

Peters, R. S. (1963). Education as initiation. In R. D. Archambault (Ed.), *Philosophical analysis and education* (pp. 87–111). London: Routledge and Kegan Paul.

Peters, R. S. (1966). *Ethics and education*. London: George Allen and Unwin Ltd.

Peters, R. S. (Ed.). (1969a). *Perspectives on Plowden*. London: Routledge and Kegan Paul.

Peters, R. S. (1969b). "A recognizable philosophy of education": A constructive critique. In R. S. Peters (1969a). *Perspectives on Plowden* (pp. 1–20). London: Routledge and Kegan Paul.

Peters, R. S. (1973). The justification of education. In R. S. Peters. (1977). *Education and the Education of* teachers (pp. 86–118). London: Routledge and Kegan Paul.

Peters, R. S. (1974). Subjectivity and standards. In R. S. Peters. (1974). *Psychology and ethical development* (pp. 413–432). London: George Allen and Unwin.

Peters, R. S. (1975). Subjectivity and standards in the humanities. In D. Nyberg (Ed.), *The philosophy of open education* (pp. 91–109). London: Routledge and Kegan Paul.

Peters, R. S. (1977). Ambiguities in liberal education and the problem of its content. In R. S. Peters (Ed.), *Education and the education of teachers* (pp. 46–67). London: Routledge and Kegan Paul.

Peters, R. S. (1983). Philosophy of education. In P. H. Hirst (Ed.), *Educational theory and its foundation disciplines* (pp. 30–61). London: Routledge and Kegan Paul.

Skinner, B. F. (1968). *The technology of teaching*. New York: Appleton-Century-Crofts.

Small, H. (2013). *The value of the humanities*. Oxford, UK: Oxford University Press.

Wittgenstein, L. (1953). *Philosophical investigations*. Oxford, UK: Basil Blackwell.

Chapter 9
Upon the Academic Philosopher Caught in the Fly-Bottle

Jean Paul Van Bendegem

Abstract Philosophy as an academic discipline has grown into something highly specific. This raises the question whether alternatives are available within the academic world itself – what I call the Lutheran view – and outside of academia (with or without support from the inside) – what I call the Calvinist view. Since I defend the thesis that such alternatives partially exist and as yet non-existent possibilities could in principle be realised, the main question thus becomes what prevents us from acting appropriately. In honour of Paul Smeyers, the fitting metaphor has to be the Wittgensteinian fly-bottle.

Introduction

The general question that has kept me busy for many years is what the role of a philosopher could be in present-day societies, if any at all. The easy answer is that such a place has been provided for, namely in academia, but that raises a number of issues that I will deal with in the first part of the next section. I will try to argue that we should look for alternatives, both within and without the ivory tower, to use the famous metaphor. I have, tongue-in-cheek, labelled the former Lutheran and the latter Calvinist. The second part of the next section deals with slow science and citizen science. The third section looks both at counter-movements and initiatives outside of academia (but sometimes with inside support), ranging from the freelance philosopher to group- and practice-oriented philosophy.

J. P. Van Bendegem (✉)
Centre for Logic and Science-Philosophy, Vrije Universiteit Brussel (VUB), Brussels, Belgium
e-mail: jpvbende@vub.ac.be

© Springer International Publishing AG, part of Springer Nature 2018   117
S. Ramaekers, N. Hodgson (eds.), *Past, Present, and Future Possibilities for Philosophy and History of Education*,
https://doi.org/10.1007/978-3-319-94253-7_9

Philosophy in the Academic Fly-Bottle

A Brief Description of Academic Research Then and Now

It is a safe hypothesis to start with that the academic world has in recent times become an extremely specific environment for its members, including that particular group labelled the philosophers. I will here focus (a) on research and less on teaching students, training future researchers, and communicating with the "outside" world, (b) on the philosophical subcommunity, and (c) mainly on the situation in Flanders. Going back in time (though not all that long), the basic research unit was a couple, consisting of the supervisor and the doctoral student.[1] The topic of research was determined between the two members of this unit and rare were the cases where the student was expected to carry out part of the supervisor's research. The aim was rather to "educate" the PhD-student to become an "independent" researcher-philosopher him- or herself. Financial support was not a core issue as means were perhaps not necessarily abundant but they certainly were not scarce.[2] This kind of situation was perfectly reflected in a *genealogical way of speaking*: if a philosopher X had to situate him- or herself in the academic philosophical world, X would typically reply that (s)he is a pupil of Y and mentor/supervisor of Z', Z″, … (all too often in simple sequential-temporal order). To be clear, this parent-child generational view has not disappeared[3] but it is no longer sufficient as a description, as it was back then.

The present-day situation has at its core the research group, involving both junior and senior researchers. More often than not this group has a research profile, i.e., a specific domain or subdomain of the philosophical research landscape, that also serves to identify it. More often than not the group is internationally connected to similar groups, although similarity has to be generously understood. It may involve inter-, intra-, trans-, and multidisciplinary collaborations. More often than not research themes within such an international network tend to be coordinated and a division of labour is established. It is not an easy matter to determine what complex of elements caused this evolution from a binary unit to a coordinated integrated group and I will focus on one element that has played a crucial role, namely the representation of the scientific environment to its practitioners. Ever since Derek de Solla Price published his *Little Science, Big Science* (see de Solla Price, 1963) we

---

[1] Exception is made for those philosophers who were associated with a famous philosopher's archive, the most famous one in Flanders surely being the Husserl archive at KU Leuven (https://hiw.kuleuven.be/hua).

[2] To take myself as an example, when I applied for a grant for a PhD-scholarship in 1979, submitted to the National Science Research Foundation (NFWO: Nationaal Fonds voor Wetenschappelijk Onderzoek), success rates were close to 50%. Today this has been reduced to about 20% in the best of cases. Having served as a member of the committee of the NWFO for philosophy for 10 years (1997–2006), I have been a direct witness of this gradual decline of funds.

[3] See, e.g., https://philosophyfamilytree.wikispaces.com/, a Wiki website that present the *Philosophy Family Tree* (consulted on 27 December 2017).

have a plethora of ways to represent a scientific community or group (see Börner, 2010 for an impressive overview) and the best known method is of course citation analysis, as it is practiced on the *Web of Science* by the former *Institute of Scientific Information*, now part of *Clarivate Analytics*.

These representations have two major effects. In the first place, it enables young researchers to plan their research more explicitly, as one can determine where the academic "superstars"[4] are and where new topics of research are being developed. But in the second place, it also enables financial sources, ranging from government, both national and supranational, to private (economic) enterprises, to make more explicit choices as to what types of research should be funded. To be more specific, more and more research in Belgium and Flanders, is guided by European research funds – ERC and Marie Curie grants, to name the top two – and their problem agendas involve primarily the exact sciences, engineering, medicine, and (some of) the social sciences. The point is not that this sort of guidance is badly or not motivated at all – after all, most of the topics address issues that are vital to all of us, climate change on top of the list – but it leads to an uneven distribution of funds across the academic disciplines and an explicitly economic view of universities. A "fine" recent example is a report, ordered by the VLIR-council[5] that represents all Flemish universities from consultancy firm Biggar Economics, in order to show that universities are economically speaking "sound" in the sense that the output in euro is greater than the input. A quote of the executive report needs, I believe, no further explanation:

> Flemish Universities undertake a wide range of valorisation activity that supports business and innovation in Flanders and beyond. This includes licensing technology and supporting the formation of new businesses (spin-off companies) as well as providing research and professional development services to businesses, offering student placements, providing access to research infrastructure and supporting science parks. (Biggar Economics, 2017, p. 3)

One of the "victims" of such policies and views is precisely philosophy as an academic discipline. A rather clear indicator is the fact that philosophy does not occur in the European research programs as a topic on its own but, in the best of cases, only as a subtopic with, in addition, a focus on ethical issues.[6] And here something strange happens: it seems that philosophy has been pushed into a situation where the dominant behaviour is a form of *mimicry*. Philosophers do their utmost best to look like (exact) scientists and that leads, among other things but most prominently, to standardisation. The focus on publications has shifted from

---

[4] For an interesting discussion, including a presentation of a formal model, concerning the status of academic superstars, see Heesen (2017), who explicitly uses this expression.

[5] VLIR stands for Vlaamse Interuniversitaire Raad – Flemish Interuniversity Council.

[6] I will not elaborate on this issue here but it is rather strange if not difficult to comprehend that philosophy of science is almost completely absent. It creates the impression that scientific methodology is not a core issue of the scientific enterprise. But at the speed that science is being reshaped and restructured, driven by economic and political forces, does it not seem a worthwhile research question to ask to what extent science still delivers what it claims to deliver?

single-authored books to multi-authored journal papers and these papers have specific formats, often imposed by the journal editors. This in turn leads to an atomisation and a strong division of labour of philosophical thinking. A typical journal paper will address one specific issue, usually critical comments on or a continuation of previous research mentioned in another paper, and add one specific element to it. To be able to understand what the topic and the discussion is about, one has to be an expert in that particular subdomain, thus increasing its inaccessibility to other philosophers in other subdomains, not to mention the "lay" audience that has little or no idea what philosophy is all about.

This brief (and incomplete) sketch illustrates that philosophy as an academic discipline has been caught in a very particular fly-bottle and to some of its practitioners this situation is no longer tolerable. The next section looks at possible alternatives within academia or, what I would like to call, Lutheran proposals.

Exploring Alternative Routes

Without any doubt, the two best known alternatives are on the one hand "slow science" (including, among others, initiatives related to "open (access) science") and on the other hand "citizen science". The former applies to all academic disciplines, thus automatically including philosophy, but the latter has found a form in philosophy that is rather special.

We are all familiar with the formulae "publish or perish" to indicate the publication pressure on a researcher in a competitive setting – and that has been transformed into "publish *and* perish" to make clear that the first formula is no longer applicable – and it seems therefore natural that a way out is to slow the process down. It would however be a mistake to assume that the label "slow science" covers a homogeneous set of approaches.[7] There are at least two interconnected dimensions that create tensions and oppositions. The first one has to do with a full or partial replacement of the scientific process. It is rather striking that *The Slow Science Academy*, considered to be the "face" of the slow science movement, proposes a complementary view. On their website http://slow-science.org/ they present their manifesto and the second paragraph reads:[8]

> Science needs time to think. Science needs time to read, and time to fail. Science does not always know what it might be at right now. Science develops unsteadily, with jerky moves and unpredictable leaps forward—at the same time, however, it creeps about on a very slow time scale, for which there must be room and to which justice must be done.

---

[7] Actually, one should not be too enthusiastic, as the term "movement" is perhaps too generous. In Rull (2016) it is claimed that (and I tend to agree): "Yet, the slow science movement is not an official organisation of scientists, nor a club or academy, and it is highly cryptic. Literature and information on slow science is surprisingly scarce" (ibid., p. 134).

[8] Consulted on 28 December 2017.

But let there be no misunderstanding for the first paragraph states the following:

> Don't get us wrong—we do say yes to the accelerated science of the early 21st century. We say yes to the constant flow of peer-review journal publications and their impact; we say yes to science blogs and media & PR necessities; we say yes to increasing specialization and diversification in all disciplines. We also say yes to research feeding back into health care and future prosperity. All of us are in this game, too.

I mentioned that the two dimensions are interconnected and this is clearly shown by the fact that the few authors who plead for a serious rethinking of the scientific process also tend to rethink the relation between science and society, and that relation constitutes the second dimension: the ivory tower on the one hand and the "open" lab on the other hand. Surely the strongest defender of such a position is Isabelle Stengers, especially in her essay *Une autre science est possible!*[9] (2013). Here the basic conception is that science, as we know it today, cannot continue in the same fashion for, quite similar to (late capitalist) economic developments, it will hit limits and, in the worst of cases, simply disappear in the form that we know it today:

> Avec l'économie de la connaissance, c'est l'économie speculative, avec ses bulles et ses crashs, qui s'empare de ce qui fut la recherche scientifique. (p. 104) ["With the economy of knowledge, it is the economy of speculation, with its bubbles and crashes, that has taken hold of what used to be scientific research", *my translation*[10]]

Putting aside for a moment questions such as the (often) utopian character of slow science, the lack of a clear support within scientific circles and the even greater lack of concrete proposals on its implementation, the question that interests me here is what role philosophy can possibly play in this rethinking of the scientific process. There is an obvious, though far too general answer: slow science involves a continuous rethinking of what science is and does and that is precisely the area of the philosopher. Although the more critically and skeptically inclined philosopher will quickly reply that replacing *philosophia ancilla theologiae* by *philosophia ancilla scientiae* need not necessarily be seen as a step forward (or, at least, requires a solid defense for the contrary). Let us compare this situation with the other alternative, namely citizen science.

Quite similar to the case of slow science, it is important to see the heterogeneity that is to be found under this label. It ranges from (a) a rather modest participation of "ordinary" citizens in scientific experiments over (b) citizens having a certain impact on the scientists' agenda to (c) society at large (co-)determining the scientific agenda. An example of (a) is pollution measurement in cities where citizens have simple measuring apparatuses[11] at home and, on a daily basis, data are collected

---

[9] The essay has also appeared in English translation, see Stengers (2017). But do note that it is not a faithful translation as a chapter has been added and some parts have been rewritten.

[10] This passage does not occur in the already mentioned English translation, hence I offer my own translation instead.

[11] This is to be understood in a very broad sense. In the case of a research project involving both the University of Antwerp and other organisations, called *AIRbezen*, the participating citizens had to

and transmitted via the internet to the scientists conducting the experiment. This is indeed rather modest for it does not involve any fundamental changes in the scientific process itself, and in managerial terms this involvement of citizens should be best described as *free out-sourcing*. Possibility (b) is more interesting for in some cases it has taken the shape of so-called "science shops" ("wetenschapswinkels").[12] Through such an interface citizens can submit questions directly to the scientists. Although the former decide what the latter should investigate, it is the latter who finally decides whether the research is worthwhile, feasible, and not too invasive into their "real" research. However, as far as (c) is concerned, again philosophers could have a role to play, namely as intermediaries between citizen and scientist. It must be equally clear that (c) at present is still to be situated in the utopian sphere. So, again the conclusion seems to force itself upon us, namely that, in the Lutheran view, philosophy does not seem to fare well. Although perhaps an exception should be made for one new and recent development *within* philosophy itself and very specific to the discipline.

As in citizen science it involves the general public but with a very specific aim, namely to investigate philosophers' intuitions. More specifically, philosophers, especially analytic philosophers, very often rely on their own intuitions when tackling specific problems within, say, epistemology or ethics. In addition, in the examples they use to support their argumentations and reasonings, they take for granted that any human being will share their intuitions. In a sense they assume that they speak for the whole population. At the turn of the century the simple idea was launched that perhaps we might take the time to check with such an "ordinary" human being or citizen whether they actually hold these intuitions. And, (perhaps not) surprisingly, it turned out that they very often did not. This gave rise to the so-called "experimental philosophy" approach.[13] It seems rather clear that a philosophical training distorts intuitions more strongly than suspected (as in nearly all academic disciplines). Ask a classical[14] logician whether from the statement "It is raining" it logically follows that "If I am the Pope then it is raining" and she will readily answer yes because the first statement has been uttered unconditionally so no condition, even funny ones like being the Pope (although there is of course at present one notable exception), can have an effect.[15] But to every non-logician such a conclusion is absurd. It is much too early to claim that experimental philosophy

cultivate for a fixed period a strawberry plant that captured the air pollution in its leaves. A more recent and similar example is the *CurieuzeNeuzen* project, once again set up with the aim to measure air pollution. See https://curieuzeneuzen.be/, consulted on 3 March 2018.

[12] See, e.g., the *International Science Shop Network* (http://www.livingknowledge.org/, consulted on 8 January 2018).

[13] See, e.g., Knobe and Nichols (2008) for an introduction and survey.

[14] I have added "classical" because in logic there are not that many intuitions that are shared by all logicians. In fact, I am tempted to believe that there are none. But the point here is that the classical logician will accept the point made as intuitively correct.

[15] In formal terms this means that from the formula q the formula $p \rightarrow q$ can be deduced, no matter what p says. In classical logic $p \rightarrow q$ can be the case even if there is no connection (of whatever sort) between p and q.

has fundamentally changed (some) philosophical practices but, even if it were so, it does not constitute a deep reconsideration of the role philosophy has to play in academia.[16]

It seems unfortunately rather clear that an "inside job" for philosophy is not to be expected soon. Or, if you like, the academic fly-bottle is a rather solid object and bumping against its walls is not very likely to have a (somewhat literal) deep impact. Let us therefore take a Calvinist view and see if we fare better there.

Philosophy in Non-academic Fly-Bottles

If within the university walls alternatives seem unlikely to develop in such a way that they actually can transform the academic world, then a different story is to be told outside of the ivory tower. Here we are faced with a heterogeneous multitude of views and approaches that do not seems to be easily classifiable. Nevertheless I do think that two main currents can be identified. A number of views direct themselves in first instance against established science and academia (and often they find supporters within), whereas the others are not directly concerned with the academic world and "simply" want to develop alternative approaches. Or, if you like, they are agnostic about how scientific knowledge is produced. The two subsections that follow explore these two main currents, keeping in mind what philosophy and their practitioners could contribute, either from within academia or from without. In the former case they could be labelled "Calvinist-in-disguise", as they try to import the outsiders' ideas into the ivory tower in order to change its internal structure. But do note that in other cases the outside movements are simply considered to be an interesting object of study and those philosophers could be labelled "crypto-Lutheran". In the latter case we talk about philosophers who have left academia, rightly deserving the label "Calvinist" without any added qualifications.

Against Academia

Counter-science and anti-science movements rarely deal directly with science itself but rather with the technological products that result from scientific research, and indirectly this can lead to a reflection on what science is all about. Once again, it is not an easy task to produce a short description of who is involved in these movements. Let me sketch briefly a case that occurred in Flanders and that became known

---

[16]There seems to be an echo here of the famous dictum, attributed to Arthur Schopenhauer (though a source is not immediately to be found), that at universities "Philosophieprofessoren" write "Professorenphilosophie". If the echo is indeed reliable then the problems sketched here related to academic philosophy today seem hardly to have changed. In biblical terms one is tempted to say that "there is no new thing under the sun" (Ecclesiastes I:9, King James version).

as "The Potato War(s)." The University of Ghent, together with BASF, had an experiment running *in vivo* on a field in Wetteren, near Ghent in East Flanders, where genetically modified potatoes were planted. On the 29th May 2011 a demonstration was held and a minor part, about 15% of the field, was destroyed. This led to a rather violent police intervention, a researcher at the Catholic University of Louvain being sacked (but reinstated later on), and finally to a lawsuit. For the topic of this chapter, it is interesting to see who the protesters were:[17] in first instance, the FLM (*Field Liberation Movement*), consisting of activists (both non-governmental organisations and scientists), further organic farmers, "ordinary" citizens, and finally the *Faucheurs Volontaires* (the *Voluntary Mowers*), a more active movement with its origin in France and to be situated within the anti-globalisation view. So quite a heterogeneous mixture.

If, in order to make a comparison, we look at the situation all over the world regarding the acceptance or rejection of evolutionary theory, usually abbreviated as Darwinism,[18] then we get a quite different picture. In this case we are in almost exclusively religious circles but, that being said, defenders of creationism or their "intellectual" counterpart, intelligent design, can be found among all creeds and beliefs. In addition, the focus is not on some technological derivatives but on school education, the main object being the introduction of religious convictions in biology courses. Given these two examples, it should be immediately clear that a further comparison with, e.g., the issue of climate change, will lead once again to a completely different picture where now political and economic forces play a major role and not so much, although indirectly and certainly not to be underestimated, religious beliefs as well.

This brings me to the question of what role philosophers can play in this particular heterogeneous mixture of topics and people concerned. Obviously, philosophers like any other citizen can join any anti- or counter-science movement, but then it is rather the citizen than the philosopher, in his or her capacity as philosopher, who is making a contribution. A more interesting development that we have witnessed in recent times, is that philosophers, with sociologists, have set a number of issues on the problem agenda of everyone involved in academia. This need not necessarily entail a reform of academic life as we know it today but it does go hand in hand with academic "reformation" in mutual support. (This is the main reason why I did not include them in section "Philosophy in the academic fly-bottle", as they are not necessarily Lutherans, to continue my tongue-in-cheek analogy, but rather Calvinists-in-disguise, as I have labelled them). All the splendid work done by

---

[17] This description is based on De Cauter (2017), p. 11 (unfortunately the paper is in Dutch).

[18] This remark about the use of the term "Darwinism" is not without its importance. It suggests that we are still dealing with the original, partially formulated theory of Charles Darwin himself, as set forth in his *Origin of Species* (1859). Thereby one denies that whole development that followed, involving the so-called *New Synthesis* or, if you like, the joining of genetics and evolutionary theory and leading to present-day discussions about the importance of epigenetics and whether or not this can be seen as a Lamarckian reformulation, integrated in evolutionary theory. In short, a scientific theory is presented as solid and unchangeable in the very same way that a literal reading of the book Genesis is presented.

sociologists of science to clarify the complex relations between science, technology, politics, economics, and society, has forced us to reconsider such cherished notions as objectivity, value-freeness, (correspondence) truth, progress, … What emerged was and is an intricate network of subtle influences, steering the mighty scientific vessel in particular directions, often economically interesting harbours, that the ship's crew is largely ignorant about.[19]

However, what emerged as well were the so-called "Science Wars". It is in the meantime a rather long history to tell with an unclear outcome and it is even not decided yet whether the wars have ended and, if so, what kind of truce has been negotiated. What has surfaced is the deep and still present tension between the exact sciences, engineering, medicine, and life-sciences on the one hand and the human and social sciences, including philosophy, on the other hand, reminiscent of the famous two (or more) cultures of C. P. Snow, itself dating back more than half a century.[20] Based on my own experience in these debates, it was often shocking to note how little all the work done in (analytic) philosophy of science over the past century was taken into account. In fact, sometimes one was left with the impression that the two parties involved were battling on different battle fields, fighting imaginary opponents.

There is however another rather specific role for philosophers as Calvinists-in-disguise (and not merely crypto-Lutherans) to play within academia, and that is to retell the history of philosophy. Again, there is no guarantee whatsoever that this will lead to changes in the structure of scientific practices today, but to formulate alternative views can be a first step. I briefly mention two examples. The first is the voluminous work of Randall Collins, *Sociology of philosophies* (1998). In it philosophers and their philosophical views are presented in terms of networks, involving societal and political elements, thereby contextualising what this or that philosopher has been thinking and writing about. In addition it is a worldwide approach involving both the East and the West. The second is the nine-volume *Contre-histoire de la philosophie* (2006–2013) by Michel Onfray. It is an impossible task to summarise this *magnum opus* but let me just mention this one example. It is quite refreshing to read about the Greek philosophers, not dominated by the famous trio Socrates, Plato, and Aristotle but by the Sophists, who accepted and defended the idea that a unique truth causes more harm than good, that discussion and argumentation are more important, that multiple, conflictual views and opinions are the basic stuff of everyday life, and so forth.

These few examples suggest without any doubt that other possibilities can be imagined but that have not been tried out yet. Actually there is a scenario that, although it comes pretty close to an "I have a dream"-type of reasoning, should be

---

[19] This is, of course, a nod to Otto Neurath's boat metaphor. It would be worthwhile to investigate how far this analogy can be continued before it breaks down.

[20] See Snow (1993). I deliberately use the word "reminiscent" because some care has to be taken in comparing Snow's views with the present-day situation. It would be unwise to state that the discussion is still the same; in fact one can argue that an inversion took place. For Snow it was the superiority of the "literates" over the exact sciences and engineering that needed to be dealt with.

considered seriously as an alternative.[21] In addition, it can be supported by recent work in network theory (so, making another link with Bruno Latour). We are all familiar with the small world hypothesis: the average distance between two people on earth is about six.[22] However, the interesting mathematical question is the inverse problem: what should the network look like to produce that average distance? The response is rather surprising: the network must have both a highly regular structure and a few random links.[23] A university with its hierarchical division in faculties and in departments and research groups satisfies the regularity requirement and the random links could be the philosophers who would thereby have a special and identifiable position in the academic network. A twenty-first century reading of a peripatetic school?

To make the connection with the next subsection it is worth mentioning that Michel Onfray was so dissatisfied with academia, which he often described as elitist,[24] that he started his own university: the *Université Populaire de Caen*.[25] Although it must be clear that this initiative implies a deep critique of academia, at the same time Onfray insists that it is independent from it and thus not much time needs to be spent on formulating such a critique. Hence the title of the next subsection.

Academia Independent

In this final part I will mainly focus on philosophy because scientific research outside of academia is mainly to be found in an industrial setting (Apple, Google, pharmaceutical companies, NSA,[26] …) and philosophy has no real part to play in this context. So perhaps the first question to ask is whether such alternatives exist? We do know of the phenomenon of the independent philosopher (or, if more

---

[21] I mention this alternative because it summarises a major part of my academic career as a teacher. Some of my courses on philosophy of science had as its major audience students from the exact sciences and engineering. Because of my double background in mathematics and philosophy, I was considered to be a "bridge" figure between their Faculties and my Faculty of Arts and Letters. This "short-cut" between Faculties made things possible that official relations, say Dean to Dean, could (or would) not.

[22] If A and B know each other, their distance is 1. If B knows C and A does not know C then the distance between A and C is 2 because one has to pass through B. It is thus the shortest distance to connect two people via "in-betweens".

[23] For a full treatment (and more) see Watts (1999).

[24] From personal experience I can testify that he rejected an offer for an honorary doctorate at my university for precisely this reason.

[25] See http://upc.michelonfray.fr/ (consulted on 2 January 2018).

[26] The American *National Security Agency* is one of the top employers of mathematicians in the US. This has actually raised some concerns with mathematicians themselves, witness this exchange in the *Notices of the American Mathematical Society*, to be found at http://www.ams.org/notices/201406/rnoti-p623.pdf (consulted on 3 January 2018), "Mathematicians Discuss the Snowden Revelations".

economic terms are to be used, the freelance philosopher) who is less focused on research itself but rather participates directly in societal debates through the old and modern media, from newspapers, magazines, and personal website, to Facebook, Twitter, and other web applications. Apart from this individualist alternative, some organised forms do exist[27] and perhaps the best known is The School of Life, set up by philosopher Alain de Botton. Putting aside for a moment the discussion about the quality of the philosophical work being done, it is quite interesting to see what the aim is:[28]

> The School has a passionate belief in making learning relevant – and so runs courses in the important questions of everyday life. Whereas most colleges and universities chop up learning into abstract categories ('agrarian history' 'the 18th century English novel'), The School of Life titles its courses according to things we all tend to care about: careers, relationships, politics, travels, families. An evening or weekend on one of its courses is likely to be spent reflecting on such matters as your moral responsibilities to an ex partner or how to resolve a career crisis.

The most striking thing surely is that de Botton not only believes that academic philosophy has lost all touch with all of our individual daily lives but also that it "chops up" our knowledge of that daily world into parts and bits that do not seem to fit that everyday world. Oddly enough, the suggestion here is that academic knowledge is not really relevant at all. How well-founded is such a harsh critique? To answer that question, it might be helpful to deal with a larger question first and that is how we see the role of philosophy (and their practitioners) in a society.

To answer such a broad question requires space and time, unavailable at the moment, so I will use the strategy of looking for elements that have to occur in whatever answer we might come up with. And I see at least two such elements: in the first place, to what extent is a society in need of reflection on itself and, in the second place, how is this reflection organised in that society? The first question can be answered in an almost trivial way: a society that does not reflect on itself has little chance of survival. However, to ask for a justification for that answer would involve considerations from evolutionary biology, human psychology, sociology, economics, and political sciences, in short, most of the human and social sciences. Speaking in quite general terms, human beings in a social network have to plan for the immediate and far future, and such plans involve these humans themselves and hence they have to reflect on how they see themselves and their social relations and thus a reflection forces itself on that society. That being said, and under the assumption that the above sketch is not reducible to a "just-so story", the follow-up question must be to what extent philosophy as such will be involved in this reflection. After all, when a person has poor health and has to observe a rather strict diet, surely this

---

[27] I am thinking here about all kinds of cultural associations that provide courses or lectures on any number of topics, including philosophy. For the situation in Flanders, Elcker-Ik, Vormingplus, Background Educations, Willemsfonds, Masereelfonds, … are perfect examples. As these organisations do not wish to "compete" with academia but rather want to be an interface between universities and "ordinary" citizens, I did not include them here.

[28] See http://alaindebotton.com/the-school-of-life/, consulted on 3 January 2018.

person will reflect on him- or herself, but that need not involve a deep philosophical reflection. So, from the necessity of reflection (unfortunately) does not follow the necessity that philosophy as we know it will be involved. Here lies, I think, a major challenge for philosophers: how to show that they are indispensable? Even if some solid answers can be provided, this still leaves us with the second question.

The second question is of a more practical nature and can be translated into a connected set of sub-questions. Does the reflection involve the whole of society or only parts of it? How do power relations relate to this reflection? To what extent is philosophy crucial and what form can/should it take? Is academic philosophy suited to the purpose or should we imagine other forms of philosophical reflection? More concretely: is there a midway between the ivory tower and the daily worries of The School of Life? That last question can be reformulated as follows: academic philosophy is characterised, as we have seen, by a very specific social structure, and The School of Life basically provides the tools for an individual to be a philosopher. What other forms of social organisation for practicing philosophy can be imagined and implemented? As it happens, that is a question that philosophers have already dealt with in the past. Often the answer was in terms of a utopian or dystopian design in words, ranging from Thomas More's *Utopia* to George Orwell's *Animal Farm*. But occasionally it was also transformed into a reality. Let me just mention the intriguing example of Walden, a commune founded by Dutch writer-philosopher-psychiatrist Frederik van Eeden[29] that existed from 1898 to 1907, inspired by Henry David Thoreau.

This rough sketch would, of course, be incomplete if I did not mention the alternative, which basically comes down to a more extreme attitude, namely a clear refusal to be involved in society. The philosopher "recluse" is of course a well-known figure, inspired certainly in Western culture through the Christian tradition, who either looks down upon material matters or instead has the gaze lifted upwards, ignoring all the misery at his or her feet. But then again such a philosopher need not be aware of any fly-bottles whatsoever, and that after all was and is the main theme of this contribution.

To conclude this section, it is clear that the Calvinist view has led us down a path where old ideas should be taken up again in order to think up or invent new ways of organising philosophical thinking (and research in some form?) in a society, away from academia. To pick up one more time the fly-bottle metaphor, the challenge is that we should in the first instance not focus on ways out of the bottle but rather imagine what other bottles are possible. And how we can travel from one bottle to another, turning every exit into a new entry.

---

[29] It would take a separate paper to show the philosophical inspiration of van Eeden, linked to the Signific Movement and such intriguing philosophers as Victoria Lady Welby and mathematicians as Gerrit Mannoury. For some history and background, see Van Bendegem (2011).

Conclusion

I admit that a lot of bottles have been mentioned, but so far I have not said that much about the Wittgensteinian origin of the metaphor, namely §309 in the *Philosophical Investigations* (1953): "What is your aim in philosophy?—To shew the fly the way out of the fly-bottle." There is a host of questions that can and should be asked about this image: Why does one not see the way out but the philosopher does? Is it indeed a matter of showing and not of telling or explaining, why was one, including the philosopher, caught in the fly-bottle in the first place? Interesting as these questions are, there is another feature that I want to stress here, and I quote the last sentence of §133: "There is not *a* philosophical method, though there are indeed methods, like different therapies". The use of the concept of therapy opens up a totally different path, namely philosophy not as (a) theory but as a set of practices. It is fitting that, if the purpose is to get out of the bottle, this chapter too should have an open end, an exit if you like, to a totally different world where philosophy becomes a way of life or dare I say a specific *Lebensform*? If so, then it is equally fitting that I stop writing here and now.[30]

References

Biggar Economics. (2017). *The economic contribution of the Flemish universities*. Brussels, Belgium: VLIR.

Börner, K. (2010). *Atlas of science. Visualizing what we know*. Cambridge, MA: MIT.

Collins, R. (1998). *The sociology of philosophies. A global theory of intellectual change*. Cambridge, MA: Harvard UP (Belknap Press).

De Cauter, L. (2017). De aardappeloorlog en zijn gevolgen: over de 'ggo-gebeurtenis' en het 'Slow Science Manifesto. *Oikos, 83*(3), 11–29.

De Solla Price, D. (1963). *Little science, big science*. New York: Columbia University Press.

Heesen, R. (2017). Academic superstars: Competent or lucky? *Synthese, 194*, 4499–4518.

Knobe, J., & Nichols, S. (Eds.). (2008). *Experimental philosophy*. Oxford, UK: Oxford University Press.

Onfray, M. (2006–2013). *Contre-histoire de la philosophie*. Paris: Grasset. (Vol.1: *Les Sagesses antiques*, 2006; vol.2: *Le Christianisme hédoniste*, 2006, vol.3: *Les Libertins baroques*, 2007; vol.4: *Les Ultras des Lumières*, 2007, vol.5: *L'Eudémonisme social*, 2008; vol. 6: *Les Radicalités existentielles*, 2009; vol.7: *La Construction du Surhomme*, 2011; vol.8: *Les Freudiens hérétiques*, 2013; vol.9: *Les Consciences réfractaires*, 2013).

Rull, V. (2016). Free science under threat. The current revival of Bernalism and the use of market-based scientific practices are undermining science as we know it. *EMBO Reports, 17*(2), 131–135.

Snow, C.P. (1993, orig. 1959). *The two cultures*. Cambridge, UK: Cambridge University Press.

Stengers, I. (2013). *Une autre science est possible! Manifeste pour un ralentissement des sciences*. Paris: Les Empêcheurs de penser en rond.

---

[30]As must be clear, this is nothing but a new metaphor, Tractarian-inspired, that is being introduced here.

Stengers, I. (2017). *Another science is possible: A manifesto for slow science* (S. Muecke, Trans.). Cambridge, UK: Polity Press (adapted translation of Stengers (2013)).

Van Bendegem, J. P. (2011). Extended review of Susan Petrilli, *Signifying and Understanding: Reading the Works of Victoria Welby and the Signific Movement* (Berlin: De Gruyter Mouton, 2009). *Historiographia Linguistica*, *38*(3), 382–388.

Watts, D. J. (1999). *Small worlds. The dynamics of networks between order and randomness.* Princeton, NJ: Princeton University Press.

Wittgenstein, L. (1953). *Philosophical investigations* (G. E. M. Anscombe, Trans.). Oxford, UK: Basil Blackwell.

Chapter 10
Postscript
Humanistic Study, Collaboration, and Interdisciplinarity: A Dialogue on the Leuven Research Community

Nicholas C. Burbules and Lynda Stone

Background Nick: The Research Community on the Philosophy and History of the Discipline of Education has been organised by Paul Smeyers and Marc Depaepe of the Catholic University of Leuven, since 1999, beginning with generous funding from the Research Foundation Flanders, Belgium (Fonds voor Wetenschappelijk Onderzoek – Vlaanderen; FWO). Since then, a group of international scholars in philosophy and history of education has convened each fall for an annual conference and working paper session – usually in Leuven, occasionally in other European cities. The conference has an annual theme, and participants prepare papers addressing that issue from their respective disciplinary perspectives. The papers are available in advance, so the sessions are organised around summaries of the papers, a brief response, and then an intensive discussion about each project. The papers are revised again after the conference and eventually published in an edited book series from Springer. The sessions are characterised by stimulating discussions, good cheer, and friendships that have grown over 20 years. Here, we reflect on the RC as an academic project, on what it can tell us about issues of collaboration and interdisciplinarity, and along the way offer a few comments about Paul Smeyers' indispensable role in conceiving and guiding the project.

Lynda: Thank you, Nick, for providing the openings of our shared chapter. I want to add a couple of ideas about the formation of the RC across its own history. There has been a core group initiated, as I understand it, by the major journal editors in philosophy of education (among others, Nicholas Burbules, for *Educational Theory*, Richard Smith, and later Paul Smeyers for *Ethics and Education*, and Paul Standish for the *Journal of Philosophy of Education*). From the original members, students have been added, as have like-minded colleagues. A few dropped out along

N. C. Burbules (✉)
University of Illinois, Urbana-Champaign, Champaign, IL, USA
e-mail: burbules@illinois.edu

L. Stone
School of Education, The University of North Carolina at Chapel Hill, Chapel Hill, NC, USA
e-mail: lstone@email.unc.edu

© Springer International Publishing AG, part of Springer Nature 2018   131
S. Ramaekers, N. Hodgson (eds.), *Past, Present, and Future Possibilities for Philosophy and History of Education*,
https://doi.org/10.1007/978-3-319-94253-7_10

the way but not many — it has been a very convivial group. One more point: while national or regional members do know about each other's academic and professional backgrounds, the principal way that all of us as international colleagues have come to know each other is through our yearly scholarly contributions. This is, first and foremost, a research group — out of which has emerged much affection and, for some members, the development of other projects.

It seems fitting that our method is a dialogue, arguably the basis of collaboration. Readers should know that Nick and I have known each other since graduate school days in which our tenures overlapped and we shared some professors. Our work as philosophers of education has evolved somewhat differently but, importantly for the international audience of this volume, we share an understanding of a national history of our discipline and of the humanities in educational research. In what follows, we also share agreement on the five topics of our dialogue, which set our reflection on the Research Community within a broader academic and thematic context. We hope that, across the five topics, a coherent thread emerges.

Humanistic Studies in Educational Research

Nick: In the U.S., humanistic studies in education are generally seen as being outside the fields of empirical sciences, such as psychology. Often, indeed, the term "research" is limited in many uses to empirical studies only; humanistic work is termed "scholarship". Philosophy and history are disappearing from education degree programs, and many who do continue this work have to justify it by linking their work to policy or other "applied" fields. The traditional ideal of humanistic study is expressed well here by the University of Humanistic Studies:

> Contemporary humanism continues to build on a rich tradition of ideas and values. Characteristics of a humanist view of life are a reliance on one's own powers of observation and comprehension, an orientation on dialogue and an aversion to dogmatism. The concepts of human dignity, justice and freedom play a pivotal role. Attaching great value to self-development, education, aesthetics and culture is also typical of a humanist attitude towards life. It is especially since the Enlightenment that humanism is explicitly viewed as a philosophy of life in which the human perspective is a defining factor in understanding and giving meaning to life and the world. (https://www.uvh.nl/university-of-humanistic-studies-2017en/about-our-university/about-humanistic-studies)

In various European traditions, and even in language, such work is not defined as outside "science" – or more precisely, science is defined as a broader way of knowing than just the narrowly empirical disciplines. The fact that the FWO funded the RC for three five-year terms shows a fundamentally different valuation of the merits of humanistic disciplines such as philosophy and history.

Lynda: The history of philosophy and history of education in the U.S. is significant for our participation in the group and in relation to our international colleagues. Several connections need to be made: to parent disciplines, to various types and levels of universities, and to a broad history of educational research. Originally, in American colleges in the 18th and 19th centuries, philosophy and history were read to train an educated class, largely of landed persons, of ministers, and even some teachers. All – primarily men – took a capstone course in moral philosophy. Can you imagine a final course like this today? As public universities were formed across the country, programs in teacher training evolved, with these disciplines required only of secondary teaching candidates. Women teachers, as is well known, first attended normal schools and only later did their curriculum and licensure became part of universities.

The preparation of these practitioners was not considered "scholarship" or "research", although their work became part of the interests of scholars and researchers. Instead, as your emphasis on empirical sciences demonstrates, a domain of educational research led by psychology rose to prominence. I agree that philosophy and history are disappearing in U.S. education institutions. Major public and private universities are lucky to have one named position in each discipline; a couple of well-known centres with more than one professor in each field do still exist. Graduate students who study philosophy of education or, more broadly, "social foundations" in flagship state universities, perhaps along with our history friends, often have appointments in teacher education.

The point of retelling this U.S. history here is that the RC has "fed our souls", or mine, at least, in home environments in which our work is marginalised, even invisible. It is notable that, in our meetings, the term "humanities" is virtually absent, due in part I think to the point that you made about a broad definition of science and of education science in the European context.

Nick: I do think that part of the comfort and appeal of the RC has been that it offers a place in which we simply do our work, among colleagues who share a sense of its value, without having to explain or justify it – or, even worse, engage in the kind of navel-gazing that often occurs in gatherings in our own country, about why we aren't more valued, why we are losing positions, and what we should be doing about it. Let me also say a bit about the ways in which Paul Smeyers and Marc Depaepe have organised and managed the group. While rigorous scholars themselves, and certainly capable of challenging or questioning ideas, they have set an example of good-natured, often humorous, engagement with the work of others. Paul in particular has always closely read the papers in advance, and often starts off our discussions with a sharp and searching comment, but also too with a tone of good humor. This sets a spirit both in manner and in substance that, I think, has come to define our ways of talking with one another. Indeed, I would say that humour is a hallmark of the RC discussions.

Lynda: I think you're right about humour; a strength of the community is taking our work seriously without taking it too seriously. This goes back to your point about navel-gazing, and the need to laugh at ourselves. Humour has been a way to learn not only across our two disciplines but also cross-culturally and cross-regionally. As an American from a vast, diverse place, I have learned a lot about different forms of diversity through bits of teasing or ribbing among our European friends.

Nick: We could have a whole chapter on humour, which I think is underappreciated as an invaluable tool of the intellectual trade: the criticism that can be expressed more gently, and indirectly, in a way that can be heard without feeling attacked; the intervention that lightens an otherwise ponderous or fraught exchange; the play on words that actually opens a question of substance; the icebreaker that helps to form a group *as* a group. We have seen all of these, repeatedly, within the RC.

Meanings of Collaboration

Nick: I think it is significant that the project was called a Research *Community*. There are various ways that collaboration played out within the group. At one level, as already mentioned, the group had focused discussions on each paper and gave the author critical and constructive feedback on how it could be improved. Further, because each year's conference had a shared theme, the entire meeting was a collaborative, interdisciplinary study on questions surrounding, e.g. publication, funding of research, the role of statistics and quantitative methodologies, and other "meta" questions about the nature, purpose, and contexts of educational research, viewed through philosophical and historical lenses. Each of these resulted in an edited volume with Springer. The RC also produced a variety of spin-off projects and collaborations, too numerous to recount here, as scholars across international boundaries discovered common points of interest through these conversations. But as a *community* we have endeavoured to create a social as well as intellectual bond – or perhaps it is more accurate to say that, for this group, those are not really separate aims.

　Lynda: I think a brief discussion of the general meaning of the term "collaboration" and of its presence in educational research will demonstrate the uniqueness of the research group. The online OED has a simple definition of "collaboration" as a group coming together to produce a product, and it names various formal and informal associations in which collaboration is often found. In U.S. educational research, collaboration in empirical studies is very common, especially in work emanating from the behavioural sciences. In educational research collaborations, participants may contribute different expertise to the problem under study. Importantly, almost exclusively, sub-groups share a disciplinary background — its language, its history, its methodology.

　Scholars in the humanities, in parent disciplines, and in education, most often write as single authors. In my view, one of the most important steps in the evolution of the RC was the establishment of a theme for each year. This actually did not happen in the first few years but its introduction is part of the genius of the founders, Smeyers and Depaepe. Several results followed from this. Having a theme guaranteed production of a book, as you have mentioned. It also guaranteed that, in order to be accepted for the meeting – through Smeyers' and Depaepe's review of abstracts – and ultimately for publication, many of us had to venture out of our comfort zones in terms of topics and subject matter. Some in the U.S., in Britain, and in Europe already had agendas in educational research, but the themes focused attention even more specifically. This was a challenge for me. Overall this move to themes, in my mind, has been one of the most important elements of the collaboration, and has made the group's work, in many ways, interdisciplinary.

Nick: Yes, in fact, the first years did not feature smooth and seamless collaboration. Philosophers and historians sometimes engaged in a bit of disciplinary jousting: philosophers pointing out that there were conceptual or epistemic underpinnings of historical arguments (which they were quite happy to illuminate); historians pointing out that philosophical work lacked context or an awareness of its socially contingent background. This sometimes led to people literally talking past one another. One year, as I recall, the two groups actually held separate sessions – thus defeating the purpose of the RC. Three things, I think, changed that dynamic. One was a change in personnel, as some participants stopped coming; another was the growth of a closer social bond, and hence a greater willingness to respect and countenance one another's work on its own terms. Paul and Marc also set a tone, here as in other ways. But the biggest shift was in identifying an annual theme or problematic that neither group could "own", and that ensured that, broadly at least, we were all grabbing at parts of the same elephant.

Lynda: Mentoring is another form of relationship within the RC that our dialogue brings to mind. It is not collaboration as typically described, but it has been significant. I can think right now of four, perhaps six, current members who have been mentored first by advisers and then by the larger group. Student or junior professor paper presentations and feedback evolved into conference presentations into publications into references for promotion and, of course, into full membership. It has been wonderful to be a part of this process.

Nick: You touch upon an aspect of the RC that is noteworthy: we have been meeting annually, in this format, for nearly 20 years. We have grown up, and grown older, together. We have gone through, and shared, many things in our "other" lives, some delightful, some painful. We have watched young students give some of their first public presentations, sometimes nervous and awkward, and we have seen these colleagues become successful professors, now with their own students and careers. (Two of them are editing this volume.) This long history has given the RC its own quality of comfort and familiarity.

Disciplinary and Interdisciplinary Work

Nick: One way to think about interdisciplinary work is that interdisciplinarity is a means, not an end. I have long believed that a better term is "problem-based research", in which what is foregrounded is the question or problem to be investigated, and then the appropriate and most useful disciplinary and methodological tools are brought to bear on addressing the problem. This basic approach has been typical of the RC, beginning each conference with a jointly identified theme and set of questions, and then leaving it to the participants how to bring their disciplinary resources to those questions. Generally, though not always, this has produced a set of papers that fit together within the theme, honouring the distinctiveness of individual and theoretical perspectives, while also bringing these into conversation with each other. This, too, is a kind of collaboration, even when the papers run in parallel. The nature of our discussions when we meet often highlights ways in which the papers relate to one another, typically in totally unplanned ways.

Lynda: There is another aspect of interdisciplinarity that perhaps characterises the philosophy group more than the history contingent. See if you agree. I have come to see the philosophers as themselves diverse, perhaps "intra-interdisciplinary". There are folks, like you, who see their work as "problem-based research". There are those who, in focusing on education, are strongly analytical and institutionally focused. There are those whose writings cross over into intellectual history. Across our discipline, members are extremely and extensively well-read. One of the principal delights of the meetings is always learning something new from such outstanding scholars. Meaning no disrespect at all, my sense is that the history group members share a theoretical history that, for many, comes out of European social-historical traditions that are different from typical Anglo-American roots. There has often been criticism of the more empirical focus of U.S. history of education.

Nick: I have not heard that at the RC, but I think this also reflects on the kinds of historians who have come from the U.S. – not historians of ideas, but not authors of narrow monographs either. Their interests in policy and theory have often opened up the kinds of broader discussions (I think for example of the session on "education-alising" social issues, or about how psychology emerged as the reigning education discipline).[1]

Lynda: This may be a good point to mention theory, a topic that continues to haunt the implicit debates of social science researchers and humanities scholars in my institution and, arguably, across the U.S.. And it is of great concern for our graduate students who want to do good work. In brief, I see members of our group sharing a view of theory as "on-its-face", that is, as embedded in the textual treatment itself. I think of the powerful, what I would call, rhetorical beauty, within papers across the philosophy and history community. We can name the authors whose work we relish reading each year. This surely differs from a view of theory as imposed on data or ideas.

International Perspectives on Educational Research and Policy

Nick: Part of what makes the RC distinctive is the international mix of scholars (in which, by the way, Americans have always been a small minority). While our colleagues are kind enough to write and discuss their papers in English, the national, cultural, and linguistic differences of our perspectives have often been an explicit topic of discussion – even to the point of what counts as a study of "education". For

---

[1] See *Educational Theory*, Volume 58, Issue 4, November 2008.

instance, a frequent theme of RC papers has been discussions of childrearing as an educational concern. U.S. university schools of education, and the research they do, are much more frequently focused on the institutional contexts of formal schooling. Family studies, and what is often termed "informal education", are clearly subsidiary concerns, often relegated to other university departments. One of the many ways in which this difference surfaces is in government policies in other countries that regulate or intervene in attempts to improve parenting – something almost unthinkable in the U.S. context, which is so much more suspicious of government interventions into the "private" sphere. Here, and in other ways, the diverse national contexts of the RC scholars highlight the differences, and the similarities, in educational policy and practices across these different contexts.

Lynda: I like the distinctions you have drawn between the international differences in what counts as education in the U.S. and other nations and regions. As you imply, the differences are due partly to cultural differences in responsibility for education and schooling: in the U.S. there are generally sharp differences between the purviews of home and school, between religious institutions and school, and especially in our federal system, between local educational control — the role of states and communities — and what a national government like ours actually does. Even with emphasis over the past several decades on standardisation and accountability, the U.S. has no national ministry of education or a national curriculum.

There are two other international differences that come to mind. One continues your point of formal and informal education in the U.S.. In my institution, a focus on cultures, communities, and families is most often found in the field of human development in education, in teacher education, and especially in psychological foundations for teaching and service professions such as school counselling. Other social science-trained researchers may turn to these topics as part of policy studies and learning sciences, two very hot arenas for research these days. The other difference takes up your point about the influence or impact of our work. We humanities scholars in education in the U.S. have virtually no voice in public educational life: sometimes writing catches the eye of someone in government, but again this is almost unthinkable. I am uncertain if my impression is correct, but I do have a sense that in the smaller nations of our international colleagues, and for those in which there is long regard for intellectual life and humanistic study, there may be more influence.

Nick: I think it was RC member Edwin Keiner who said that the true international language of educational research is "broken English". There are at least two ways to look at that. One is the creative syntax that can occur when an idea formulated in one language is expressed in another. This can lead to confusion and misunderstanding – sometimes laughter. But when words that don't have exactly the same meaning are used across languages, this sometimes opens up new possibilities for rethinking, especially for keywords (in English) like "education", "science", and "knowledge" – words that have different and sometimes multiple equivalences in other languages. What can get "broken" is the assumption that the English denotations and connotations of such words are universal.

Lynda: The topic of an education science continues to interest me. First, as you point out, terms have different meanings in different languages. Moreover, scholarly and research traditions internationally also differ and this is the arena that I ponder. Finally, there is the strategic use of terms such as "education science" for funding. The RC's leaders have been geniuses at working through conceptions and requirements to benefit our group and its longevity. I doubt if I could have ever done this with such rigour and grace. As a member, I am eternally grateful for the opportunities their skills afforded us.

Individual and Group–Based Research

Nick: One characteristic of humanistic studies, noted in the earlier quote, is that inquiry is strongly linked with an individual voice, style, and point of view. As you mention, the major works of philosophy and history are almost always written by one person, in a distinctive voice. This touches again on the theme of collaboration. Very few RC papers have been co-authored (unlike research in other disciplines where multiple authorship is standard practice, including work that is sometimes termed "Big Science", which might have dozens or even hundreds of co-authors). As we have discussed, collaboration within the RC takes other forms. It is a group of very strong and accomplished individuals, and that, too, is what gives it its character.

Lynda: I concur about the very strong and accomplished individuals who have comprised the core community. As a humanist scholar, I have always prized individual style and experimentation and have found the group supportive of my own and similarly conceived orientations to scholarship. For example, in the RC, philosophers and historians often draw on multiple sources for papers: educational narratives, journalistic writings, classical texts, "new" scholarly fields and traditions, all come to mind. At any given meeting around the central topic, there is a stimulating diversity of approaches. Building on now-available archives, in recent years, for instance, wonderful photographs have been used. Both groups, we should emphasise, develop major points that evidence supports; the point for humanistic scholars is that multiple kinds of evidence are valued.

Nick: You raise a very suggestive point. One change from the early days of the RC is the much more common use of PowerPoint and/or visual slides as part of the presentations. One question is the use of graphical information as "data" for content analysis; a slightly different question is the use of graphics as part of the process of presenting a talk. I think we have only begun to scratch the surface of multimedia scholarship within the RC, though across the humanities disciplines more broadly this has been an area of exploration and experimentation. We have seen this mainly from our historical colleagues; but what would a philosophical argument look like, for example, rendered graphically? (As I recall, you presented a paper on outliers and rhizomes at the RC using this approach – you even had a picture of ginger root!)

Lynda: More importantly your own response to that paper — an outlier in itself. With feedback and further development, the result was a paper of which I am particularly proud that appeared in a special journal issue under your editorship.[2]

Since this section is about individual work, a further issue and distinction between national and international practices concerns promotion and tenure. I am constantly in awe of the scholarly acumen, the depth of reading and writing, of our international peers. I also worry about a kind of anti-intellectualism among our U.S. researchers — skills yes, studies that have some impact, sure, but not the intellectual background for what I would like in creative, imaginative research. Maybe this is a whine, a navel gaze to which you referred previously, a conversation for another time perhaps.

Nick: Let me reflect briefly in closing on this dialogical form as itself also a manner of collaboration. Our memories and perspectives on the RC are parallel but not identical; we recall different things or recall the same things differently, we have compatible but different theoretical stances toward the issues of discipline, knowledge, and scholarship. We have different voices, exhibited here, but voices in conversation with each other. I know we both hope that in this we have presented an homage to the style and tone of the RC, and to our good friend and colleague Paul Smeyers.

---

[2] See *Educational Theory*, Volume 61, Issue 6, December 2011.

Appendix: List of Selected Publications

Articles in Internationally Peer-Reviewed Academic Journals (English)

Smeyers, P. (1990). On Broudy's "The uses of schooling". *International Review of Education, 36*, 261–263.

Smeyers, P. (1992). The necessity for particularity in education and child-rearing. The moral issue. *Journal of Philosophy of Education, 26*, 63–74.

Smeyers, P. (1993). On what we really care about in child-centeredness. *Philosophy of Education, 48*, 141–144.

Smeyers, P. (1994). Some radical consequences for educational research from a Wittgensteinian point of view or does almost anything go? *Philosophy of Education, 49*, 139–147.

Smeyers, P. (1995). On the unavoidability of power in child-rearing. Is the language of rights educationally appropriate? *Studies in Philosophy and Education, 14*, 9–21.

Smeyers, P. (1995). Education and the educational project. In an atmosphere of post-modernism. *Journal of Philosophy of Education, 29*, 109–119.

Smeyers, P., & Marshall J. (1995). The Wittgensteinian frame of reference and philosophy of education at the end of the twentieth century. *Studies in Philosophy and Education, 14*, 127–159.

Smeyers, P. (1995). Authentic selves and education. *Philosophy of Education, 50*, 273–277.

Smeyers, P. (1995). Initiation and newness in education and child-rearing. *Studies in Philosophy and Education, 14*, 229–249.

Smeyers, P. (1995). Education and the educational project. Do we still care about it? *Journal of Philosophy of Education, 29*, 399–411.

Smeyers, P., & Marshall J. (1995). Philosophy and education: Accepting Wittgenstein's challenge. Epilogue. *Studies in Philosophy and Education, 14*, 345–348.

Smeyers, P. (1996). Educating ethically: Culture, commitment and integrity. *Studies in Philosophy and Education, 15*, 147–157.

Smeyers, P. (1996). Back to the individual. On the educational importance of commitment. *Journal of Philosophy of Education, 30*, 471–478.

Smeyers, P. (1998). Some questions about the activity-passivity dimension in Frankfurt's position. *Ethical Perspectives, 5*(1), 22–30.

Smeyers, P. (1998). Child-rearing and parental 'intentions' in postmodernity. *Educational Philosophy and Theory, 30*, 193–214.

© Springer International Publishing AG, part of Springer Nature 2018   141
S. Ramaekers, N. Hodgson (eds.), *Past, Present, and Future Possibilities for Philosophy and History of Education*,
https://doi.org/10.1007/978-3-319-94253-7

Smeyers, P. (1998). Assembling reminders for educational research. Wittgenstein on philosophy. *Educational Theory, 48,* 287–308.

Smeyers, P. (1999). 'Care' and wider ethical issues. *Journal of Philosophy of Education, 33,* 233–251.

Smeyers, P., & Levering, B. (2000). Educational research: Language and content. Lessons from the Low Countries. *British Journal of Educational Studies, 48,* 70–81.

Blake, N., Smeyers, P., Smith, R., & Standish, P. (2000). Precarious work. *Educational Philosophy and Theory, 32,* 339–349.

Smeyers, P., & Verhesschen, P. (2001). Narrative analysis and philosophical research: On the nature and the frame-work for the criteria of qualitative educational research. *International Journal of Qualitative Studies in Education, 14,* 71–84.

Smeyers, P., & Lambeir, B. (2001). *Carpe diem.* Tales of desire and the unexpected. *Journal of Philosophy of Education, 35,* 283–299.

Smeyers, P. (2001). Nietzschean doubts. Wittgensteinian musings. *Philosophy of Education, 56,* 115–117.

Smeyers, P. (2001). Qualitative versus quantitative research design: A plea for paradigmatic tolerance in educational research. *Journal of Philosophy of Education, 35,* 477–495.

Blake, N., Smeyers, P., Smith, R. & Standish, P. (2001). Unnecessary supplement. *Studies in Philosophy and Education, 20,* 433–441.

Lambeir, B., & Smeyers, P. (2003). Nihilism: Beyond optimism and pessimism. Threat or blessing for education at the turn of the century. *Studies in Philosophy and Education, 22,* 183–194.

Burbules, N., & Smeyers, P. (2003). The later Wittgenstein and ethics. Invigorating questions challenging the outlook on education. *Philosophy of Education 2002,* 248–257.

Lambeir, B., & Smeyers, P. (2003). Dangerously one-sided, frightfully wrong. On education, individuals and twenty-first century society. *Studies in Philosophy and Education, 22,* 325–328.

Smeyers, P., & Smith, R. (2003). Two dogmas of measurement. *Measurement: Interdisciplinary Research and Perspectives, 1,* 279–285.

Gogolin, P., Smeyers, P., Del Dujo, A.G., & Rusch-Feja, D. (2003). European Social Science Citation Index – A chance for promoting European research. *European Educational Research Journal, 2,* 590–609.

Smeyers, P. (2004). *Simply the best?* On the pitfalls of full humanity. *European Educational Research Journal, 3,* 807–812.

Smeyers, P., & Hogan, P. (2005). The inherent risks of human learning. *Educational Theory, 55,* 115–121.

Smeyers, P. (2005). Idle research, futile theory, and the risks for education: Reminders of irony and commitment. *Educational Theory, 55,* 165–183.

Smeyers, P. (2005). The labouring sleepwalker: Evocation and expression as modes of qualitative educational research. *Educational Philosophy and Theory, 37,* 399–415.

Smeyers, P., & Burbules, N. (2005). "Practice": A central educational concept. *Philosophy of Education 2005,* 336–343.

Smeyers, P. (2006). What philosophy can and cannot do for education. *Studies in Philosophy and Education, 25,* 1–18.

Smeyers, P. (2006). 'What it makes sense to say'. Education, philosophy and Peter Winch on social science. *Journal of Philosophy of Education, 40,* 463–485.

Smeyers, P., & Burbules, N. (2006) The changing practices and social relations of education. *Educational Theory, 56,* 363–369.

Smeyers, P., & Burbules N., (2006). Education as initiation into practices. *Educational Theory, 56,* 439–449.

Smeyers, P. (2007). On dogmas and bridge-building in educational research. *Studies in Philosophy and Education, 26,* 571–576.

Smeyers, P. (2007). Present still, the integrity of the educator. *Philosophy of Education 2006,* 462–464.

Vanobbergen, B., & Smeyers, P. (2007). On Cioran's criticism of utopian thinking and the history of ducation. *Educational Philosophy and Theory, 39*, 44–55.

Depaepe, M., & Smeyers, P. (2007). On historicized meanings and being conscious about one's own theoretical premises – A basis for a renewed dialogue between history and philosophy of education. *Educational Philosophy and Theory, 39*, 3–9.

Smeyers, P. (2007). Research in and on higher education: Are scholars and scholarship utterly dispensable? *South African Journal of Higher Education, 21*, 415–426.

Smeyers, P. (2008). Transgressing the dichotomies of *Bildung* and socialization. Is initiation into practices an alternative? *Zeitschrift für Pädagogische Historiographie, 14*, 35–37.

Ramaekers, S., & Smeyers, P. (2008). Child rearing: Passivity and being able to go on. Wittgenstein on shared practices and seeing aspects. *Educational Philosophy and Theory, 40*, 638–651.

Smeyers, P., & Burbules, N. (2008). Introduction. Wittgenstein's legacy for education. *Educational Philosophy and Theory, 40*, 585–590.

Smeyers, P. (2008). Qualitative and quantitative research methods: Old wine in new bottles? On Understanding and interpreting educational phenomena. *Paedagogica Historica, 44*, 691–705.

Smeyers, P., & Depaepe, M. (2008). A method has been found? On educational research and its methodological preoccupations. *Paedagogica Historica, 44*, 625–633.

Smeyers, P. (2008). On the epistemological basis of large scale population studies and their educational use. *Journal of Philosophy of Education, 42*, 62–86.

Bridges, D., Smeyers, P., & Smith, R. (2008). Educational research and the practical judgment of policy makers. *Journal of Philosophy of Education, 42*, 5–14.

Smeyers, P. (2008). Child-rearing: On government intervention and the discourse of experts. *Educational Philosophy and Theory, 40*, 719–738.

Depaepe, M., & Smeyers, P. (2008). Educationalization as an ongoing modernization process. *Educational Theory, 58*, 379–389.

Levering, B., Ramaekers, S., & Smeyers, P. (2009). The narrative of a happy childhood: On the presumption of parents' power and the demand for integrity. *Power and Education, I*, 83–93.

Smeyers, P. (2009). More than a logical point: From consciousness to responsiveness. *Philosophy of Education 2008*, 399–401.

Smeyers, P. (2009). Education, educational research, and the 'grammar' of understanding. A response to Bridges. *Ethics and Education, 4*, 125–129.

Smeyers, P., & Waghid, Y. (2009). Initiating the debate. Educational research: On tensions, expectations, and policy. *South African Journal of Higher Education, 23*, 1065–1071.

Waghid, Y., & Smeyers, P. (2010). On doing justice to cosmopolitan values and the otherness of the other. Living with cosmopolitan scepticism. *Studies in Philosophy and Education, 29*, 197–211.

Smeyers, P. (2010). Empathy, paternalism and practical reason. Philosophy of education and the ethics of care revisited. *Journal of Philosophy of Education, 44*. 171–180.

Smeyers, P., & Waghid, Y. (2010). Cosmopolitanism in relation to the self and the other: From Michel Foucault to Stanley Cavell. *Educational Theory, 60*, 449–467.

Smeyers, P. (2010). Compulsory schooling: Shifting the focus on particular issues. *Philosophy of Education 2009*, 163–165.

Smeyers, P. (2010). Child-rearing in the 'risk' society. On the discourse of rights and the 'best interests of a child'. *Educational Theory, 60*, 271–284.

Smeyers, P. (2010). State intervention and technologization and regulation of parenting. *Educational Theory, 60*, 265–270.

Smeyers, P. (2010). Revisiting philosophy of education. *Teoría de la Educación. Revista Interuniversitaria, 22*(1), 91–116.

Smeyers, P. (2010). Monitoring the educational system? *Zeitschrift für Pädagogische Historiographie, 16*, 110–111.

Smeyers, P., & Burbules, N. (2011). How to improve your impact factor: Questioning the quantification of academic quality. *Journal of Philosophy of Education, 45*, 1–17.

Smeyers, P. (2011). Transdisciplinarity? On discipline, method and the danger of a new homogenization of educational research. *European Educational Research Journal, 10,* 143–147.

Smeyers, P. (2011). On what education is for. *Philosophy of Education 2010,* 214–216.

Smeyers, P. (2011). Philosophy of ... Philosophy and ... Taking the conditions we find ourselves in seriously. *European Educational Research Journal, 10,* 292–301.

Smeyers, P. (2012). Review of Yusef Waghid, Conceptions of Islamic Education: Pedagogical framings. *Studies in Philosophy and Education, 30,* 91–98.

Waghid, Y., & Smeyers, P. (2012). Beyond democratic citizenship education: Making an argument for religious freedom through an extended ethic of care. *Journal of Education, 53,* 117–132.

Smeyers, P. (2012). Chains of dependency: On the disenchantment and the illusion of being free at last (Part 1). *Journal of Philosophy of Education, 46,* 177–191.

Smeyers, P. (2012). Chains of dependency: On the disenchantment and the illusion of being free at last (Part 2). *Journal of Philosophy of Education, 46,* 461–471.

Postma, D. W., & Smeyers, P. (2012). Like a swallow, moving forward in circles. On the future dimension of environmental care and education. *Journal of Moral Education, 41,* 399–412.

Smeyers, P., & Depaepe, M. (2012). The lure of psychology for education and educational research. *Journal of Philosophy of Education, 46,* 315–331.

Waghid, Y., & Smeyers, P. (2012). Reconsidering *ubuntu*: on the educational potential of a particular ethic of care. *Educational Philosophy and Theory, 44* (Special Issue), 6–20.

Waghid, Y., & Smeyers, P. (2012). Taking into account African philosophy: An impetus to amend the agenda of philosophy of education. *Educational Philosophy and Theory, 44* (Special Issue), 1–5.

Smeyers, P. (2012). Moral perception and judgment and a truly radical change of social practices. *Ethics and Education, 7,* 199–205.

Smeyers, P. (2013). Making sense of the legacy of epistemology in education and educational research. *Journal of Philosophy of Education, 47,* 311–321.

Smeyers, P. (2014). Education *in/for* non-violence: Messages for believers and non-believers. A response to Hanan Alexander and Yusef Waghid. *Ethics and Education, 9,* 79–83.

Waghid, Y., & Smeyers, P. (2014). Re-envisioning the future: Democratic citizenship education and Islamic Education. *Journal of Philosophy of Education, 48,* 539–558.

Smeyers, P., De Ruyter, D., Waghid, Y., & Strand, T. (2014). Publish yet perish. On the pitfalls of philosophy in an age of impact factors. *Studies in Philosophy and Education, 33,* 647–666.

Smeyers, P., & Fendler, L. (2015). Revisiting the Wittgensteinian legacy. Perspectives on representational and non-representational language-games for educational history and theory. *Paedagogica Historica, 51,* 674–690.

Fendler, L., & Smeyers, P. (2015). Focusing on presentation instead of representation. Perspectives on representational and non-representational language-games for educational history and theory. *Paedagogica Historica, 51,* 691–701.

Dekker J., & Smeyers, P. (2015). Material culture and educational research: An Introduction. *Paedagogica Historica, 51,* 671–673.

Smeyers, P., & Depaepe, M. (2015). Die Forschungsgemeinschaft "Philosophy and History of the Discipline of Education" Ein Rückblick. *Zeitschrift für Pädagogik, 61,* 623–342.

Smeyers, P. (2016). The rise of data in education systems: collection, visualization and use. *History of Education, 45,* 122–127.

Smeyers, P. (2016). Neurophilia: Guiding educational research and the educational field. *Journal of Philosophy of Education, 50,* 62–75.

Smeyers, P., & Depaepe, M. (2016). Introduction: Educational research: Discourses of change and changes of discourse. *Journal of Philosophy of Education, 50,* 6–7.

Hemelsoet, E., & Smeyers, P. (2016). Understanding Roma 'practices'. Prompting educational research to surpass 'what is the case' to 'what needs to be done'. *Teoría de la Educación. Revista Interuniversitaria, 28*(2), 201–224.

Roets, R., Smeyers, P., Vandenbroeck, M., De Bie, M., Derluyn, I., Roose, R., Vanobbergen, B., Bradt, L., & Van Gorp, A. (2017). Du choc des idées jaillit la lumière: thinking with Eric Broekaert's integrated and holistic paradigm of education. *Therapeutic Communities: The International Journal of Therapeutic Communities, 38,* 169–176.

Articles in Peer-Reviewed Academic Journals (Dutch and German)

Smeyers, P. (1981). De predictieve waarde van proefexamens voor de eerste kandidaturen psychologie en pedagogische wetenschappen aan de K. U. Leuven. *Pedagogisch Tijdschrift, 6,* 117–127.

Smeyers, P., & De Keyser, C. (1981). Aansluiting van secundair en tertiair onderwijs. *Pedagogisch Tijdschrift, 6,* 158–163.

Smeyers, P., Van Gool E., & De Keyser C. (1983). Een analytische wijsbegeerte van opvoeding en onderwijs. Twee Angelsaksische bijdragen tot de 'Philosophy of Education'. (I). Een studie van het werk van I. Scheffler en R.S. Peters en van hun opvatting over 'Philosophy of Education'. *Pedagogisch Tijdschrift, 8,* 66–73.

Smeyers, P., Van Gool E., & De Keyser C. (1983). Een analytische wijsbegeerte van opvoeding en onderwijs. Twee Angelsaksische bijdragen tot de 'Philosophy of Education'. (II). Een studie van het werk van I. Scheffler en R.S. Peters en van hun opvatting over 'Philosophy of Education'. *Pedagogisch Tijdschrift, 8,* 125–134.

Hellemans, M., Masschelein, J., & Smeyers, P. (1985). Der Sozialwissenschaftler als Interpret. *Phänomenologisch-pädagogische Verhandlungen, 7,* 9–22.

Smeyers, P. (1985). Hirst's 'Forms of Knowledge'. Een epistemologie als basis voor de selectie van curriculuminhouden. *Pedagogische Verhandelingen, 8,* 82–89.

Smeyers, P. (1986). Een Wittgensteiniaanse duiding van de discussie omtrent Freinet of klassiek lager onderwijs. *Pedagogisch Tijdschrift, 11,* 3–14.

Smeyers, P. (1987). Opvoeding een initiatie in vanzelfsprekendheden. Een Wittgensteiniaans-Lacaniaanse duiding van het opvoedingsconcept. *Pedagogisch Tijdschrift, 12,* 81–93.

Smeyers, P. (1987). Inspirator en eminent vertegenwoordiger. R.S. Peters' impact op de "Philosophy of Education". *Pedagogisch Tijdschrift, 12,* 183–191.

Smeyers, P. (1987). Nogmaals, geen psychologisch maar een wijsgerig perspectief. Bedenkingen bij Spieckers kanttekeningen op mijn 'Opvoeding een initiatie in vanzelfsprekendheden'. *Pedagogisch Tijdschrift, 12,* 176–177.

Smeyers, P. (1987). Over de relatie tussen filosofie, theoretische en normatieve pedagogiek. *Pedagogische Verhandelingen, 10,* 37–46.

Smeyers, P. (1988). Wat is dat toch, wijsgerige pedagogiek? Over het statuut en het object van een door Wittgenstein geïnspireerde filosofie van opvoeding en onderwijs. *Pedagogisch Tijdschrift, 13,* 23–46.

Smeyers, P. (1988). Is het doel van de opvoeding zoek? Bedenkingen over de aard van opvoedingsdoelen n.a.v. een 'kommunikationstheoretische Wende'. *Pedagogisch Tijdschrift, 13,* 441–453.

Smeyers, P., & Levering, B. (1989). Persoonlijke verantwoordelijkheid als pedagogische basiswaarde aan het einde van de twintigste eeuw. *Pedagogisch Tijdschrift, 14,* 132–140.

Smeyers, P. (1989). Over de methode van de wetenschappelijke pedagogiek. *Pedagogisch Tijdschrift, 14* (Speciaal Nummer), 9–14.

Smeyers, P. (1991). Het verlangen naar zekerheid en geborgenheid. Enkele wijsgerig pedagogische beschouwingen over opvoeding en onderwijs in de multi-culturele samenleving. *Pedagogisch Tijdschrift, 16,* 125–138.

Smeyers, P. (1992). Over zijn en behoren in de wetenschappelijke pedagogiek. Een bijdrage vanuit de taalfilosofie als filosofie van een praxis. *Pedagogisch Tijdschrift, 17,* 139–160 .

Smeyers, P. (1992). Opvoeding en onderwijs. Over initiatie en de mogelijkheid van kritiek. *Pedagogisch Tijdschrift, 17,* 270–288.

Smeyers, P. (1992). Over macht en liefde in de opvoeding. *Comenius, 12,* 301–325.

Smeyers, P. (1993). Charles Taylor en de hernieuwde aandacht voor het authentieke individu. *Pedagogisch Tijdschrift, 18,* 268–287.

Smeyers, P. (1993). Inleiding tot "Opvoeding, democratie en nationalisme". *Pedagogisch Tijdschrift, 18 (Speciaal Nummer),* 5–7.

Smeyers, P. (1993). "Much ado about nothing?" Mag het, kan het en/of moet kinderopvang misschien? Enkele wijsgerig-pedagogische beschouwingen over de inzet van het debat. *Pedagogisch Tijdschrift, 18*, 399–416.

Smeyers, P. (1994). De opvoeder na het postmodernisme: integriteit en particuliere betrokkenheid. *Pedagogisch Tijdschrift, 19*, 305–331.

Smeyers, P. (1995). Paul Hirsts epistemologische reflecties over de inhoud van het onderwijs. Bijna juist, steeds de provocatie waard. *Pedagogisch Tijdschrift, 20*, 65–74.

Smeyers, P., Spiecker, B., Steutel, J., Levering, B., Van Haaften, W., & Snik, G. (1995). Discussie: C.J.B. Macmillan. *Pedagogisch Tijdschrift, 20,* 199–216.

Smeyers, P. (1996). Over "vertrouwen" en "zorg" als morele en als pedagogische basisconcepten. *Pedagogisch Tijdschrift, 21,* 48–68.

Smeyers, P. (1996). Een feministische visie op ethiek en pedagogiek: Nel Noddings' Ethics of Care. *Pedagogisch Tijdschrift, 21,* 69–80.

Smeyers, P. (1997). Ethiek als expressie: een uitweg voor de pedagogiek? *Pedagogisch Tijdschrift, 22,* 149–169.

Smeyers, P., & Levering, B. (1998). Over de toekomst van het Nederlands als taal voor wetenschappelijke publicaties in de pedagogiek. *Comenius, 18,* 77–88.

Smeyers, P., & Levering, B. (1998). Inleiding tot "Interpretatief onderzoek in pedagogiek en onderwijskunde. Voorlopige balans en hernieuwde plaatsbepaling van de kwalitatieve benaderingswijze". *Pedagogisch Tijdschrift, 23,* 177–180.

Smeyers, P. (1998). Recht doen aan de eenheid van taal en wereld. Pedagogisch interpretatief onderzoek: *Pedagogisch Tijdschrift, 23,* 181–201.

Smeyers, P. (1999). Het ongrijpbare verlangen. Pedagogische bespiegelingen over en voor het individu. *Comenius, 19,* 245–261.

Smeyers, P., & Masschelein, J. (2000). De pedagogiek en de representatiecrisis. *Pedagogisch Tijdschrift, 25,* 209–212.

Smeyers, P., & Masschelein, J. (2000). Contouren en uitwegen van de representatiecrisis in de pedagogiek. *Pedagogisch Tijdschrift, 25,* 213–232.

Smeyers, P., & Lambeir, B. (2001). *Carpe diem*, verlangen en nihilisme: zegen of onraad voor opvoeding bij de eeuwwende. *Pedagogisch Tijdschrift, 26,* 87–107.

Smeyers, P., & Levering, B. (2001). Nieuwe vorm, andere inhoud. Toch postmoderne wijsgerige pedagogiek. *Pedagogisch Tijdschrift, 26,* 213–232.

Lambeir, B., & Smeyers, P. (2002). Spijt over wat niet is geweest. Opvoeding en ... van nu af *moet* je gaan. *Pedagogisch Tijdschrift, 26,* 57–74.

Levering, B., & Smeyers, P. (2002). Repliek. *Kwalon. Tijdschrift voor Kwalitatief Onderzoek in Nederland, 7,* 36–37.

Levering, B., Ramaekers, S., & Smeyers. P. (2004). "Als ze maar gelukkig zijn". De integriteit van ouders in het geding. *Pedagogisch Tijdschrift, 29,* 39–53.

Books As (Co-)Author (English)

Blake, N., Smeyers, P., Smith, R., & Standish, P. (1998). *Thinking again: Education after postmodernism.* New York: Bergin & Garvey.

Blake, N., Smeyers, P., Smith, R., & Standish, P. (2000). *Education in an age of nihilism.* London: Falmer Press.

Smeyers, P., Smith, R., & Standish, P. (2007). *The therapy of education.* Houndsmills, Basingstoke: Palgrave Macmillan.

Peters, M., Burbules, N., & Smeyers, P. (2008). *Showing and doing: Wittgenstein as a pedagogical philosopher.* Boulder, Colorado: Paradigm Publishers.

Smeyers, P., & Smith, R. (2014). *Understanding education and educational research.* Cambridge: Cambridge University Press.

Books As (Co-)Author (Dutch)

Lambeir, B., Postma, D. W., Levering, B., & Smeyers, P. (2003). *Hoezo pedagogisch?* Amsterdam: SWP.

Lambeir, B., Levering, B., Smeyers, P., & Vanobbergen, B. (2006). *Zonde van de tijd. Zeven opstellen over opvoeding*. Amsterdam: SWP.

Books and Special Issues As (Co-)Editor (English)

Smeyers, P. (Ed.). (1994). *Identity, culture and education* (Papers of the fourth biennial conference). Leuven: International Network of Philosophers of Education.

Smeyers, P., & Marshall J. (Eds.). (1995). *Philosophy and education: Accepting Wittgenstein's challenge*. Dordrecht: Kluwer.

Crawley, F., Smeyers, P., & Standish, P. (Eds.). (2000). *Universities remembering Europe. Nations, culture and Higher Education*. New York: Berghahn Books.

Peters, M., Marshall, J., & Smeyers, P. (Eds.). (2001). *Nietzsche's legacy for education: Past and present values*. Westport: Bergin & Garvey.

Blake, N., Smeyers, P., Smith, R., & Standish, P. (Eds.). (2003). *The Blackwell guide to the philosophy of education*. Oxford: Blackwell.

Smeyers, P., & Depaepe, M. (Eds.). (2003). *Beyond empiricism. On criteria for educational research*. Leuven: Leuven University Press.

Smeyers, P., & Hogan, P. (Guest Eds.). (2005). The inherent risks of human learning. *Educational Theory, 55*(2).

Smeyers, P., & Peters, M. (Guest Eds.). (2005). *James Marshall. Educational Philosophy and Theory, 37*(3).

Smeyers, P., & Peters, M. (Eds.). (2006). *Postfoundationalist themes in the philosophy of education*. Oxford: Basil Blackwell.

Smeyers, P., & Depaepe, M. (Eds.). (2006). *Educational research: Why 'What works' doesn't work*. Dordrecht: Springer.

Smeyers, P., & Burbules, N. (Guest Editors). (2006). The changing practices and social relations of education. *Educational Theory, 56*(4).

Smeyers, P. (Guest Editor). (2006). Voices of philosophy of education. *Studies in Philosophy of Education, 25*(1–2).

Depaepe, M., & Smeyers, P. (Guest Editors). (2007) Refuge in theory. *Educational Philosophy and Theory, 39*(1).

Smeyers, P., & Depaepe, M. (Eds.). (2007). *Educational research: Networks and technologies*. Dordrecht: Springer.

Smeyers, P., & Depaepe, M. (Eds.). (2008). *Educational research: The* educationalisation *of social problems*. Dordrecht: Springer.

Smeyers, P., & Burbules, N. (Guest Editors). (2008). Wittgenstein's legacy for education. *Educational Philosophy and Theory, 40*(5).

Bridges, D., Smeyers, P., & Smith, R. (Guest Ed.). (2008). 'Evidence-based education policy': What evidence? What basis? Whose policy? *Journal of Philosophy of Education, 42*(Supp.).

Smeyers, P., Depaepe, N., De Coninck-Smith, N. (Guest Editors). (2008). Focusing on method. *Paedagogica Historica, 44*(6).

Depaepe, M., & Smeyers, P. (Guest Eds.). (2008). Educationalization. *Educational Theory, 58*(4).

Smeyers, P., & Depaepe, M. (Eds.). (2009). *Educational research. Proofs, arguments, and other reasonings: The language of education*. Dordrecht: Springer.

Bridges, D., Smeyers, P., & Smith, R. (Eds.). (2009). *'Evidence based educational policy': What evidence? What basis? Whose policy?* Oxford: Blackwell.

Smeyers, P., & Waghid, Y. (Guest Eds.). (2009). The state of Higher Education in South-Africa: Fifteen years since democracy. *South African Journal of Higher Education, 23*(6).

Smeyers, P., & Depaepe, M. (Eds.). (2010). *Educational research. The ethics and aesthetics of statistics.* Dordrecht: Springer.

Smeyers, P., & Depaepe, M. (Eds.). (2013). *Educational research: The attraction of psychology.* Dordrecht: Springer.

Smeyers, P., Depaepe, M., & Keiner, E. (Eds.). (2013). *Educational research: The importance and effects of Institutional spaces.* Dordrecht: Springer.

Smeyers, P., & Depaepe, M. (2014). (Eds.). *Educational research: Material culture and the representation of educational research.* Dordrecht: Springer.

Smeyers, P., Bridges, D., Burbules, N., & Griffiths, M. (Eds.). (2015). *International handbook of interpretation in educational research* (Part one). Dordrecht: Springer.

Smeyers, P., Bridges, D., Burbules, N., & Griffiths, M. (Eds.). (2015). *International handbook of interpretation in educational research* (Part two). Dordrecht: Springer.

Dekker, J. J. H., & Smeyers, P. (Guest Eds.). (2015). Educational historiography: (Re-) Presentations, realities, materialities. *Paedagogica Historica, 51*,(6).

Smeyers, P., & Depaepe, M. (Guest Eds.). (2016). Discourses of change and changes of discourse. *Journal of Philosophy of Education, 50(1).*

Smeyers, P., & Depaepe, M. (Eds.). (2016). *Educational research: Discourses of change and changes of discourse.* Dordrecht: Springer.

Smeyers, P. (Guest Ed.). (2017). Section: Postmodernism and education. In M. Peters (Ed.), *Encyclopedia of educational theory and philosophy.* Dordrecht: Springer. (online) https://link.springer.com/referencework/10.1007%2F978-981-287-532-7

Smeyers, P. (Ed.). (2018). *International handbook of philosophy of education.* Dordrecht: Springer.

Books and Special Issues As (Co-)Editor (Dutch and German)

Hellemans, M., & Smeyers, P. (Hrgs.). (1986). *Phänomenologische Pädagogik. Methodologisch und Theoretische Ansätze.* Leuven: Acco.

Smeyers, P., e.a. (1993). (Eds.). Opvoeding, democratie en nationalisme. *Pedagogisch Tijdschrift, 18 (Speciaal Nummer).*

Hellemans, M., Masschelein, J., & Smeyers, P. (Eds.). (1994). *The school: Its crisis. Eduquer après la République.* Leuven: Acco.

Smeyers, P. (Eds.). (1994). *Heeft de school nog een vormingsproject?* Leuven: Acco.

McCarty, L. Prior, Farber, P., Smeyers, P., & Büyükdüvenci, S. (Guest Eds.). (1996). *Studies in Philosophy and Education, 15* (1–2).

Smeyers, P., & Levering, B. (Eds.). (1998). Interpretatief onderzoek in pedagogiek en onderwijskunde. Voorlopige balans en hernieuwde plaatsbepaling van de kwalitatieve benaderingswijze [Themanummer]. *Pedagogisch Tijdschrift, 23*(5–6).

Levering, B., & Smeyers, P. (Eds.). (1999). *Opvoeding en onderwijs leren zien. Een inleiding in interpretatief pedagogisch onderzoek.* Amsterdam: Boom.

Smeyers, P., & Masschelein, J. (Eds.). (2000). Postmoderne tendensen in de pedagogiek. De pedagogiek en de representatiecrisis. *Pedagogisch Tijdschrift, 25*(3–4).

Smeyers, P., & Levering, B. (Eds.). (2001). *Grondslagen van de wetenschappelijke pedagogiek. Modern en postmodern.* Amsterdam: Boom.

Smeyers, P., Ramaekers, S., van Goor, R., & Vanobbergen, B., (Red.). (2016). *Inleiding in de pedagogiek, deel 1. Thema's en basisbegrippen.* Amsterdam: Boom.

Smeyers, P., Ramaekers, S., van Goor, R., & Vanobbergen, B., (Red.). (2016). *Inleiding in de pedagogiek, deel 2. Grondslagen en stromingen.* Amsterdam: Boom.

Supervision of Doctoral Theses

Verhesschen, P. (2001). *Revelatie en transformatie: Narrativiteit als paradigmatische instap voor pedagogisch onderzoek.*

Ramaekers, S. (2003). *Beyond certainty and scepticism: A philosophical investigation of educational theory and practice from the position of Wittgenstein, Nietzsche and Cavell.*

Postma, D. (2004). *Because we are human: A philosophical inquiry into discourses of environmental education from the perspective of sustainable development and man's caring responsibility.*

Simons, M. (2004). *De school in de ban van het leven. Een cartografie van het moderne en actuele onderwijsdispositief.*

Lambeir, B. (2004). *The educational cyberspace affaire: A philosophical reading of the relevance of information and communications technology for educational theory.*

Smedts, G. (2008). *Thinking about parents in the age of parenting. A philosophical reading of what it means to be a parent in times of the Internet.*

Allewijn, P. (2009). *Gedeelde opvoeding op het kinderdagverblijf? Een onderzoek naar de samenwerking en afstemming tussen ouders en pedagogisch medewerkers.*

Decoster, P. (2016). *From cinema education to the onmipresence of digital screens.*

Printed by Printforce, the Netherlands